Now You See It, Now You Don't:

Using Empty Space in Self Defence

Rick Wilson

Photographs by Chris Beaton

River Illustrations by Makayla Alook

Edited by BD Wilson

WARNING

Some of the techniques and drills contained in this book are extremely dangerous and could cause injury or death. It is not the intent of the author, publisher or distributors of the book to encourage readers to attempt any of these techniques or drills without proper professional supervision and training. Attempting to do so can result in severe injury or death. Do not attempt any of these techniques or drills without the supervision of a certified instructor.

The author, publisher and distributors of this book do not make any representation or warranty regarding the legality or appropriateness of any technique contained in this book.

Specific self-defence responses illustrated in this book may not be justified in any particular situation in view of the totality of circumstances or under the law for the applicable jurisdiction.

The author, publisher and distributors of this book do not make any representation or warranty regarding the effective application of any technique contained in this book due to the totality of circumstances that pertain to any self-defence response.

The author, publisher and distributors of this book disclaim any liability from damage or injuries of any type that a reader or user of information contained in this book may encounter from the use of said information.

Consult a physician before engaging in the techniques and drills contained in this book and only under supervision of a certified instructor.

This book is presented for academic study only.

Acknowledgements

I need to thank my family for their support and in particular my wife, Andrea, who puts up with my obsession with self-defence.

I need to acknowledge that this book would not be in any kind of publishing shape without the hard work and patient effort of my daughter, BD Wilson.

This book, as was the last one, is only understandable with the illustrations. The photographs are done by my friend Chris Beaton. This book took more effort and creativity to find the right shots to highlight the use of empty space. His suggestions and efforts in multiple photo shoots made this book what it is.

Of course, I would look pretty silly in the pictures without my training partners, who not only helped by showing up to a number of photo shoots, but also were also a huge part in developing and discovering the material you will see in this book: Rav Ruparain, Stan Tubinshlak, Adam Ahmed and Paul Hunter.

When I needed a couple of illustrations of a river my wonderful and talented granddaughter, Makayla Alook, stepped up to draw them for me.

I would thank Rick Bottomley for all his sharing with me over the years and the tremendous effort he put into reviewing this book, all of which made it so much better, but since I dedicated this book to him that would just give him a big head.

I also want to thank my friend, Randy King for taking the time away from what has become a very busy and successful seminar schedule to write the foreword for this book – Thanks Randy.

Dedication

I have a lot of people to be thankful for in my life, but I don't think I could dedicate my first book on a pure martial principle to anyone other than my good friend, long time training partner and Taiji instructor, Rick Bottomley.

A long time ago in a dojo not so far away, I asked Rick B. what he thought of the class I had just taught. He said that it was a class taught by a strong guy teaching strong guy techniques (jamming). Then he asked, "what is that small woman on the end of the line going to do with them?"

"Die," was my answer and that lead to a very long discussion about how to avoid going force on force.

The next time I taught and asked him what he thought, he responded that he was shocked because I was teaching what we had talked about. I said "Well, yeah I was listening." He said no one else ever had, and from that moment on we have listened to each other, discussing and exploring principles for a few decades now to improve what we do.

That discussion not only set my path in martial arts but brought me to this very book. Although, Rick B. jokingly says I see things that aren't there but seem to make things work....

Thank you, Rick Bottomley, for making me better at this oddly complex, but simple stuff. I would not be the martial artist I am today without our friendship.

Contents

Foreword

Rick Wilson's brain is a wondrous place that I always want more access to and this book is a great window into it. The way he sees things is unlike any other I have met and the way he can weaponize and transfer that mindscape is amazing!

Now You See it, Now You Don't is straight up proof of that. Rick takes a concept that, let's be honest, can sound pretty close to a McDojo life video and hacks out the new age mumbo jumbo and gives you real ways to use it to your advantage. I was fortunate enough to play with some of the concepts in the book with Rick while he was writing it. After the session I viewed not only self protection but the world much differently, and you will too.

There is a reason that I call Rick a dark wizard. (Now I am not saying he is Voldemort… but I have never seen them in the same room, and really how "real" is his nose?) The way he can take high level conceptual material and then break it down and weaponize it in a situation always astounds me.

Have fun reading this book and playing with the material… and maybe don't let Rick near any babies that have a "chosen one" vibe.

Stay safe.

— Randy King Edmonton, AB 04April2018

KPC Self Defense, Randy King Live, Talking to Savages, Violence Dynamics.

Introduction

A long while back in a discussion with Rory Miller, we asked each other why many skilled people weren't using empty space. Why no one, other than us (and my friend, Rick Bottomley), seemed to talk about using empty space in self-defence. It was as if many talented people were unaware of this principle.

This had me looking at the martial artists who impressed me and, while there was always a lot and their styles varied, the one consistent factor was their use of empty space. Others would use speed or power to execute a technique, but the best used empty space.

Even those using it weren't talking about it, however, and so I had to ask if the concept was missed in teaching or in learning? My research brought me to the conclusion: it's both. Now I will never say that no one out there teaches using empty space specifically, because the martial arts world is too vast, but while most proficient martial artists do it and some will give an indication of its use, I often see practitioners explaining how to a technique saying "do this" and then they actually do something different where they use empty space. I have not seen it taught as a separate concept (other than in my first book, Watch Out For The Pointy End.)

What do I mean by empty space and how does it relate to self-defence?

Not to seem too flippant but empty space is just that: space that is empty. Let's say you were trying to catch an elevator to get to an important meeting, but the doors were closing. You would never think of trying to slam through one of the doors to get inside. No, instead you would turn your body sideways to fit through the space between the closing doors, the empty space.

That seems like a simple enough concept, but many times when you look at a self-defence application they are trying to move directly through the Aggressor's structure, to slam through the elevator doors. If you are bigger or stronger this may work, and very often this is the case, like in the story told in the dedication of this book. Going between the doors doesn't require you to be bigger or stronger.

Empty space has many applications. If I want to move a person and decided to press directly down on their shoulder, how much effect do you think I would have? Again, unless you're a lot bigger or stronger than they are, you would have no effect at all. However, behind their shoulder is nothing – empty space – and if I push their shoulder back into that empty space they are far more likely to move.

These two concepts are the bare bones of using empty space in self-defence. The essence is to never go force on force. To never try to overwhelm their structure where it is the strongest but always where it is the weakest. To never try to move them through their structure but move them where they have no structure.

I have found that I use some form of empty space all the time, and most often I am layering, or stacking, uses of empty space to increase the efficiency and effectiveness of my self-defence. Therefore, in this book I am going to offer you the gift of this extraordinary principle and I certainly hope it brings an "aha" moment for you. Often, once you are aware of it, you see where it is and where it isn't and see it in what you already know.

I'm going to use a number of thought processes, and I will start with a specific one that will run throughout the book to help explain and mentally demonstrate the principles. If you choose to accept and practice empty space, it will enhance your martial arts in surprising ways. I believe this principle separates great martial artists from common ones. It is a principle and therefore not restricted to one style or one system. It applies to all.

Occasionally (okay maybe more than occasionally) my teaching approach can strike people as odd, but I assure you in the end it all comes together for the practical purpose of self-defence. I had a student, Stephen Robertson (Author of *Go For Shakedown*), who was a helicopter pilot in the Canadian armed forces. One night he was late to class and came in as we were doing an odd drill. I paused and asked if he wanted to know what we were up to and he said, "No, I don't need to because I know at some point tonight I'll go okay, we did that drill because it makes this work!"

Everything I do serves a martial and self-defence purpose. If it didn't, why the heck would you do it? Okay we could think of a few health reasons and so on, but for me this is about self-defence and my drills, no matter how odd they may seem at first, relate directly to how to use things for that end.

There is an old story about a man going to a sword master to ask to be taught. The old master invited him in and offered to make tea. As the old man prepared the tea slowly and with precise movements the would-be student began to tell the master all about sword fighting to show off his knowledge. Finally, the tea was ready and as the old master poured the tea into the would-be student's cup, he kept pouring. He poured so much it began to over flow and spill. The would-be student jumped back out of the way demanding to know what the old master was doing. The old master smiled and explained: "You are like this cup, so full of what you think you know nothing more can be poured in. It will only spill out on the floor wasted. If you wish to learn from me, then you must first empty your cup."

That story is the most important thing when taking on a new thought process. You must empty your cup and get every other martial thing you've doing out of your head and set it aside. For example, moving into empty space "uses" footwork but it is "not footwork." Footwork is the technique to get there and empty space is the principle.

Much like my first book, this one is a manual to train you how to use empty space for self-defence. As much as I appreciate books that present general principles, but as a practical martial artist I always want to know how to learn (train) the principle not just what it is. Just how I look at things.

A while back I saw where a person who had done my seminar on "Fighting in Empty Space" had posted a comment on a forum on how it was presenting how to think differently. Another forum member jumped all over him, posting that in real assaults there is no time to think therefore thinking was all wrong, and, if you carry that through, fighting in empty space must then be wrong as well. The commenter was correct that there is no time to think in an assault, but he was wrong to dismiss what was being said. I see three zones of training: Learning, Conditioning and Testing. When you are in the Learning Zone, which is where most seminars are, there is all kinds of time to think. In fact, you have to think because you are learning new things. (For details on the Three Zones of Training see Addendum 1 at the back of this book.)

In this Learning Zone you are about to enter I am going to ask you not only to think, but to think in a particular way. This is so you can understand and learn about empty space, and through learning and understanding you will be able to see and feel what I am trying to pass on. Once you can see and feel empty space you can give it over to your deeper brain where tactical habits can be held, allowing yourself to explore using empty space without thinking.

I use a lot of visualization in the book to try and teach what you need to know and experience to understand empty space. I use different visualizations because I never know which one will strike a chord in you, the reader. Everyone is different and what makes perfect sense to one doesn't to another. Therefore, while solving the maze is the main thought process, I will be introducing you to others as well.

Once you begin to see and feel empty space you will just do it and do it all the time: no thinking involved, no visualization involved. Of course, this takes work; nothing in self-defence comes without putting in the work.

So, do not panic about being asked to think during these drills because that too will pass. But you need to think to perform the drills and you need to work the drills to learn.

Therefore, this book will present drills and techniques to illustrate using empty space in self-defence, but they are merely a delivery system not what is being delivered. With practice you will see how to use empty space in self-defence, and you will see how it is used, or should be used, in the techniques you already know.

As I said in my knife defence book, I believe understanding why things work is more important than any technique because when chaos hits nothing may look like it did in training and you cannot fix, modify, adapt and adjust something if you have no idea what makes it work. So, in training, always look for and understand the why.

The Analogy of Solving a Maze

I wanted to find a way to introduce and help people start to see and use empty space in self defence and make it easier to understand and process.

My experience in educating people, particularly adults, is that if they can make a logical connection between what you are teaching and something they already know then the learning pace accelerates.

This brings us to the concept of solving a maze. Pretty much everyone has solved a maze. We have all sat down at a piece of paper with pencil or tablet in hand and looked at the puzzle of a maze in front of us. This task is a perfect analogy for beginning to understand the basics of using empty space in self defence.

A maze is an organized group of lines that we have to navigate through. We know we cannot cross or touch a line (that's cheating) but rather we must move between those lines — in and through the empty space — to find our way to a treasure, to escape, or both.

A maze requires you to look for and use empty space.

The concept of solving a maze is simple and we easily grasp the goals and guidelines. It is this concept we want to keep in mind as we modify it for self-defence. Solving a maze and using empty space for self defence are not all that different in application as you will see.

Solving the Maze

A maze is a set of lines you cannot cross and must find your way using the empty space between the lines.

Each maze has a task for you to complete and, as said above, in most case they will be one of three goals.

The Three Goals of Solving a Maze

1. Find treasure

2. Escape

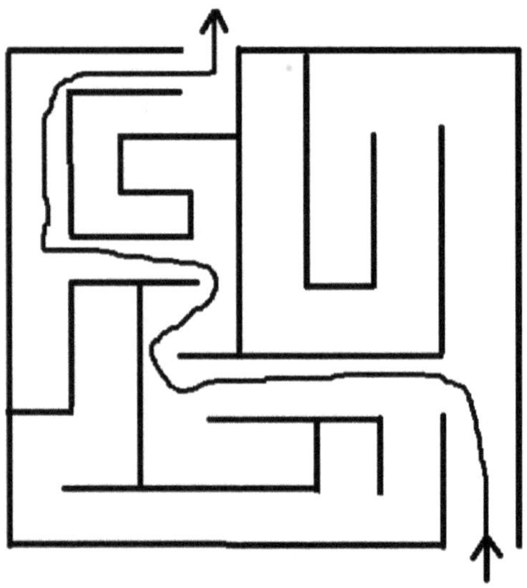

3. Find treasure then escape

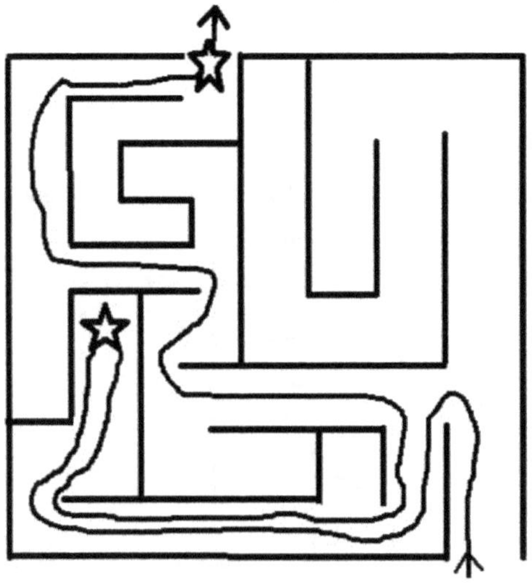

When you solve a maze, there are some very clear rules. You cannot simply draw a line from where you are directly to where you want to be. You must find your way through the open/empty spaces of the maze without crossing a line or getting continually stuck in a blind alley.

Guidelines:

- You cannot cross a line.
- If you hit a blind alley back out and go somewhere else.

The concept of hitting a blind alley in a maze and immediately changing your path is important, because you want to train yourself to quickly sense when you are trying to move through the Aggressor's structure, not using empty space, and change immediately. Going against the structure of a bigger stronger Aggressor is not good self-defence (hence this entire book).

One of the things I have always found about solving a maze that makes it easier is to look at the goal and then work backwards to the start positions. The simple fact is there are less incorrect pathways from the goal than from the start and you can often see them a little easier. This works in applying fighting in empty space as well.

Think about being in a crowded room and wondering how to get out fast if there were to be a fire or other emergency. What is the first thing you do? You look for the exits. You don't look through the crowd first to see if that path leads you to an exit. Once you have located the exit you then look back from there to where you are to see the best and clearest path. You look for the way to work through the maze of people and things. You look for the empty space.

A helpful approach:

- Look backwards from the goal (treasure, escape, or both) to where you are.
- There are less missteps when looking back from the goal to you.

When you look at a maze at first all you see is are the lines that form the corridors and twists and turns and block your way. However, to solve the maze you change that focus to look for the open/empty spaces between you and your goal. You no longer look at all that stands between you, but rather at the clear path that gets you to your goal.

We can (and will) apply this to a person where their structure creates the lines of the maze.

We can (and will) apply this to a room with obstacles between us and the door to escape.

We can (and will) apply this to all movement.

We can (and will) apply this to manipulating the Aggressor.

We can (and will) apply this to striking.

In this process of learning to solve the maze we need to keep in mind this is just a learning tool and that there are martial goals. Each goal of solving a maze equate directly to a goal in counter assault:

Solving the Maze	Counter Assault
Find treasure	Acquire a target
Escape	Movement
Find treasure then escape	Manipulate them

These three areas encompass most areas of fighting. We're also going to cover many more additional uses of empty space in close quarters counter assault, and manipulating the Aggressor but these are the three major ones.

Let's Sum Up

One of the ways to wrap your head around empty space and looking for it is to use the same process you would when solving a maze. You want to look for and travel through the empty spaces of the maze. You will find that obstacles and an Aggressor's structure are similar to a maze's lines. To go beyond an intellectual understanding, you will need to have a tactile experience to feel what empty space is all about.

Learning to See Differently

I want you to use your mind which is your most powerful weapon in self-defence. I want to affect how you see and how you think and, therefore, how you act.

This teaching approach requires the student to set aside all preconceived ideas of what "is." They cannot look at a drill and say oh that's just footwork. They must see it differently. They must think of it differently. They must feel it differently. It has to go beyond the intellectual into the tactile. I am not trying to get all mystical here; it has nothing to do with mystic magical energy, but rather using your mind and its deep connections throughout your body. If they can do this, they will acquire the principle in a very short period of time and then it will simply take looking for it in everything they do and drilling the process.

The only way to do this is to provide drills that allow you to experience the difference between not using empty space and using empty space. That will be our focus to start.

Let's begin with a simple drill, but one that can be highly effective in showing the difference between not focusing on empty space and focusing on it.

The Obstacle Drill

In a room big enough to set out obstacles such as striking pads, chairs or tables, spread them around leaving enough space between them for you to walk. The pattern can be as simple as the picture below showing striking pads on the floor.

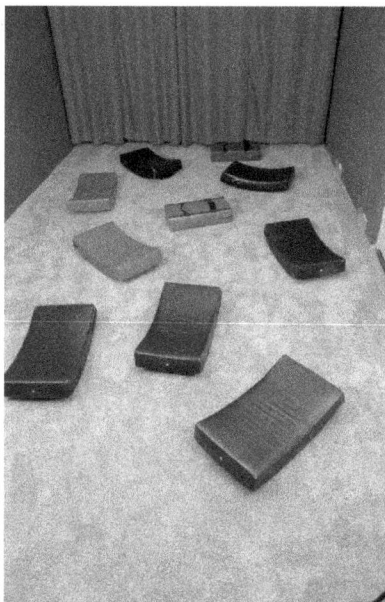

Part One

Take a moment and look all around, focusing on each obstacle, seeing it, seeing where it is in the room. Look from one to another.

Take a good long look at them. **Focus on them.**

Now walking as fast as you can move between them. **Keep your focus on the obstacles.**

Keep your eyes on the obstacles.

Walk through them for about a minute.

Stop and take some time to think about how you moved.

- Did you move smoothly, or did you stumble or hesitate?
- Did you bump into any obstacles, even a little?
- Did you touch any as you moved?
- How comfortable were you moving between them?
- Do you think you could go faster? If so, try again, a little faster, but keep it safe.

NOTE: There are no correct answers to these questions because the answers are what you felt or didn't feel.

If you react like others I have done this with, however, then walking through while focusing on the obstacles means your mind is entangled in them and you stumble a little, hesitate and walk awkwardly through them. When you focus on the obstacles your mind makes them seem almost larger or more than they are making it harder to move through them.

Below are altered pictures of the obstacles in the picture above, to give a visual representation of what focusing on the obstacles will do to your perception and how it will shrink the space you see and move in.

Part Two

You can use the same set up of obstacles or move them for a clean slate.

Take a moment to look at the room, but this time, **do not look at the obstacles:** look at the space between them.

See all the empty space between the obstacles.

See the paths between the obstacles.

Do not pay any attention to the obstacles, only look at the space between them.

The obstacles form the maze; the obstacles are the lines of that maze.

To walk through that maze you look between the lines for the empty space and the clear paths

Now walking as fast as you can move between them keeping your focus on the empty space, the open pathways.

Walk through them for about a minute.

Stop and take some time to think about how you moved.

Ask yourself the same questions as before.

- Did you move smoothly, or did you stumble and hesitate?
- Did you bump into any obstacles even a little?
- Did you touch any as you moved?
- How comfortable were you moving between them?
- Was it easier than the first time?
- Do you think you could go faster? If so, try a little faster, but keep it safe.

Take a moment and compare how the two thought processes and focus affected how you were able to move.

When your mind is tuned to the empty space between the obstacles that empty space becomes the focus and the obstacles smaller and less important, making it easier to move through them. You do not become entangled in the obstacles and can therefore easily move between them.

Below are altered pictures of the obstacles in the picture above to give a visual representation of what focusing on the empty space will do to your perception and how it will expand the space you see in between the obstacles and move in.

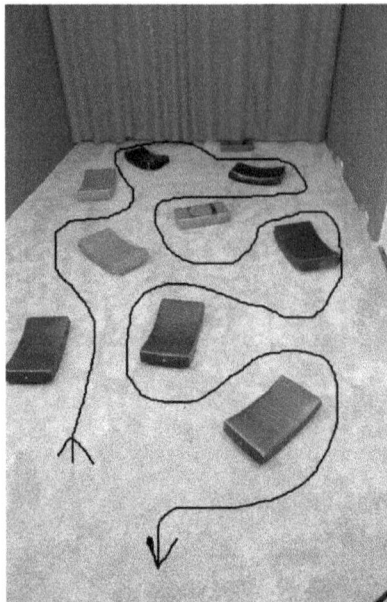

We are going to see the theme of using empty space providing the added benefit of us not becoming entangled in what the Aggressor (once we get to self defence), is doing or attempting to do to us. One difficulty in self-defence is the fact that it is very hard to not focus on what a person is doing when they are trying to take your head off, but you need to find a way to not become entangled and stuck in the box they have designed. When you shift your focus to empty space it gives your mind something else to focus on, which can allow people to not become entangled with what the Aggressor is doing.

Let's Sum Up

This simple drill illustrates for us how focusing on the lines of the maze hinders what we want to do and how focusing on empty space enhances what we do. We want to stop focusing on the obstacles and start focusing on the empty space, to stop focusing on the lines and see the empty space to move through the maze. Look at the first picture again: you can see it is just a simple maze to find your way through. Pause before you move on and really contemplate how different focusing on the empty space allowed you to move through that maze compared to focusing on the obstacles. This is the first lesson and the first awareness of how different using empty space can make things.

Take a Moment

Based off the last drill, I want you to take a moment and do a few small mental exercises, to start to look for and to see the empty space.

Drill One: Take a Moment to See - 1

Teaching ourselves to see and use empty space can also be done when we are not training.

Part One

If you are in a spot where this will work safely then proceed. If not, then wait, because this is something you can do at different times during your day and at different locations. In fact, it is something I want you to start doing until seeing and using empty space is simply "what you do."

Wherever you are stand still for a moment.

Look around you.

See the objects around you.

See the exits.

See the people (if there are any.)

Does focusing on those things draw your attention to them?

Just as in the last drill if we focus on the objects or people that is what we become fixated on.

Part Two

We want to shift our thinking to looking at that maze for the empty spaces.

Shift your focus and look for and see all the space between the objects and the people.

For example, see the path through the maze to get to an exit.

As stated above, this is an exercise you can work on at any time as you go about your day start to see the empty space between objects and people and think of moving through that empty space. You do it anyway, just make it a little more conscious. It also is a nice situational awareness drill.

I once read an old story about the founder of Aikido, Morihei Ueshiba O'Sensei. When he had become elderly people grew concerned about him, so when he was visiting a city to give a seminar they appointed caretakers. O'Sensei, having a mischievous side, used to take great delight when getting off a train at a station to slip effortlessly through the throngs of travelers without touching them or slowing down, all the time leaving his panicked caretakers in the dust, bumping into people. Clearly, he could see, find and use the empty spaces between the travelers.

Drill Two: Take a Moment to See - 2

Part One

Have a partner stand off to your side at an angle (arms down at their sides), say 45 degrees on your left front as in the picture below.

First look right at your partner and see if you can tell how doing that, looking right at them, draws all our attention to them. You can look directly at them or in your peripheral vision as long as they are your focus.

See how by focusing on them they almost see to take up more space, to be larger than they are as shown in the **altered image** below:

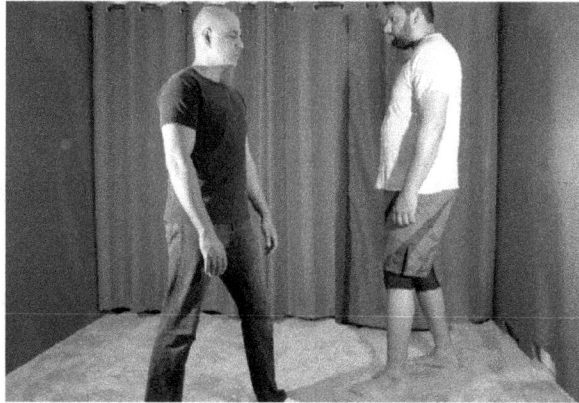

Part Two

Next, don't focus on looking at your partner but shift your focus to look at all the empty space around them. Once again you can look towards them, but this time, whether looking directly or in your peripheral vision, do not focus on them but the empty space around them.

Notice how by shifting your focus off of your partner and to the empty space all around them they are less important and can even seem smaller or to take up less space as shown in the **altered image** below.

Have them move into different spots but still within your view and repeat the process.

The purpose here is to distinguish the difference in what you "see" between fixating on your partner and looking for all the empty space.

An important point to note is that even while looking for the empty space you still know where your partner is, but they are not your focus.

Part Three

Have your partner take a spot within your view but this time with their arms up in guard position.

Again, the first step is to focus on your partner and focus on their guard position. This time look right at them. Once again take note that by focusing on your partner, particularly their guard position that image takes up all your focus and they can seem larger than life as shown in the **altered image** below.

Part Four

Next, again shift your focus to look not only at all the empty space around them but also in-between their guard as well. Note how by not focusing on your partner and their guarding position it opens your perception up to all the empty space around them making them seem smaller and less significant as shown in the **altered image** below.

Take a moment to compare the two ways of seeing basically the same thing.

What are the differences you perceive or feel?

Part Five

Have your partner extend their arm halfway through a strike to your head.

Look at your partner and focus on them. Concentrate on them. See how by focusing on them you make them seem larger than they are as shown in the **altered image** below.

Part Six

Now focus even more on the incoming strike itself. Look right at the fist coming for you. See how by focusing on the strike itself shifts the image even more making that incoming strike even larger and more significant than it is as shown in the **altered image** below.

Part Seven

Now, once again shift your focus to look at all the empty around that strike. Look around and past the incoming fist. Make the empty space your focus and see how that shrinks your partner's importance and how the empty space now seems larger making your partner smaller as shown in the **altered picture** below.

Take a moment to compare the two ways of seeing basically the same thing.

What are the differences you perceive or feel?

Part Eight

Have your partner slowly move around you (but still within your view) and slowly throw strikes at your head and body.

They are **NOT** to land a strike.

You do not move or attempt to stop them, just see the constantly changing location and the continuous strikes.

Look at the strikes focus on them; focus on your partner's body.

Part Nine

Next, repeat Part Eight but once again, shift your focus to look at all the empty Space around the strikes, around your partner.

Take a moment to compare the two ways of seeing basically the same thing.

What are the differences you perceive or feel?

Drill Three: Seeing the Empty Space Options

As your partner throws a lead hand strike I want you to look at the empty space around them. Look at all the space open around their guard and their strike and even the empty space behind you. See your options for avoidance as highlighted in the picture below.

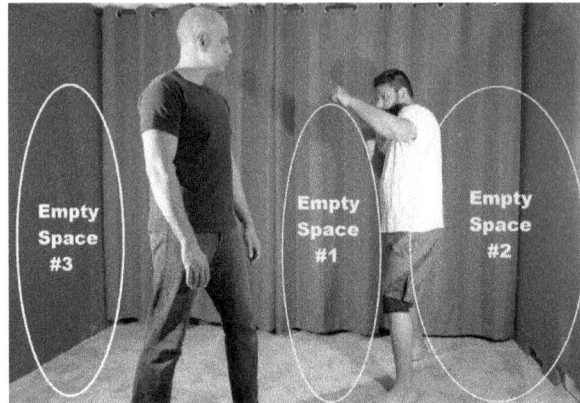

The picture above shows three options of empty space. Empty space #3 is behind us and while we could (or may need to) retreat backwards it leaves us still in the same position with the Aggressor; therefore, not the best strategic option. Empty Space #1 and #2 allows us to move to the side of the Aggressor; however, as pointed out with Empty Space #3 not all empty space is equal. If we shift to the left as the strike comes in it places us in line of your partner's power hand. Therefore, Empty Space #2 is a better option.

With a simple rotation, step and slide of your feet you can move towards Empty Space #2 avoiding the strike and opening up and entirely new venue of empty space to use. This avoids any clash or going force on force.

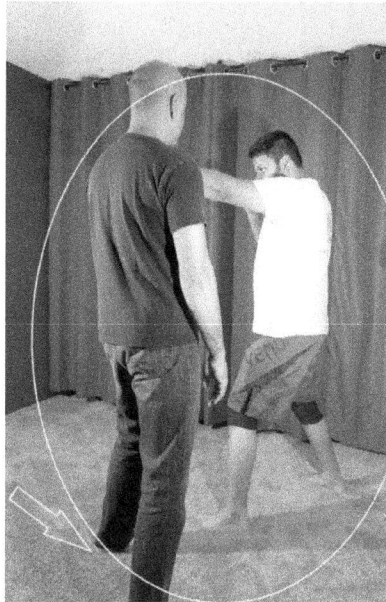

The only time you will lose sight of empty space is if you get entangled in their strike and begin to focus on the strike itself rather than the empty space around it.

What you choose to focus on changes what you see and what you perceive changes what you do.

We need to pause between looking at our partner and fixating on what they are doing and shifting our focus to looking for the empty space around them and notice the difference. This will become vital in the more active drills to come.

We need to relate this in our minds back to solving a maze. You won't solve the maze by looking at all the lines blocking your way, but you will solve it by looking at all the empty space that leads you to your goal. If we want to side step to avoid an incoming strike then focusing on the lines of the maze — the strike — will not accomplish that goal. Instead, we want to focus on the space between the lines of the maze: the empty space.

Again, as you move throughout your day take just a moment now and then to see that there is always empty space. Try and make seeing empty space a constant thing, a habit.

Let's Sum Up

The point of these drills is to open your awareness to see the things around you just as you would when looking at a maze. We do not want our focus drawn away from empty space, so we must practice seeing it in a very non-threatening way to begin. You can work on this anytime by looking around you and seeing the empty space between the lines of the maze we walk through every day. Make it simply a part of your normal view of the world. This is often a beneficial and fun thing to do when moving through a crowd like O'Sensei.

Finding the Treasure

It is important to move slowly in the drills for this chapter for a number of reasons: first you are learning to see differently and slowing down will allow that, and second if you go fast your partner, whose job is to simply stand there as you perform the drill, will instinctively move, thus negating the drill.

In the obstacle drill, we touched on how focusing on the lines of the maze entangles us and prevents us from achieving our goals with ease. We've touched on just trying to see empty space as we move through our everyday life, and how to see and move around an Aggressor. Now we will begin to focus on the use of empty space when we are in a conflict with an Aggressor.

We will introduce this through using empty space to increase the efficiency and effectiveness of our striking. The Aggressor's guard or cover position is just like the lines of a maze, we need to ignore the lines and see the path between the lines to the treasure (targets).

Drill One: See the Treasure

The purpose of this drill is to introduce seeing targets in different manner.

Pretty much every martial artist has trained targets through some form or another. Combinations are taught to flow from one set target to another based on the historical success of that pattern. We want to go beyond mechanical combinations to see where targets have been, are, and will be, and we want to see the path back from the targets to our weapons. We have to see the empty space between our target and our weapons. This drill takes repetition to ingrain and often means a lot more once you have worked the other drills in this book and the whole picture of using empty space has been seen I recommend coming back and reworking this drill.

If we think back to the maze analogy, finding a treasure is what we are doing. We need to see through the lines of the maze to the treasure and see how to move through the empty space between the lines to get there.

Too often all we see is their guard. In fact, my long-time training partner and Taiji instructor, Rick Bottomley, would teach people to spar pointing their fist at their opponent looking right over it like a gun sight. This wasn't just to have a good cover position, but also because it drew their opponent's attention to the fist aiming right at them. It entangled them in the lines of his maze.

Part One

Get into a fighting stance.

Your partner, the Aggressor, stands in front of you with their hands in guard position. Their job is to remain still throughout the entire drill. A hard job I know but someone has to do it.

Note: This is a drill, it is not real and does not represent self defence it is merely a teaching tool.

Look at your partner's guard, focus on their arms and the position the arms are in.

KEEPING your focus on their guarding arms, slowly reach out and touch targets rotating to touch one way then the other. Keep rotating and touching targets as you focus on their guarding arms. Every time you rotate touch a target. Do not rotate and touch, rotate back to position, then rotate again and touch. Instead, rotate left and touch with right hand and immediately rotate right and touch with left hand.

Keep your focus on their guard and their fists aimed at you.

Take a moment to think about how that went.

- Did your hand go straight to the target without hesitation?
- Did you bump into or brush their guarding arms?
- How did it feel?

What you can find is that by focusing on their guard position and the fists pointed at you that you often do not cleanly strike passed their guards as shown in the following pictures where you clash instead of smoothly flow through the maze.

Part Two

Have a partner stand in front of you again in a guard position, only this time ignore the guarding arms and shift your focus and attention to the space around them, in-between their guarding arms, behind them, beside them and under them.

Their arms in defensive positions are just like the lines in the maze. You see them but there is no need to focus on them. They are just lines of a maze and we need to see our way between them.

To seek a treasure or to translate that to a martial approach to strike a target we need to find our way through that maze to the target (i.e. the face).

When we look at a person in a guard position in front of us, just as with a maze, at first all we see is what forms barriers between us and what we want: those pesky lines.

Now shift your focus and what you are looking at, to the space that is open and empty. No person, no matter how large, can occupy all space. There is always empty space.

Look to a treasure/target: ears, head, shoulder, solar plexus, groin, knees, thighs, shins, etc. and THINK back along the path from the target to your striking tool, in this drill your hands. See all the open targets areas as show in the picture below.

See the empty space. See your target. See the path back from the targets to your weapons. See the way through the maze to your targets (the treasure in the maze.)

People often comment when sparring there were no openings, but that isn't true. Now our partner may not allow us to hit all the open targets, but why is it we don't see them?

Just look at all the open targets as shown in the picture below. Again, seeing a target and hitting it in a real conflict are two different things; however, looking at the picture below you can see ALL the options open to us. When in a conflict we somehow think the person is well guarded when in fact there are plenty of targets. It isn't that there were no openings but rather we were entangled by focusing on their guard.

Now, seeing all the empty space between you and all those targets, begin to slowly reach out and touch targets rotating and touching with each rotation just as in Part One, only this time through empty space.

DO NOT SIMPLY DO COMBINATIONS – SEE THE TARGET AND "SEE" THE PATH TO YOUR WEAPONS – FOLLOW THE PATH BACK.

Every time you rotate see the path from another target to your weapon.

See the empty space.

Never cross a line.

Do not touch their guard.

See back from the target to your weapons.

Once again, the unreal part of this drill is the fact the partner who is being targeted doesn't move (but this is a drill it is not real.)

Take a moment to think about how that went. Ask the same questions.

- Did your hand go straight to the target without hesitation?
- Did you bump into or brush their guarding arms?
- How did it feel?
- Was it easier?

Compare how the first run through focusing on their guard (the maze) felt and went in comparison to the second run through focusing on the empty space between the lines of the maze (their guard.)

Drill Two: Interlude drill

This drill adds an additional thought process for striking that I think blends with empty space and striking very well. It can take striking to a different level, so if you give this an attempt and it doesn't add anything for you then leave it for now. Return once you've finished all the drills in this book to redo it.

One partner stands in front of the other with their hands at their side. They are to remain motionless.

The other partner also stands with their hands at their side.

You see the path from a target on your partner to your hand. (This is just like looking backwards through the maze from the treasure to your starting point, like from the exits to where you are in a room.)

Do not move yet but think of the path and then think of your hand already having followed that path and already being ON the target.

Now you get to move, but simply think your hand is there on the target and put it there.

No, once again I am not trying to by mystical here but rather to engage your mind in a different way. The purpose of this is drill is multiple. We want to remove from our thought process as much time as we can between seeing and knowing where the target will be and our strike being there.

We know (or should know) where our weapons are at all times. We are hunting treasure/targets, so you need not concern yourself where your weapons are. Focus on the target and the empty space back from the target to your hand (or foot, or elbow etc.) and simply be on the target.

If you get it right the partner standing and presenting targets will perceive the strikes very differently than before. Again, no magic or mysticism here. This is using our minds to improve performance by removing tells.

You can repeat the drill with your partner holding their arms in guard position.

Now back to our regular programming.

Drill Three: See the Treasure in Motion

The purpose of this drill is to take all of the above into motion and see through the maze as it moves, but first we are going to once again see how it is to do the drill without using empty space.

Part One

Your partner takes a guard position only this time your partner moves around and moves his guard positions, BUT they are not actively trying to block your strikes. They are arbitrarily moving their guard positions around to give you more to deal with.

This is important because you are moving slowly so anyone can block your strike. Your partner is just moving their guard position around, they ARE NOT purposely interfering with what you are doing.

On the flip side this will be hard for your partner to do, so keep the speed down and allow them to do their job or else your speed will kick in their instinct to block which will not serve the purpose of this drill.

Look at the guard position and the lines protecting them. Keep your focus on their guard.

As you keep your focus on their guard, move, rotate and with every rotation try to touch a target slowly.

Take a moment to think about how that went.

- Did you touch the targets you wanted?
- Did you run into their guard?
- Did you find it hard to get passed their moving guard?

Part Two

I want your partner to take a step back away from you and, just as they might shadow boxing, begin to move and shift their guard around as they did in the first drill.

I want you to watch them move and look to see the empty spaces between their guards and how even in movement it is still there. Watch how it shifts. Watch how and where the empty space appears as they move.

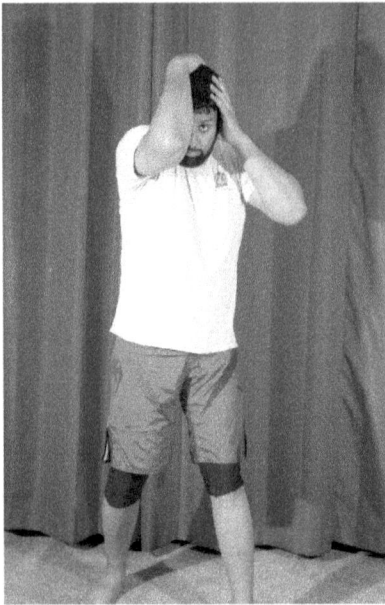

Part Three

Now step back close to your partner and as they move their guard around pay no attention to their guard but look at that constant empty space from the target to your weapons. Empty space exists between and around their guard positions. Begin to slowly rotate and touch targets every time you rotate.

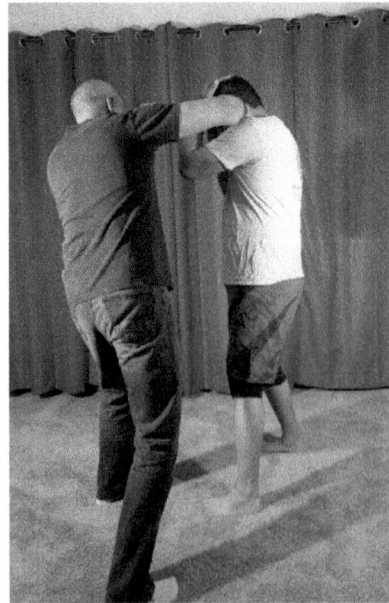

Take another moment to think about how that went.

- Did you touch the targets you wanted?
- Did you run into their guard?
- Did you find it hard to get passed their moving guard?
- How did it compare to when you focused on their guard position?

Drill Four: Second Interlude Drill: Setting Your Own Maze Just an Additional Step

The purpose of this drill is to implant the fact that while you are striking you are often open; however, you can set up guards to inhibit the counter strikes of the Aggressor. You can entangle them by giving them a line of maze (your guard) to focus on as you strike them.

Repeat Part Three of the last drill, seeing the empty spaces from the targets back to your weapons and touching targets. This time, however, check that as you touch their target you are setting up your own maze lines between your partner's weapons and targets on you. Give them something to focus on.

Setting your own lines means that as your strike finds the target they do not have a clear path from one of their weapons to an obvious target on you. Unless they have also trained to see their way through empty space, setting a maze line can help prevent a counter strike.

Let's Sum Up

We are taking our ability to not focus on the lines of the maze and to focus on the empty space between those lines to get from the treasure (targets) to our weapons. By adding in a partner, we take a slight step towards a more real setting where a person, representing an Aggressor, forms the maze. We must not focus on them and their guard, but on the empty space from the targets to our weapons. One factor you need to survive an assault is the ability to be indifferent to what the Aggressor is doing, so you do not become entangled. Once you become entangled, you are doing what they want, which is never a good strategy for surviving an assault. One excellent way to not become entangled is to shift your focus off the lines of the maze to empty space, to shift your focus from their guards to seeing your targets and seeing the empty space back to your weapons. By doing this your focus is now on something that will enhance your chance of survival.

Fill the Empty Space

We're going to talk about moving now. I've said that moving using empty space is like drawing a line through a maze, not touching the sides, and like turning sideways to slip between the shutting elevator doors. Both of these are true, but to fully use moving and empty space we also have to go past that and think about the space we're going to occupy.

It is fine to move to empty space and that accomplishes moving in a manner that does not fight their force; however, what we are able to do next will depend on whether you have moved through and to empty space or whether you have filled and taken over that empty space.

Drill: Fill the Empty Space

Part One

Face your partner both of you in a ready guard position.

Note the empty space on either side of your partner and recall that the outside moves us away from their power hand; therefore, Empty Space #2 shown below is safer.

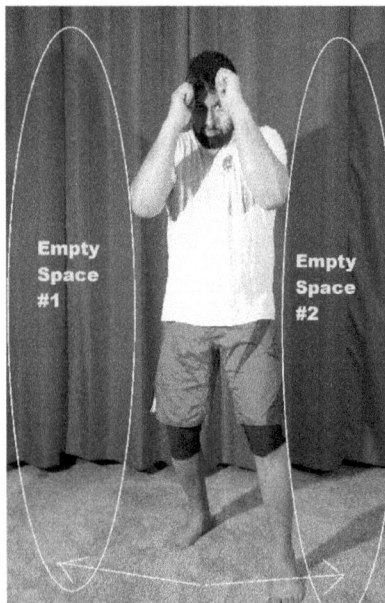

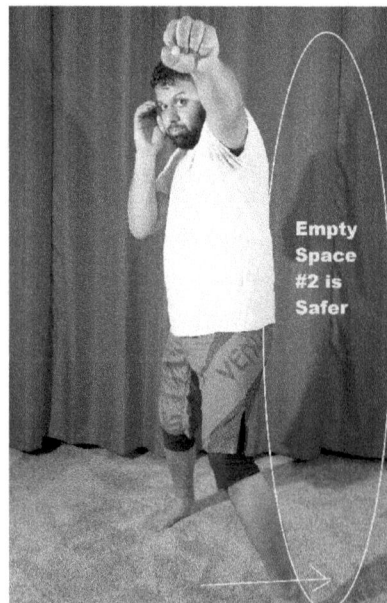

Your partner slowly slides in with a lead hand strike (in other words, left lead hand strike from a left foot forward stance).

All I want you to do is simple side step to the right to avoid the strike in any fashion you'd like. The picture below shows one option, moving to the side (Empty Space #2) to avoid the strike and place yourself off line to the Aggressor.

Do it a few times.

Take a moment (as always) to think about how it felt.

- Did you feel in a strong position at the end?
- Did you feel you were in a strategically better place?
- Did your movement seem to have an effect on your partner or did they seem ready to throw the next strike?

Ask your partner how they feel. Are they comfortable with how you moved or are they intimidated?

Remember how that felt.

Part Two

Have you partner take a step back away from you and you take a step back.

Your partner will again slowly slide forward with a left lead hand strike, however this time not at you, but instead into the air with space between you and them. This way you may observe what they are doing from in front of them.

As they move and strike, I want you to look to the outside of the striking arm beside their body.

Watch and see that pocket of empty space.

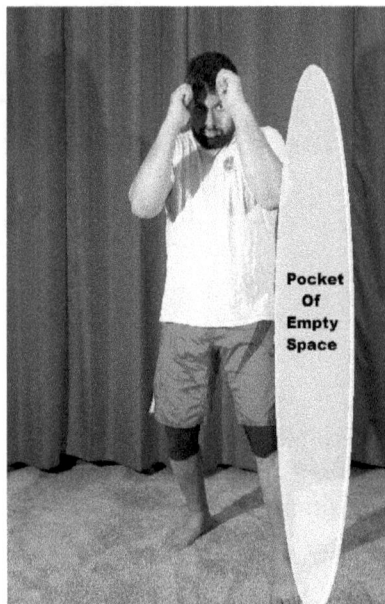

Pocket Of Empty Space

As they strike, visualize yourself moving into the empty space, taking it over, filling that pocket, making that space yours.

Visualize yourself moving in to take over and fill that empty space a number of times.

Own that space.

FILL
The
Pocket
Of
Empty
Space

Part Three

Now: Have your partner get closer and slide in slowly throwing the strike at you.

Make what you visualized real.

See the empty space, the pocket, and move into that space filling it, taking it over, and making it yours.

I've tried to visually emphasize in the picture below that I have moved in and taken over that pocket of empty space. It belongs to me.

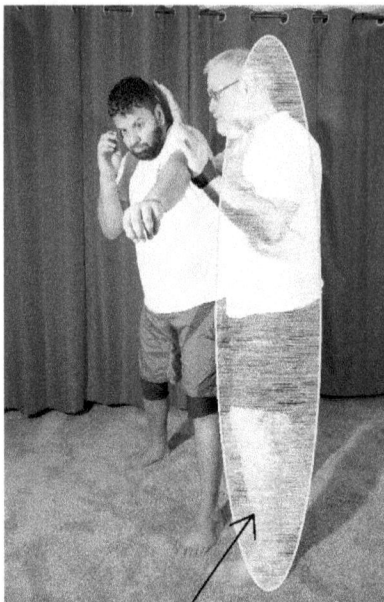

Repeat a number of times.

Once again take a moment to evaluate how that felt.

- Did you feel in a strong position at the end? If so did it feel stronger than when you simply side stepped?
- Did you feel you were in a strategically better place?
- Did your movement seem to have an effect on your partner or did they seem ready to throw the next strike?

Ask them how they feel.

- Are they comfortable with how you moved or intimidated?
- Did they feel different form when you simply side stepped to avoid the strike?

Remember how side stepping felt and compare it to how this felt.

- How are they different?
- Which do you feel gives you the self-defence advantage?

Think for a moment on how two movements, basically the same (stepping to avoid a strike,) can feel so different.

Part Four

Take a moment with your partner and have them slowly throw a different strike and repeat the process:

1. First focus on the strike
2. Step to avoid
3. Visualize moving into empty space.
4. Actually fill the empty space.

Run through a number of different strikes.

Again, I believe the mind is your most powerful weapon. I truly want you to focus on visualizing it as a pocket of space and I want you to see the path from it to your position, and I want you to slip into and fill that entire pocket. I want you to fill and own that space.

This is how you should move from now on.

Let's Sum Up

This drill introduces the fact that filling empty space is something more than just footwork. Occupying empty space takes it over and owns it. You and your partner should have felt very different when you moved in and occupied empty space rather than just stepping to avoid a strike or even stepping into empty space to avoid a strike. We could call stepping into empty space Level One and occupying empty space Level Two. While Level One is good, Level Two will be more effective.

Entering and Attacking Empty Space

In filling the empty space so far, we have dealt with a straight line of incoming force. Here we are going to deal with a curved incoming line of force, specifically the looping sucker punch that is actually still a common assault today.

We're going use empty space on a looping hook punch to improve the effect of a common entry.

Part One: Seeing the Empty Space

Have your partner take a step back and throw the looping right sucker punch as you observe it from a slight distance. Feel free to move around and watch it.

Look for the empty space pocket between their arm and their body.

See that empty space.

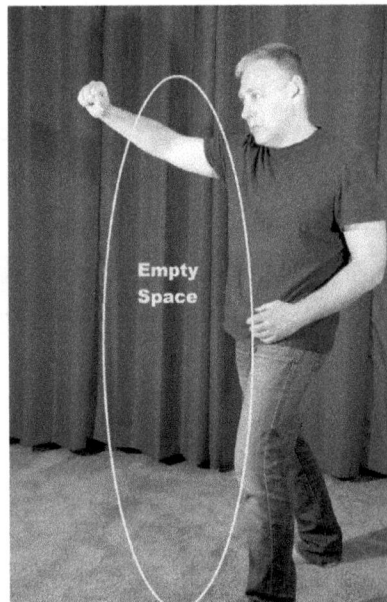

Part Two: Intercepting in the Empty Space

Now you know where the pocket of empty space is in-between the incoming arm and their body.

Stand back as your partner throws that looping right sucker punch and visualize yourself stepping in to occupy that pocket of empty space. Picture yourself stepping in and filling that pocket of empty space.

Now you need to actually do it. As the strike comes in (starting once again slowly) step into that empty space with your intercept, using a common entry described in the next section.

The Common Entry

Your partner slowly begins to throw the looping hook sucker punch (right hand) at your head.

With both arms raised in a guard position, slide forward to meet the incoming strike with your right arm impacting their right shoulder and torso, and your left arm impacting their incoming arm.

NOTE: This entry has been used by multiple styles for as long as martial arts and people fighting have been around.

Try this a few times and think about how it feels.

Try it with the strike a little harder and faster, but keep it safe.

Even though we are using the empty space pocket and filling it, this entry performed as describes meets force on force as shown in the pictures below with lines indicating where your force is going.

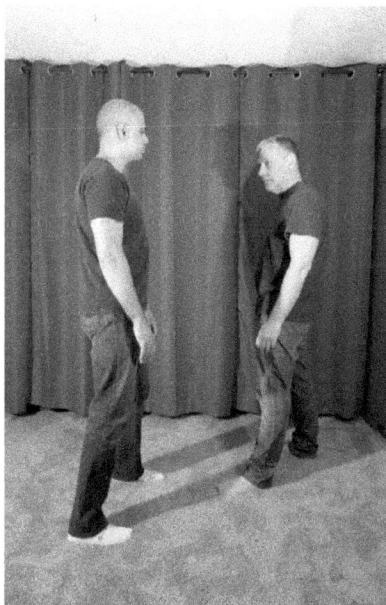

Think about how it went:

- Did you stop the incoming strike?
- Did you feel impact when you did so?
- How safe did you feel?
- How would it feel against someone much larger than you?

Picture the biggest strongest athlete you can and ask if yourself if it would work going force on force with them.

Remember your answers.

Part Three: Attacking Empty Space, Step 1

You are going to step into that empty space pocket again, but this time we want to see something else, so we are going to get your partner to help us out.

Just as in Part Two, your partner will throw a slow looping right sucker punch and you will step into the pocket of empty space and intercept it. AND THEN both of you will freeze in that spot right at the moment of intercept.

Once you are frozen at the intercept point, I want you to look and see if you are facing the attacking partner.

In the picture below, you've moved off their line of force but still the majority of the intercept is into the Aggressor's structure. We want to change that, because going into their structure means you must overcome it to survive.

ASK: Are your feet pointed at them and is your right intercepting arm pointed into their shoulder and structure?

Now, look to your left just beyond the striking arm. What do you see?

You should a bunch of empty space beyond their arm.

Rotate left so that your right arm is in contact just off the shoulder joint, so their body is not behind it, only empty space is.

You should now be facing empty space rather than your partner.

Even though we entered that pocket of empty space before and directed our force, we need to move directly towards empty space rather than driving straight into their structure; therefore, we rotate farther to truly face empty space as shown in the picture below.

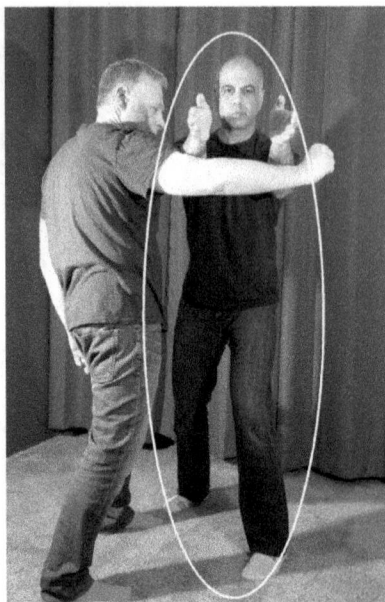

Try the incoming strike slowly again, but this time do not just move into empty space, but do it so you end facing empty space.

Try then try it with the strike faster but stay safe.

Ask yourself again the questions:

- Did you stop the incoming strike?
- Did you feel impact when you did so?
- How safe did you feel?
- How did it feel compared to Part One?

Part Four: Attacking Empty Space, Step 2

You are stepping into empty space.

You are now truly and fully facing empty space at the end of the move.

Your contact with the Aggressor's body is into empty space.

So now let's take attacking empty space to another level.

If in your intercept your hands are not open, I want you to do this with open hands.

As you come in to intercept, as you move into empty space, as you rotate to face empty space, as you contact the Aggressor, I want you to "THROW" your fingers over the contact points into empty space, very much like throwing a dart. But KEEP your elbows down.

Do not throw your arms, just throw your fingers as if you were flicking water off of them. Throw them over the arm into empty space. Keep your elbows down.

Look at this picture again and see the fingers thrown over like darts into empty space.

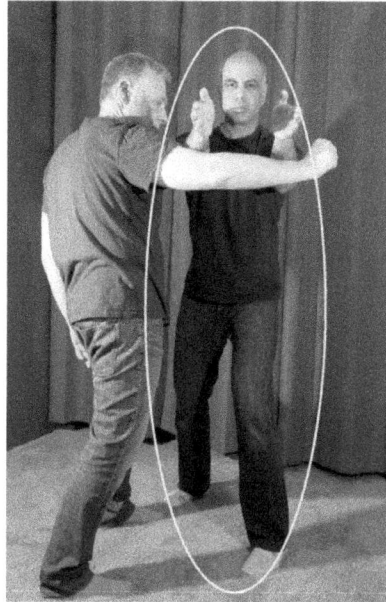

Ask yourself again the questions:

- Did you stop the incoming strike?
- Did you feel impact when you did so?
- How safe did you feel?
- How did it feel compared to what you have done so far?

Take a moment after this drill to review all the uses of empty space contained in that simple intercept.

Let's Sum Up

In this drill, we see that empty space is not only applicable to linear lines of incoming force, but also curved lines. It also introduces us to looking beyond one move using empty space and onto seeing the next action into empty space. The last part of the drill also shows that we can use moving into empty space aggressively to affect the Aggressor, attacking empty space.

Connect to Them

At this point we have introduced moving through empty space, entering and attacking through empty space and moving to occupy empty space. Now we'll look at a slightly different use of empty space.

Once we close with an Aggressor, occupying empty space, we may then need to connect to them in order to manipulate their structure.

While we will also use empty space to manipulate them (as in find the treasure and escape the maze), there is another way to use empty space to enhance any manipulation of their structure. First though, to manipulate them we need to secure connections that do not fail.

To connect to an Aggressor, or rather to a piece or part of an Aggressor, we need to make sure there is no empty space between our connector and the part of the Aggressor we are connecting to. We need to eliminate any empty space in the connection.

Part One

Same as a previous drill (Fill the Empty Space) we will have our partner slowly throw a lead hand strike at us as we move to fill the empty space on the outside of their striking arm. Once you are behind them, place your right hand on their right shoulder slightly hooking over it. If they are too tall you can also hook their hip in the same manner as illustrated for their shoulder (pictures below).

With just you hand resting on their shoulder try to feel how connected you are to them.

- Is there space between your hand and their shoulder?
- Does the connection feel loose?

In most cases, you will find there is empty space in your connection as shown in the picture below.

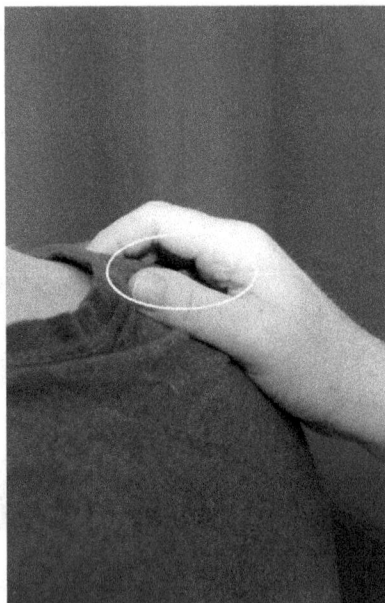

While we are not Geckos and lack their setae (foot hairs) to attach to surfaces, the thought process of how close a Gecko's foot must merge with a surface to create the intermolecular bonding of the Van Der Waal forces is something we can use. A Gecko has hundreds of tips off each setae, spread like a spatula to press to a surface and form a bond. We want to think in this same way to eliminate empty space and form a bond.

Now, hook your hand onto their shoulder. In your mind think of expanding your palm and fingers into their shoulder, not squeezing the shoulder but rather squeezing out any empty space between it and your hand. Occupy all the space between your hand and their shoulder without pushing.

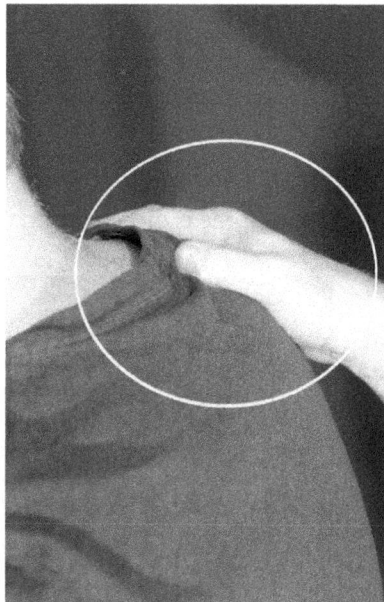

How does the connection feel now?

- Can you feel any space still between your hand and their shoulder?
- Does the connection feel more secure?

If done correctly you are making their shoulder part of your structure which, although done using empty space, leads to the principle of Bone Slaving.

> **Bone Slaving:** Bone Slaving is when we take possession of one of the Aggressor's body parts and we connect it to us, making their bones, their skeleton, our bones, and our skeleton into ONE STRUCTURE so that when we move our skeleton, theirs is moved too.

Have your partner slowly throw that lead hand as you move and fill and take over the empty space to the outside and place your hand on their shoulder, this time eliminating any empty space to form an "air tight" seal between your hand and their shoulder.

Repeat a few times.

Note this movement, while it can be done, is simply a tool to demonstrate this use of empty space and the next use of empty space. I'm not promoting it as a self-defence technique.

Part Two: Use the Empty Space All around You

Repeat the movements of the last drill, but now, once you're connected to them take a moment and press that connection into them, into their structure.

I want you to find their structure and where pulling on them goes directly into it making all your efforts pointless, thus experiencing not using empty space. Note in the picture below how when you pull along their structure all your force is directed into their base.

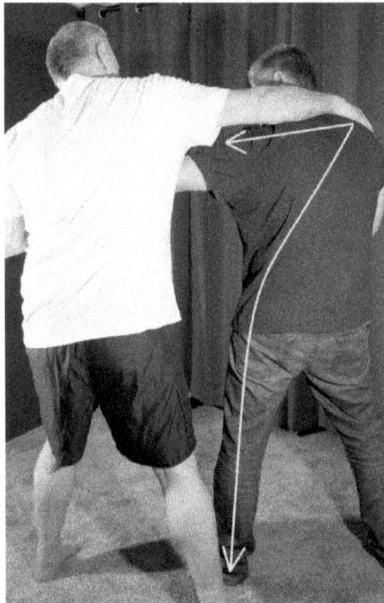

Can you feel how solid their base is?

Can you feel how hard it would be to attempt to pull them through their base?

Now take a moment to observe that behind your arm and hand and body is empty space.

Read through this before trying it: you are going to use that empty space just as you would the space between the lines of a maze. You will step back into empty space. You will bring along your arm and hand, which is now connected to their shoulder, dragging their shoulder backwards out into the empty space behind them. As you step your foot back into empty space, and as their shoulder is dragged out into empty space, pivot on your left foot to add a rotation to the step and drag.

NOTE: Do not think of pulling their shoulder. Simply step back and because they are now part of you (Bone Slaved) and you are moving into empty space they will come without effort.

CAUTION: Hang on to your partner as you may be surprised at how quickly they are moved.

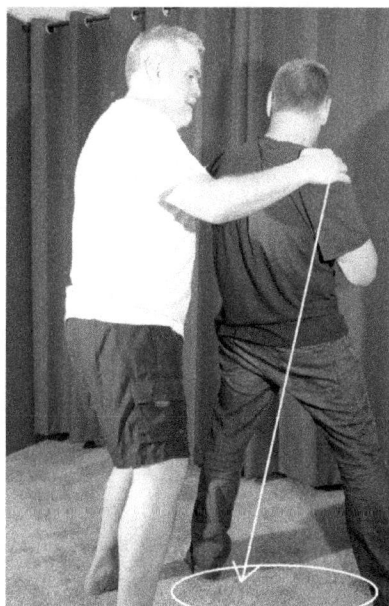

Let's Sum Up

When we talk about using empty space, we mean to make as much use of empty space as we can to gain any advantage, to increase our efficiency and our effectiveness. By eliminating the small amount of empty space in our connection to the Aggressor we find another use of empty space. It is an action we want to think of like that of a Gecko sticking to a wall. Once we have that connection we can move again into empty space, manipulating the Aggressor's structure as we move. This is where we begin to see stacking the uses of empty space. Not complicated, as the same movements simply make use of multiple applications of empty space.

Stepping Into Empty Space

In the previous chapter, we worked on connecting to the Aggressor. Now we want to use that as we show why ending facing empty space can prevent you from becoming entangled, by allowing you to immediately move into empty space.

Let's return to the movements we have already performed and see two different applications of stepping into the empty space we are facing.

Lead Hand

Your partner slides in with that committed lead hand strike and we fill the empty space beside it, but this time not as deep as we did in "Connect To Them". We still step to the outside of their right arm, but this time we have stepped only far enough that our left arm is at their right shoulder.

NOTE: Leaving the arm extended to work this principle is not real and is only to illustrate this use of empty space because if a striker is smart, they will never leave their arm, they will always retract it. (There are ways to catch and trap that lead hand strike, but that's for another book.)

You are at the outside of their right arm facing empty space.

Connect to their arm with your hands. Remember to connect by taking empty space out.

Carefully and slowly step into the empty space in front of you, right through their arm.

If you do this correctly you will be placing an arm bar on their arm. Careful not to hyper-extend your partner's elbow and injure them in this drill. They are cooperating.

Here we have used moving into empty space after connecting with the Aggressor's body to manipulate them by going directly through that body part. Since the arm had no structure to block your step, it should have been easy to manipulate the arm and therefore the Aggressor.

Look at the stacking of empty space use:

- Your left arm (closest to them) is shearing (cutting) over their arm into empty space. (Highlighted in the picture below by my pointing with the index finger.)
- Your left arm is coming back towards you but shearing (cutting) over the arm into empty space. (Highlighted in the picture by my pointing with the thumb.)
- You are stepping with your centre into empty space.

Shearing: Shearing is cutting through a piece of the Aggressor. Moving an oblique angled force like a wedge (which is driving through part of the Aggressor to empty space.)

All this happens in one sequence which ends with you rotating into empty space and dropping your partner to the ground with the extended arm bar.

Here is the sequence again without out the helpful but incorrect hand positioning. (Note the shearing or cutting is done with the edges of the wrist and not the flat portions.)

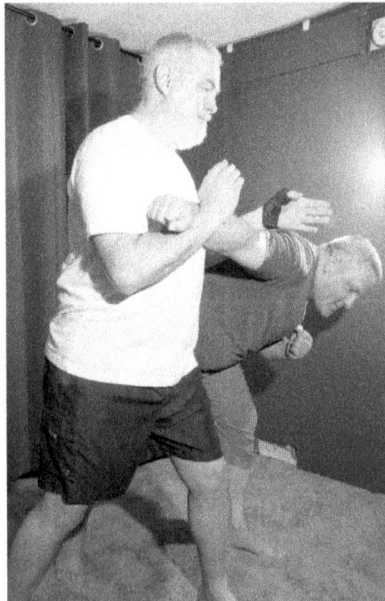

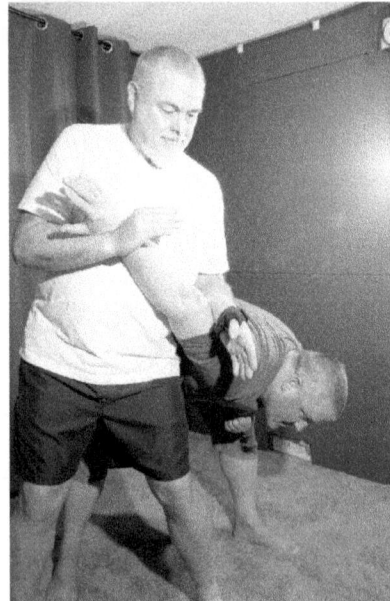

Looping Sucker Punch

Now let's return to that looping sucker punch and the intercept using empty space.

We left it where you are stepping into the empty space between the Aggressor and their arm. You ended facing empty space, and you have thrown your fingers over into empty space using it to attack.

You are now in contact with the Aggressor and facing empty space.

You are facing empty space and you are connected to their arm, so now you will use both those factors.

Since we are facing empty space we are simply going to step forward into it. Because we are moving into empty space you should be able to do it with ease.

Once again, look at all the empty space being used:

- Your arms are shearing into empty space.
- You are stepping into space.

Your left hand folds over and traps the Aggressor's arm. Your right arm moves forward and shears (cuts) through their right arm at the elbow joint.

BUT, let's not forget you are connected to their arm and their arm is between you and empty space.

Because you are connected to their arm, as you step into empty space, rotate to your left which pulls the Aggressor off their base and they will drop into empty space (fall.)

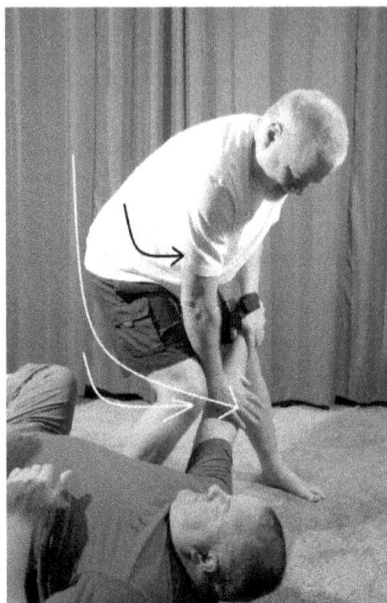

Let's Sum Up

We have learned that connecting to the Aggressor and then stepping, whether backwards or forwards, into empty space moves them. We have learned we can step through their arm, through empty space to further manipulate the Aggressor. It makes sense then to end our movements whenever possible facing empty space, because it makes the next logical step to be into that empty space. If we end facing the Aggressor, we often find our next move is directly into them and we will become entangled and end up in a force on force struggle. By ending facing empty space we avoid becoming entangled.

Get Out of Blind Alleys

This topic needs to be covered before we move further on and remembered for the balance of the journey so let's consider this another Interlude Drill.

If you recall the guidelines for solving a maze the second one was:

> If you hit a blind alley back out and go somewhere else.

This is an important concept for using empty space because sometimes we err and do not go into empty space and sometimes the Aggressor shifts on us blocking our use of empty space. Stuff happens in chaos, or luck rears its head, and if we do not recognize that we've lost the use of empty space immediately, then we make futile attempts to make something work that has a lower percentage chance to do so. We need to learn to feel that empty space has gone — we've hit the blind alley in the maze — and must abandon that path and move on.

Drill: Get out of Blind Alleys

Have your partner throw a left lead hand strike.

As they throw the lead strike move into the empty space on the outside of their left arm beside and behind them (occupy it) just as we have before in Fill the Empty Space.

Use your right hand to connect to their shoulder (or hip if they are too tall), just as you practiced in the chapter on "Connect to Them" by removing empty space between your hand and their shoulder (or hip.)

NOW, consciously press that connection into them, into their structure attempting to move them by forcing them through their structure.

I have tried to highlight the running into a wall in the picture below by adding the "wall" visually.

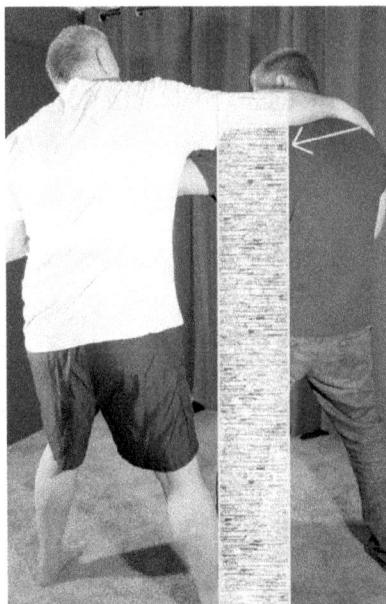

The moment you feel that resistance of moving into their structure IMMEDIATELY change your movement and step back into empty space taking them with you.

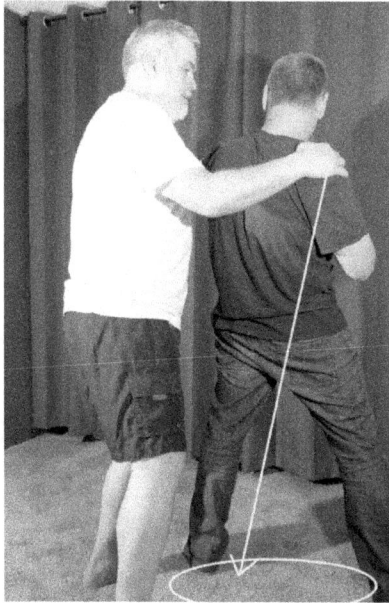

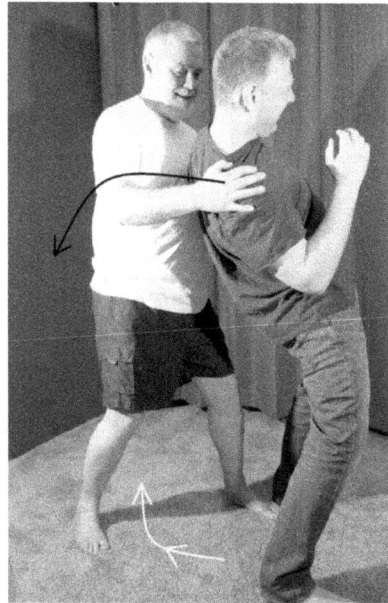

Work it a few times to begin to sense immediately when you've hit that blind alley and learn to let it go and switch to a better direction into empty space. Focus on the speed at which you feel resistance and change from pulling into their structure to taking them into empty space.

Focus on learning that pulling their shoulder into their structure is like moving into a blind alley of a maze. You don't stand there wondering if it will change or hoping that the alley will magically open up giving you a path way. No, you simply back out quickly and look for empty space to move through.

It is the same when manipulating a structure. If you begin to move and they don't, and you feel that resistance, then you have mistakenly moved into their structure. Rather than trying to overcome it with strength, simply redirect and move into empty space. This will become much more important now as we expand manipulating their structure.

Let's Sum Up

This drill highlights training to quickly abandon attempting to move someone through their structure, because the chances of success have dropped. We need to immediately back out of blind alleys and find another path to empty space.

Voids

Human beings are bipedal; therefore, no matter how they stand they will have voids, or unbalance points created by empty space.

What is a void?

Void: An area where the person has no brace, spots of empty space on the ground.

When we are standing, a brace is usually a leg.

When on the ground, a brace is any part of our body in contact with the ground.

If you press into a person, into their structure, a brace, they are stable and can inhibit you from moving them. (Recall the feeling from the last Chapter on Getting Out of Blind Alleys.)

If you press them into empty space, then they must move. If we do this correctly they will fall, and we want them to fall into a void.

We want to move their centre off their base, which disrupts their balance, either allowing us to take them down or to create a moment where they are distracted enough for us to strike.

Of course, the best strikes take place AS you disrupt their balance.

There are two types of voids.

Major Void: Major Voids are found in front and behind the braces. These are areas where the Aggressor cannot brace themselves unless they move their brace. Major Voids are the most easily accessed.

Minor Voids: Minor Voids are areas out to the side of your base, past a brace and off the base area. To make use of these voids you MUST move the Aggressor's centre off their base and out over a Minor Void. These are not as easily accessed as a Major Void because it requires that you move the Aggressor's centre first.

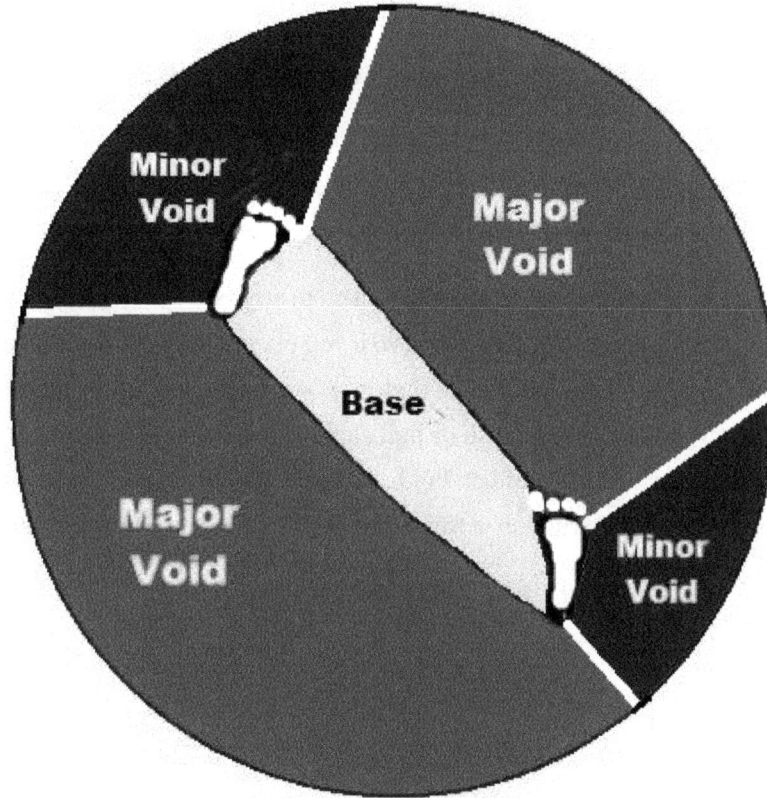

Drill One: Identifying the Major and Minor Void Change Over Points

The first part of training voids is to learn how to recognize where the Major Voids are.

To do this you must first feel the difference and change-over points from a Major Void to a Minor Void.

Have a partner take a neutral stance (feet about shoulder width apart beside each other.)

Up until now we have separated trying to do things without empty space and with empty space, but for this drill they will be mixed. You are looking for the differences.

Start right in front of your partner and lightly push on them. The person being pushed is not fighting back. They will NOT shift to prevent the push. They are simply the "Meat Puppets" for this drill.

Try it.

Work your way all around your partner.

Where did they move the easiest and where it was hard to move them?

Take a moment to consider what you learned.

How to Take Advantage of the Major Voids

Here is a quick way to see where to press or pull on to access the Major Void and to take advantage of it. As we said, people stand on two legs, so if you place a stick (or draw a line) from one foot to another and then, from the middle of that line, at 90 degrees draw another line straight out (perpendicular) you can simply push or pull along that perpendicular line. If they do nothing to adjust they will move into the Major Void. This will also be important later in the chapters on Moving the Treasure, Destruction of Structure, and Striking into Empty Space.

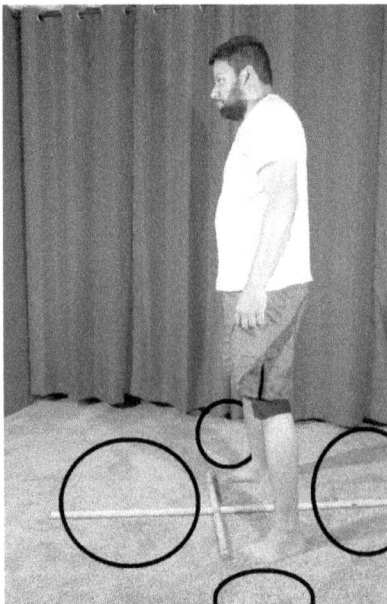

Here, if Adam does not move his feet it is very easy to topple him over by pressing along that 90 degree line to his base as shown below.

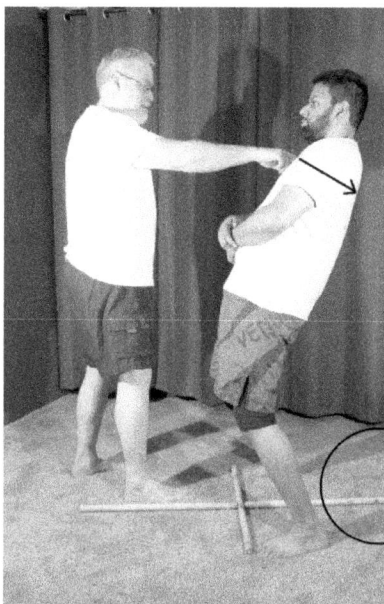

Move behind your partner and push them forward. Again, note how easily they are moved.

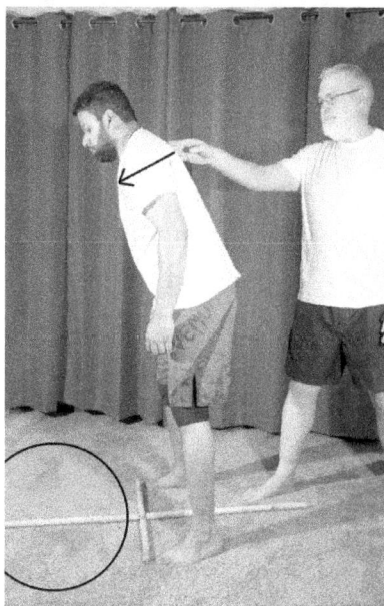

Take note that the push above was along the 90 degrees line to their base. This is important, because it enhances using those Major Voids.

In application using the Major Void, you use empty space to move your partner off their structure and over the front or rear Major Void, and then continue to rotate your body and arms to let gravity take them into that void.

Here is the mental aspect I want you to use for this. I want you to think of those Major Voids, both front and back, as whirlpools or sink holes depending on which visualization works best for you.

When you intend to use those voids for a take-down (as we will in the next chapter) I want you to think of those voids as drawing you to them and sucking your partner into them.

How to Take Advantage of the Minor Voids

Move to one side of your partner and push into their structure to feel the block of resistance.

Pushing them towards a Minor Void meets with resistance and shouldn't move them at all without a lot of force being applied.

While it is preferable to dump a person into the easier Major Void, you can make use of the Minor Voids by using empty space to manipulate our partner's structure to access them.

The problem with pressing towards a Minor Void is their leg. We have to get them up onto and then over that leg before we can dump them into the Minor Void. Press up on your partner's arm into the empty space just above their head and keep pressing until you feel them balanced on that leg and begin to extend out over the Minor Void.

Here you won't use the visualization of a whirlpool or sink hole but rather a cliff.

The Minor Void is a cliff, but you have this protective barrier in our way. Just as they have protective barriers in place at the Grand Canyon to stop people from going over, your partner's leg is a protective barrier stopping you from throwing or pulling them off the cliff.

What do you need to do to get them over that barrier?

1. Raise their centre.
2. Move their centre over their brace and out over the Minor Void.
3. Pull or push to drop them off the cliff and into the Minor Void.

To use a pull into empty space to get them over the barrier you only have to think of it like shoving or pulling them off a cliff.

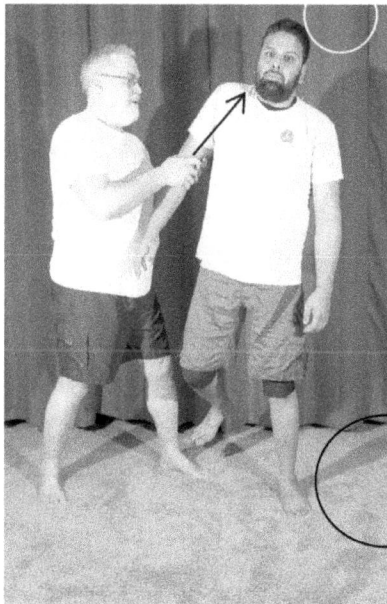

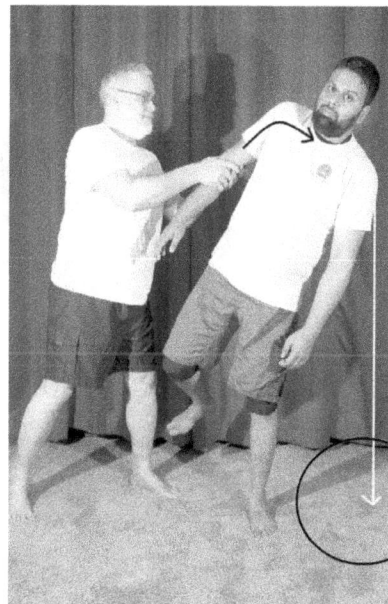

Move to the other side and repeat first pressing into their structure.

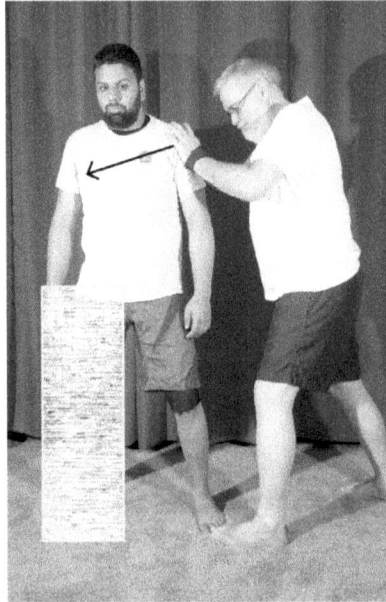

And then pushing up into the empty space just above their head bringing them onto their leg and out over the Minor Void.

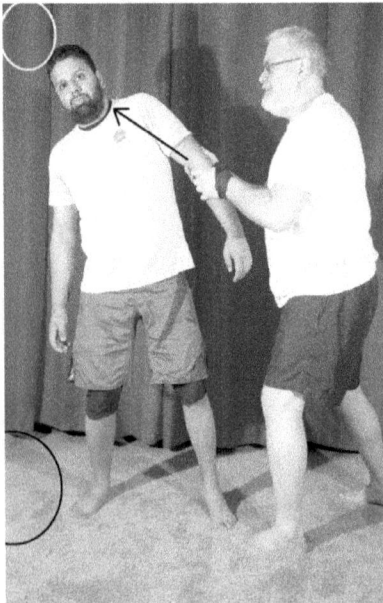

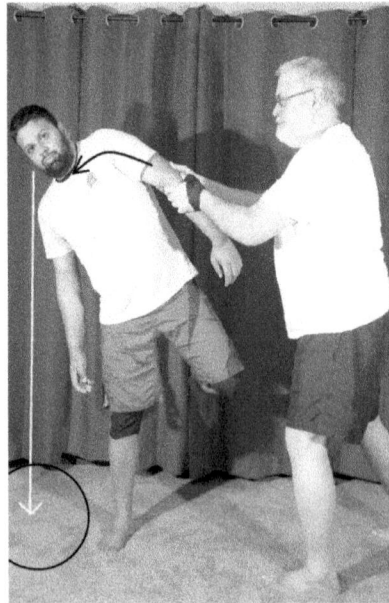

Drill Two: Repeat This Drill Pulling on Your Partner

Start right in front of your partner and lightly pull on them. The person being pulled is not fighting back. They will NOT shift to prevent the pull. They are simply the "Meat Puppets" for this drill.

Move around your partner inch by inch pulling on them and feel where they move easily and where they do not.

You should find that pulling into the Major Void is easy and you are moving them into empty space.

Pulling them towards a Minor Void should meet with resistance and shouldn't move them at all without a lot of force being applied.

But, if when pulling towards a Minor Void you pull them UP onto the bracing leg first then they will more easily be pulled into the Minor Void. (Up and over the barrier and over the cliff.)

Continue pulling and note the angles on your partner's stance when things become easy.

I hope everyone noted that when you pull up or push up you are doing so into empty space....

Let's Sum Up

Voids are pocket, or target areas, of empty space that we can use to take an Aggressor down. Knowing where the Major and Minor Voids are is required for takedowns, but you also need to know how to use them and how to mentally enhance that use through the visualization of whirlpools and cliffs.

Moving the Treasure through Empty Space

In some games of the maze, when you move through empty space to find a treasure, once you've found it you have to escape with it. You use empty space to get to the treasure and then you use empty space to move it, and, of course, you use empty space to then escape. A trifecta of empty space use.

We have begun to look at manipulating the Aggressor by attaching to a piece of them, eliminating empty space to make that connection even better and then using empty space to move both ourselves and the part of the Aggressor we have attached to. Here we'll take a closer look at that.

There are ways to set up the situations and positioning we're going to use, but for now we won't do anything dynamic. We will simply take the position needed. There are many ways we could end up in these positions.

Drill One: Elbow Take-down

Part One

As always, we need to experience trying to do an elbow take-down without using empty space.

Have your partner stand in front of you with their arms at their sides.

Bend their right arm up at the elbow to 90 degrees.

You can use the Clamp from my book *Watch Out For The Pointy End* (as shown in the pictures below) or grip their wrist with your left hand and place your right forearm over the inside of their elbow joint.

Put your weight onto your right forearm and drop it onto their elbow joint.

Pull down directly into their structure (their structure is represented by the block out area in the picture below because it is like trying to pull them through a solid block.)

Examine what happened and what both of you experienced.

- Did you manipulate their structure at all?
- If you did, did it take effort and strength?
- How did they feel about your attempt?

Keep that result in mind and now try it a different way.

Part Two

You can use the Clamp from my book *Watch Out For The Pointy End* (as shown in the pictures below) or grip their wrist with your left hand, place your right forearm over the inside of their elbow joint again.

Begin to step backwards into empty space taking their arm with (remember you've connected to it) you. Pull it along, extending it out into empty space away from their body.

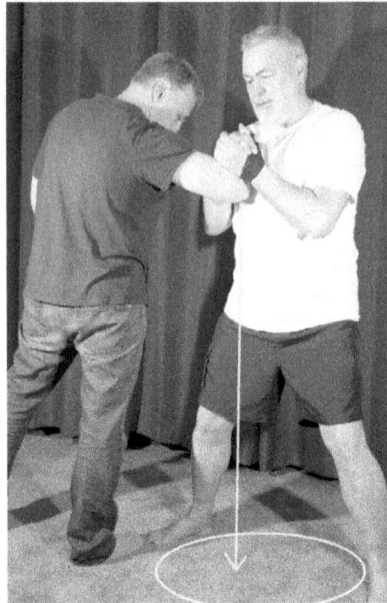

If you do this slowly you will see two things:

1. Empty space will begin to appear between their elbow and their body which means it is disconnecting from their structure.
2. As you step back, taking their arm with you, it will extend out away from their body and over empty space, a Minor Void. You have them hanging out over the cliff.

You need to see empty space between their elbow and their torso, and empty space beneath their arm.

When you see that their arm has been extended away from their body then their elbow should no longer have their structure under it. Their elbow is now out over the Minor Void.

Continue your step back into empty space and now press (drop) your weight onto their elbow down into that empty space of the Minor Void. You can add a rotation to your left as you drop onto the elbow.

If you simply take an elongated step backwards, the drop onto the arm will happen because your centre has dropped due to the lengthening of your stance.

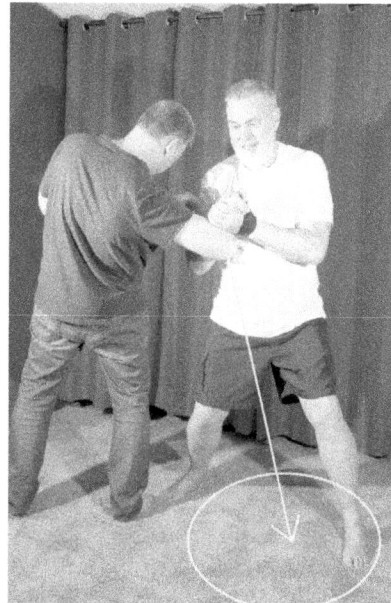

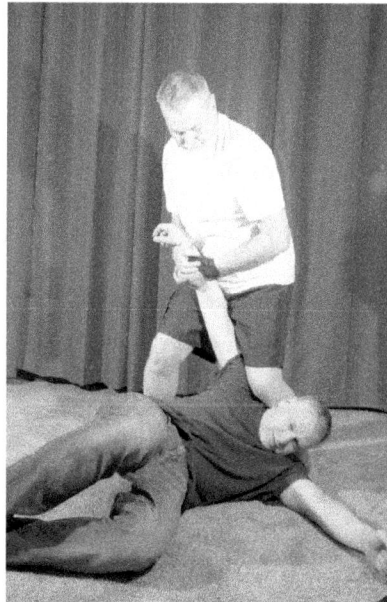

Examine what happened and what both of you experienced.

- What happened to their structure?
- Did they go down?
- Did it take effort?

- How did your partner feel?
- How did it compare to your first attempt where you did not use empty space?

This is our first example of using empty space to manipulate the Aggressor's structure.

Drill Two: Head and Arm Take-down

Let's look at another take-down, but this time we run into a problem, in that we are standing right where we need empty space to be.

Part One

The Head and Arm Take-down is a simple maneuver. You hook behind the head with a hand (e.g. your right) and with your other hand (e.g. your left) you grip their wrist (e.g. their right arm's wrist.)

Now you simply, and simultaneously, move your right hand to six o'clock on a clock face and your left hand to twelve o'clock on a clock face. This action drops their head downward and launches their arm upwards creating a spiral that can, if done correctly, take them down.

Once again let's try it without implementing empty space.

Step close to your partner and put your hands in position and attempt the movement.

NOTE: Remember we are just getting into this position to show how empty space can be used; however, if you think back to the entry on that looping sucker punch you can see how you might end up in this position.

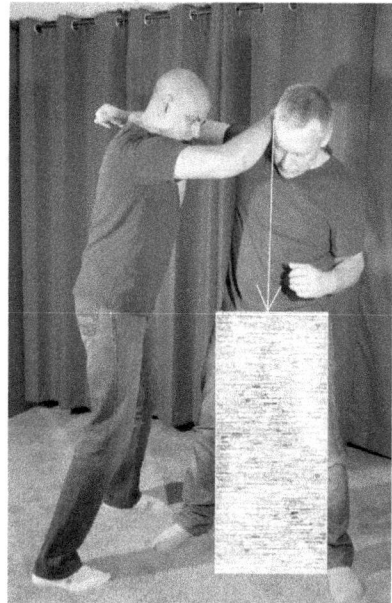

Examine what happened and what both of you experienced.

- Did it work?
- Did you meet resistance?
- What stopped you if it failed?
- If it worked did it take effort?
- How did your partner feel as you tried this?

There are a number of resistant points you may have found:

1. The head was hard to move.
2. The arm was hard to move.
3. Once you started to move the head and arm it was still hard to press the head down because you were in the way.

These three points will be eliminated by using empty space.

We are going to perform this in one easy step, and I do mean step.

Part Two

We are going to use empty space on every part of this to make it much easier to perform.

I am going to describe what needs to be done, but everything needs to happen simultaneously.

You are going to take your right foot and step backwards, rotating to your right into the empty space behind you, and then (if necessary) take another step back with your left foot. (If you happen to have your back against a wall for some reason then move; this isn't the take-down for that situation.)

As you step back, your right hand which is hooked behind their head (from their right side) is going to move in a horizontal line which will move the head off their torso and into empty space.

NOTE: One mistake often in this take down is to immediately try to drag the head down. Don't. Instead the first movement should be not downward but horizontal to move the head forward and off its structure. (This is just like when we moved the elbow out and away from the body to get it off structure.)

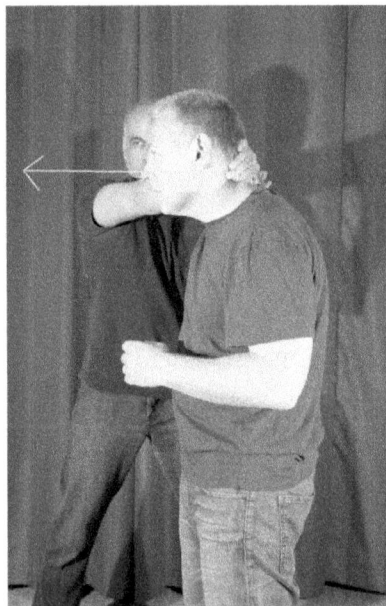

As you step back your left arm will press forward, to your partner's rear, which will move their right arm out into empty space, again taking it off structure

As well, you will be vacating the space in front of your partner opening a hole of empty space, a Front Major Void.

As you step back, rotate your arms moving your right to six o'clock on the clock face and your left to twelve o'clock on the clock face. Move them through the empty space you have created. Note the first picture the light circle on the floor is the original empty space but as you step back you enlarge it represented by the dark line. That is your target – the Major Void, the whirlpool you want to drop them into.

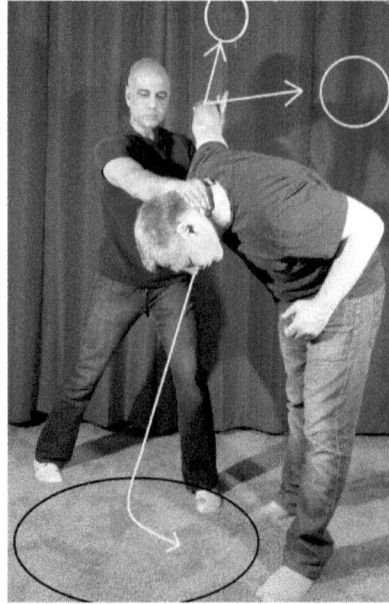

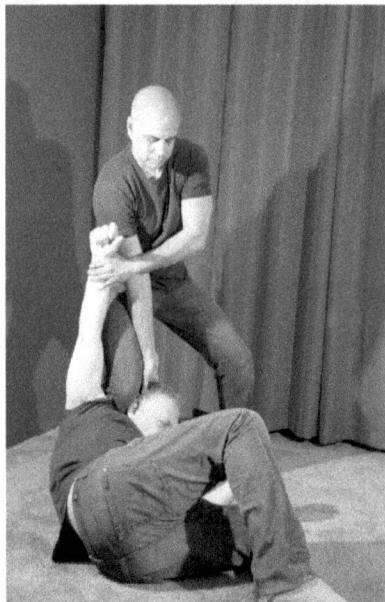

Now, did they spiral and go down?

Did you feel the same resistance as before?

Moving the head and the arm into empty space and off their torso removed their ability to use body strength and structure to resist. By vacating the spot in front of them you created empty space to drop them into.

Compare the two attempts and work on them slowly so you can feel where there is resistance and where there is not.

How did your partner feel this time?

If we need to use empty space sometimes we need to move ourselves and create it.

Drill Three: Head Take-down

There is a take-down taught in some security courses that works but takes effort. If we alter it to use empty space, then that effort disappears.

Part One

Your partner has, due to circumstances (perhaps a body blow), been bent over in front of you.

One take-down that is taught is to grip the head and press it down towards their feet into their structure.

What happens in this take down is the press overloads their structure (sometimes painfully) and they collapse. The problem is because you are overloading their structure it takes pressure and power and if you do not have enough to overwhelm their structure (they are bigger and stronger) then it can fail. It also requires them to be able to remove their structure in a way that allows them to collapse.

There is also a danger (perhaps of liability) that you can damage their neck.

Try it but be careful of your partner's neck.

Once again, the image of a block has been added to the photos below to show your partner's structure.

Examine what happened and what both of you experienced.

- How did it feel?
- Did you succeed? Try a few different sized partners.
- Was it easy or did you have to use strength?
- How did they feel as you tried?

Part Two

Okay now let us alter this so we can use empty space from this position to achieve the goal of putting them on the ground.

Again, your partner has ended up bent over in front of you and you grip their head.

Instead of pressing into their structure we will use empty space.

Stepping backwards you pull their head forward and off their structure. Once again, the first moments of your movement should pull the head along a horizontal line and off their base (their structure.)

You have now elongated them out and off their base over empty space, the Front Major Void, just as we did their arm in the elbow take down but this time with their torso and using a Major Void instead of a Minor Void.

Continue to step back and begin pulling their head on an angle to the floor. Keep stepping back and pulling to the floor through empty space until they are taken down. Let that Whirlpool of the Major Void suck them in and to the ground.

Examine what happened and what both of you experienced.

- How did that feel?
- Did you succeed?
- Was it easy?
- Was it easier than the other take-down?
- How did your partner feel this time?

Did you note how we once again removed ourselves to open the empty space we needed just as in the Head and Arm take-down?

Note: I am not saying if that other take-down works for you to stop using it. I am giving an alternative using empty space particularly for those who find that take-down hard, or impossible, to do on a larger person.

Drill Four: Arm Clear

Let's bring back that looping sucker punch where previously we stepped through their arm to manipulate the Aggressor. We could do that again, but this time we will move the arm through empty space to manipulate them.

Therefore, rather than step through the arm we are going to use the fact that it is extended and therefore is over empty space and we can grab that treasure to drive it downward and to our right.

As we drive the arm down and to the right by rotating, our rotation also moves us out of the way. We then step to empty space and rotate in the direction we are manipulating their arm.

Note the circle indicating the empty space you are going to move the arm through as you rotate.

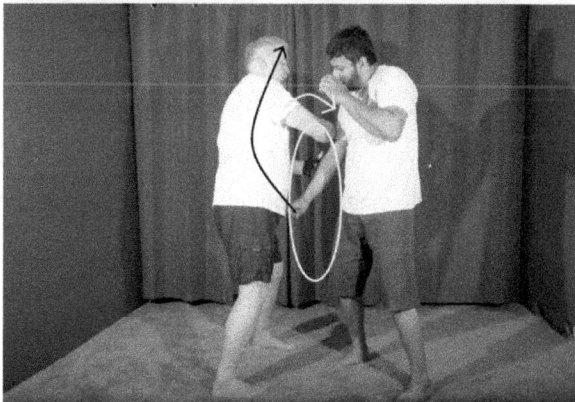

If done correctly you will find that driving the arm down and to the right as we step into empty space and rotate to our right, we will not only move the Aggressor's arm, but often the Aggressor's body as well. Regardless of if they moved, we have moved to the outside and into a strategically better position with this action.

As you sweep their arm, keep it moving upwards which opens the space between you and you can fill that space as you move in.

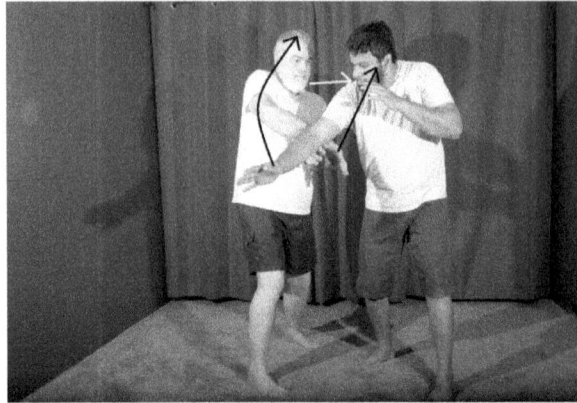

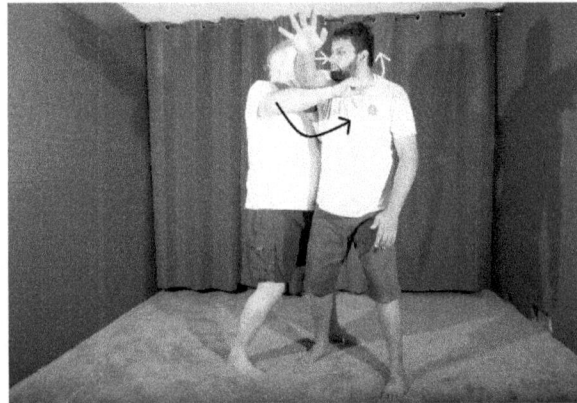

Once you have the positional advantage you can choose how to end the encounter: escape, strike or manipulate and control. In the example below, you use the momentum to slip in and apply a head and arm choke.

Let's Sum Up

In this section, we looked at a few important issues. When we want to move the Aggressor, we do so by taking them into empty space. If where we want to take them is already occupied by us, then we move out of the way and open up the empty space we need.

We also introduced something very important. I have found that often those teaching self defence are bigger stronger men and that may be because some of the professions that require self-defence attract big strong guys. However, being big and strong can (not always) mean strength is a part of the techniques used. What we learned here was, if we are struggling with making a particular, or mandated, technique work, it may be because the way it is being done requires strength. To have the technique succeed we need to look at it to see where we can use empty space to make it work or to adapt it into to something that works for us.

Leading into Empty Space

We are not going to go into details on the principle of leading, but we will touch on it here because this principle makes use of empty space. In fact, without using empty space, you cannot lead.

Leading is done by making the Aggressor do more than they want to do.

Drill One: Hand Pad

A simple example of leading can be done by holding a hand pad and having your partner slide forward and strike the pad as hard as they can.

In fact, have them do that a number of times: slide forward hit the hand pad as hard as they can, step back and reset and repeat.

At some point, just as they are about to hit the pad begin to move it, keeping it slightly ahead of the strike. (This can be done by rotating away from the strike.)

You are rotating into empty space and continuing to move the pad into and through empty space.

Observe what happens to the partner throwing the strike.

Most often they keep trying to catch up to the pad to the point of over extending themselves and taking themselves off balance.

You can see in the pictures above how overextending can disrupt their structure and positioning.

People like to be successful. When they have almost hit the pad, they have the tendency to really want to hit it, and therefore keep going past the point they should.

Simple enough right? You certainly need timing to lead and not get hit (the hand pad of course could represent your face), but what else do you need?

Why, yes empty space.

To lead you must move, to move you need empty space. If you cannot move you cannot lead; therefore, to lead you need empty space.

Leading is done by allowing the part of you that you want to lead to "fall" into empty space. Thinking of that pad falling back and around into empty space is a handy visualization you might want to play with.

This is one of the elements in my book on knife defence. When there is a real intent to stab and you begin to move ahead and out of the way of the strike then the person tends (nothing is 100% guaranteed) to follow and go farther than they wanted. At least, when the person attacking with the knife has an actual intent to stab and not to "point spar."

Drill Two: Avoid the Pointy End

Watch the leading into empty space used in the example below. (Here, I also rotate myself into empty space to avoid the knife.)

Note: If you want to know what to do next after you have avoided the knife, see my book *Watch Out For The Pointy End*.

Let's Sum Up

While leading is a principle unto itself, it cannot be done without empty space to fall into. The thought of falling into empty space to lead is a very useful one when learning what leading feels like.

Working in Close Quarters and a Jar of Marbles

Now we are going to take this into a more realistic assault distance. Most assaults happen up close and personal. So, we are going to step in and look at the empty space that exists even when you are in bad breath range and how we can use it for self defence.

These are the first steps in close quarters and we will adjust and improve as we progress in this book.

There will be two aspects of empty space covered as we deal with close quarters in this chapter:

1. Using empty space as always to strike, move and manipulate.

2. Eliminating empty space to control.

We'll start with using empty space to strike.

Drill One: Striking

The first thing we need to do is once again experience this as not using empty space.

Part One

Clinch up with your partner in bad breath range in any manner.

I want one person to follow the instructions and the other to just be a meat puppet for now, alternate and each take a turn.

One partner maintains one hook and guard position and then simply freezes in space and doesn't move.

The other person focuses on the hook and the guard position. Focus on them and think about how they are right there.

Now try to strike. (You can release your hook to strike.)

- How did it feel?
- Was it hard?
- Did you find your focus on the hook and the guard drew you to them?

Remember there are no correct answers to these questions because the answers are what you felt or didn't feel.

Part Two

Now, take the same positions only this time pause a moment to see that although you are close to your partner there is still empty space between you. There is still empty space to your partner's guard hand side. You still have empty space to strike through.

Take the time to see the empty space and then keep focused on the empty space.

Their hook, their guard are irrelevant to you moving through empty space.

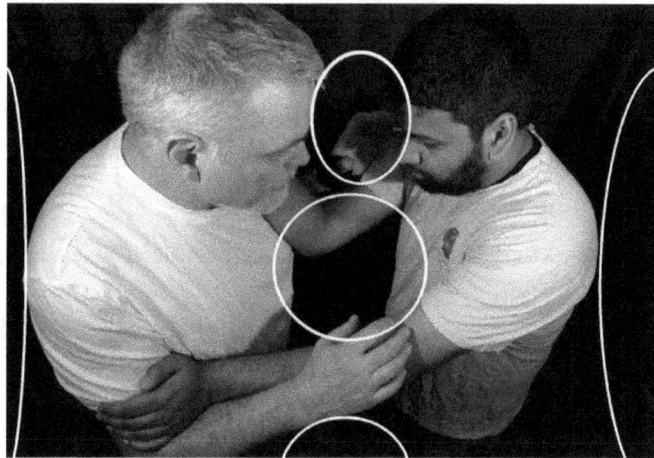

You can release your hook to strike

See your target, see the empty space, see your path to your target, strike your target through empty space. Don't be afraid to move and open that path of empty space wider.

Play with it.

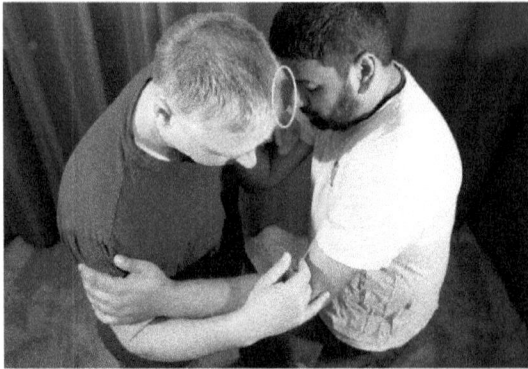
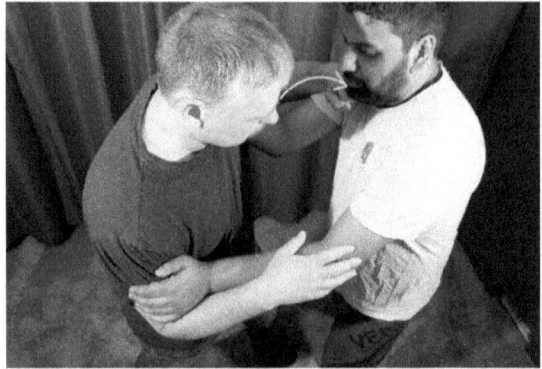
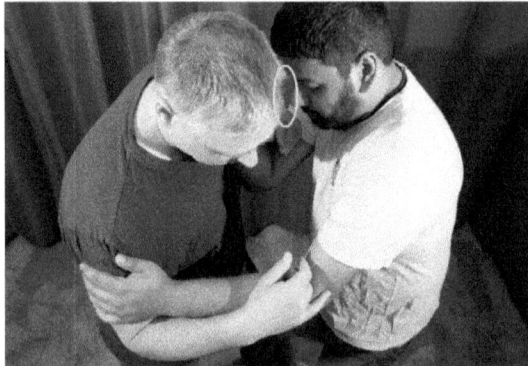
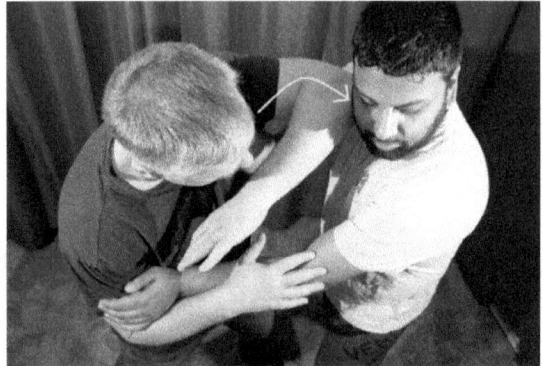
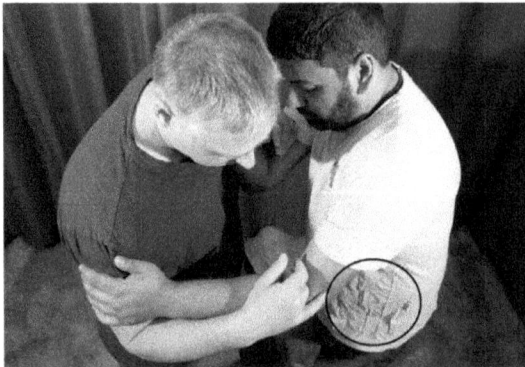
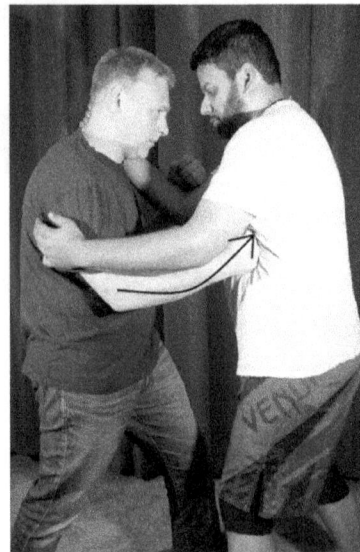

Think about how it went.

- How did it feel?
- Was it hard, as hard to strike as before, or easier?
- Did you find your focus on empty space drew you to it?

You should find that once you realize the Aggressor's structure is just like the lines of a maze then all you have to do is stop focusing on them to see the paths of empty space to your targets.

Drill Two: Move and Strike

Part One

Take the same clinch position.

Focus again on their hook and their guard.

Keep your focus on their hook and guard and try to move and strike at targets. Just as before rotate and try to touch targets on every rotation.

- How did it feel?
- Did you feel constrained?
- Did it feel limited?
- Did you think to move?

Once we clinch with a person we often become entangled in their lines of the maze and forget that nothing says we cannot move through the maze. We get to move!

Part Two

Take the same clinch position. Play with moving through empty space and finding targets. This time their maze lines are irrelevant to you. Simply see the space all around you can move in and how that opens up even more space for you to strike through.

Don't be afraid to move yourself to open up that empty space into a wider pathway.

Remember you can release your hooking hand. Remember you have more tools to strike with than your hands. Elbows can roll over barriers through empty space to strike.

Use the same movement as you did a moment ago but simply use that movement to strike through empty space. Move, rotate, strike. Touch targets on every rotation.

- How did that feel?
- Was it easier?
- Did it become even easier once you began to move?

Look at the clinch in the picture below. While we are close there is a lot of space I can actually rotate in and through. Even though we are close there are a lot of different paths to strike.

The lines on the floor in the pictures below show the direction you want to (then have) rotated.

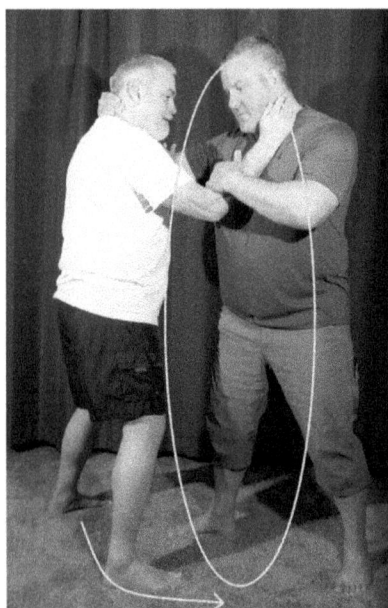

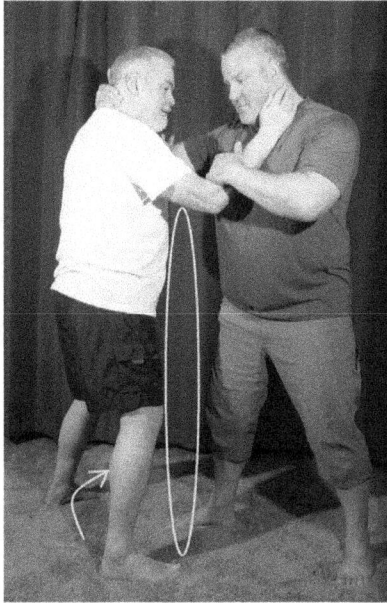

As you can see from the pictures above, you can rotate and strike because, even though you are close, there is space.

Drill Three: Move and Manipulate

Clinch with your partner again and connect to part of them, then move yourself and that piece of them through empty space to disrupt their balance.

The same empty space can be used to rotate and affect the Aggressor's structure. Notice that this time you are not only moving yourself through empty space but also a piece of the Aggressor.

A small note on the manipulation above: you can see in the pictures that I fully rotated to empty space, which also takes his elbow to empty space. If you do not then you are still fighting their structure and that move will either fail or require strength to pull off.

Think over these results before we add to the drill and then move on to the second way to use empty space in close quarters.

Drill Four: Putting It All Together in Movement

We are going to repeat moving and striking, adding in one factor.

Before we get there, I need to stress this drill is to be done slowly.

One partner is hooking and holding, the other partner (the meat puppet) has the toughest job here. Because we are moving slowly they would be able to stop anything their partner is doing, but that isn't the drill.

In this drill, they are to be annoying with the hook and move the guard hand around BUT not in a deliberate attempt to block their partner's strike.

The partner doing the moving and striking has to STAY SLOW because if they exceed a fight response speed the meat puppet will (and should) respond by blocking and we do not want that.

We will, of course do the drill two different ways.

Part One

Take a moment to see the obstacles and barriers they have placed on you and between you. Stay focused on them. As they move you focus on what they are doing and placing in your path as you move around and strike.

Reflect on how that went.

Part Two

Pause and take a moment to see the empty space between you, around you, and stay focused on the empty space. As they move focus on the empty space that still exists or is being created by their movement as you move around and strike.

The interference and the moving guard add back in a slight touch of reality for you to ignore and be indifferent to as you focus on empty space.

Drill Five: Eliminating Empty Space to Gain Control

We have talked about moving through, into and filling empty space when we move, and now we are going to take that farther in close quarters to gain control over a clinched position.

Part One

Take the same clench position and without getting into a Sumo match use slight pressure on each other to feel the level of control you each have.

Take a moment to note the level of control you had and how it felt.

Now we will engage your mind again.

Part Two

Picture a jar filled with marbles. The sides of the jar represent you and your partner, and the marbles represent the connections between the two of you.

In between all the marbles is empty space. Control lies in this empty space.

Imagine pouring a thick liquid into the jar slowly (whatever works for you honey, syrup, molasses, oil, and so on. I like honey.) Watch how it seeps and oozes into the empty space between the marbles until it fills all the empty space.

Take the clinch position again.

You (only one of you) are going to visualize that jar of marbles and that your partner is part of that jar. Feel all the empty space between the marbles.

Now close in on your partner playing the role of the honey seeping into the empty space. Fill that empty space.

It is important to note that the honey doesn't move the marbles. Instead, it fills in the spaces. You must take the same approach. You are not trying to move the Aggressor; you are trying to fill the spaces in between the marbles (you and your partner) without alarming them.

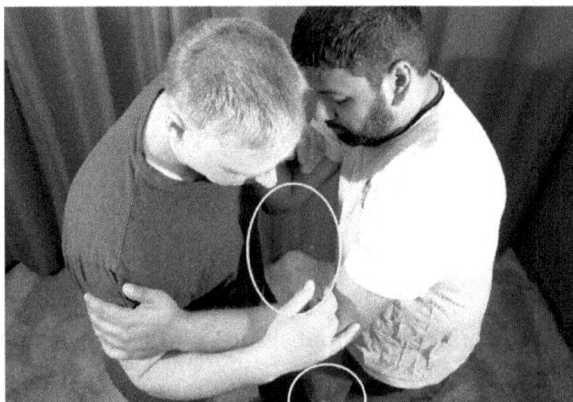

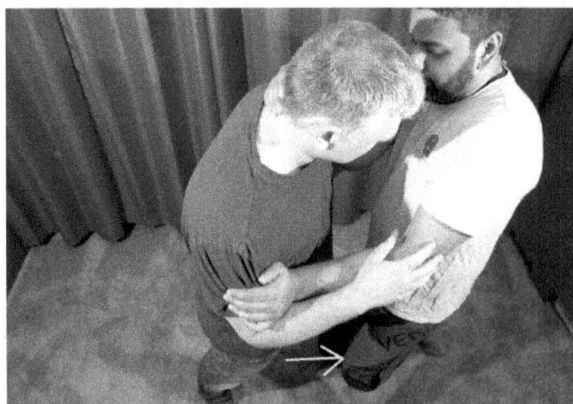

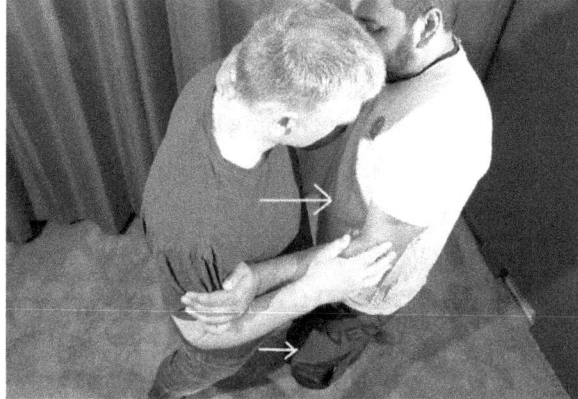

Now, once you have filled that jar of marbles with honey — slipping into to all the empty space between the marbles — use slight pressure to feel the level of control you have. (Again, without getting into a Sumo match.)

- How much control did you feel you had?
- Was it different?
- How about your partner?
- How did they feel about their level of control compared to the first time?

Empty space serves many purposes and taking over that empty space can give us positional control.

This principle carries over anywhere you want to take control of their structure. Yes, even on the ground. One common factor people feel when a high-level player is on top of them is that they weigh far more than they should. They have eliminated all the empty space so that you take on all their mass.

Drill Six: Merging, Eliminating Empty Space, Connect to Them and Close Quarters

If you recall the section on "Connect to Them" we have another element of using empty space we can add for control in Close Quarters.

When you take the clinch position, run through the slight pressure drill first with neither filling the jar.

Take turns playing at filling the jar with honey before you take the next step.

Finally, each of you in turn eliminates space in their connections just as we did in "Connect to Them" and then fill the jar and try the pressure drill again.

Take a moment to play the pressure game mixing up who is doing what, but don't get competitive or else you will revert back to muscling and lose everything covered in Close Quarters so far.

Drill Seven: Merging Eliminating Empty Space, Connect to Them, Close Quarters, and the Voids

Wow, that sounds like an awful lot to do at once, but when you know how to do each of them then it is no more complex than what you were doing before, only far more effective.

When you fill all the space and connect to the Aggressor in Close Quarters you will have seeped in and filled the space. Most importantly, you've filled the space underneath them. Your centre is now in control and you should, once you have filled all the empty space, know you are now in control of their balance and can move directly into them.

What? Directly into them?

This must sound like a contradiction to what we have been talking about. However, if you think back to the Voids, once you have control of their balance you can make use of the Voids.

You have taken control of their balance and have, often, two options:

1. You can move directly into their centre (at a 90 degree angle) driving them towards a Major Void and allow your force and their imbalance to topple them into that sink hole of the Major Void.

2. You can use the fact you are now filling underneath them to drive towards their centre, but upwards to take them up over the safety barrier and drop them off the cliff of the Minor Void.

Let's Sum Up

Here we removed some of that empty space between us and our partner because in real assaults they are more often up close and personal. We looked at the fact that even when close, there is still a lot of empty space to find our way through and to strike through, as long as we focus on the empty space and not the maze. We also found a visualization to eliminate the empty space between us and the Aggressor when we want to control them. Filling that jar of marbles is something you will want to ponder and play with.

Using Empty Space on Lower Limbs

Up until now when manipulating our partner's structure, we have focused on their upper structure, but applying the use of empty space also works on the lower limbs and in particular the knees.

When we want to collapse a knee, it can be difficult. We can use force and slam the knee on the side, perhaps collapsing it and also damaging it, but what if we don't want to do damage?

When would we want to manipulate their knee instead? Pretty much anytime we connect with an Aggressor, but here is an example. An Alberta Sheriff tactical instructor I was teaching used what I am about to explain when teaching a group of recruits. Their job was to put a person onto the ground and place him in handcuffs. He had his back braced against a wall and his job was to resist. They were not being successful. She stepped in and with one motion of her knee the guy collapsed to the ground leaving the recruits just a little in awe of her.

Here is the best way to learn it.

Drill One: Testing

Part One

Have your partner stand well balanced and structured.

You kneel down by the outside of one of their knees.

Grip their knee between your hands.

First press forward and backward, then gently to the side feeling how stable they are.

NOTE: Once again I will add a visual "block" in the picture below to show you are working against their structure.

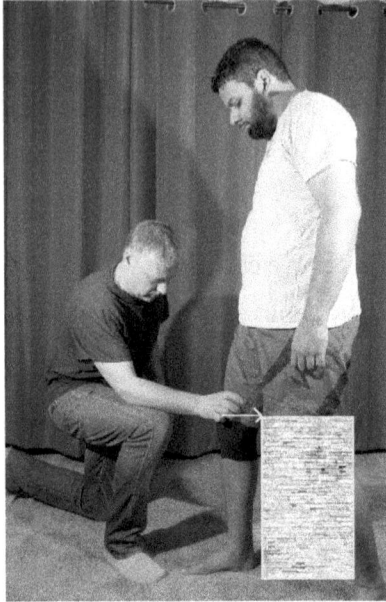

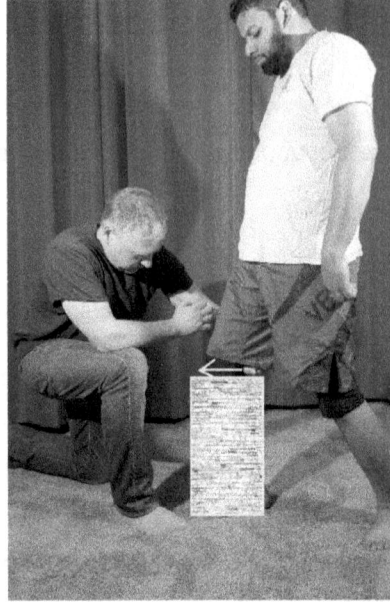

Pressing to the side of the knees should feel weaker, but not easily bendable. Careful not to injure your partner.

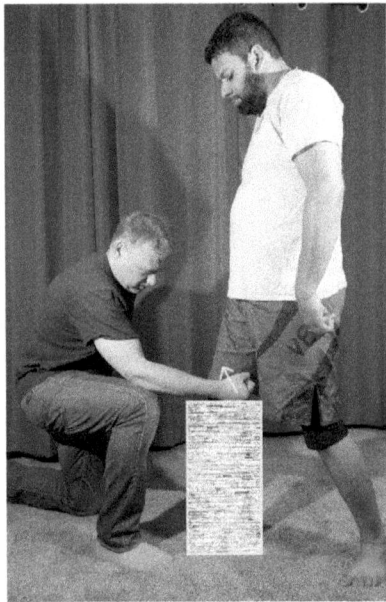

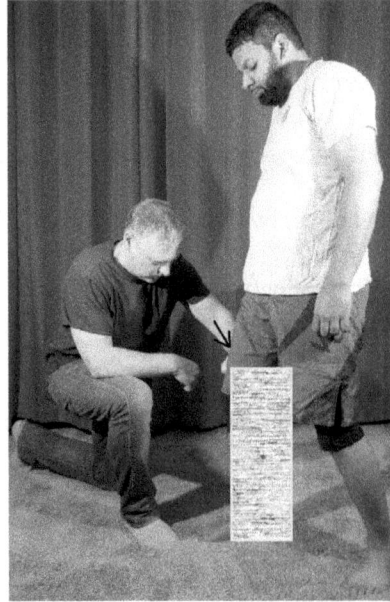

Part Two

This time move the knee in a circle moving it outward and towards the front and then outward to empty space.

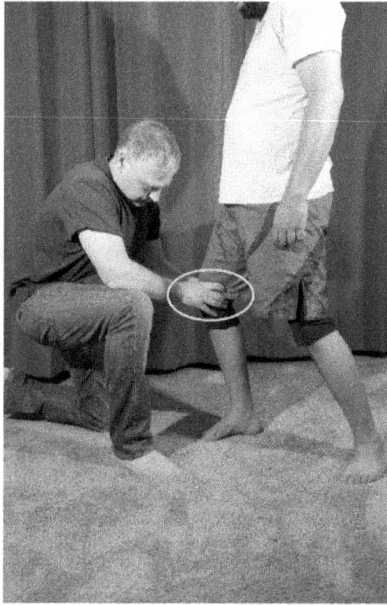

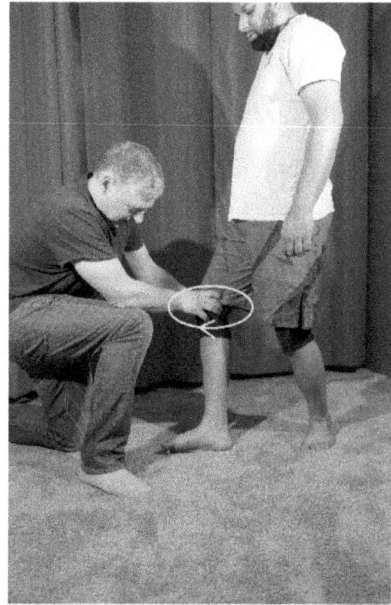

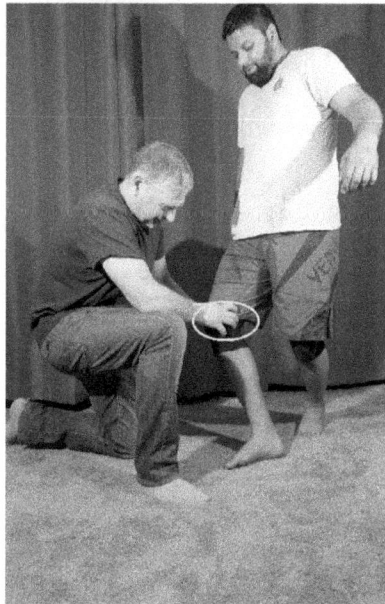

You can also circle the knee inward and then back to buckle the knee. Again, you are moving the knee to empty space

See how that makes a difference?

Usually you get about half a circle drawn when the leg collapses.

Drill Two: Applying the Knee Circle

You can circle your partner's knee with yours when in close quarters, which is what the Sheriff Instructor did to put the man on the ground.

I also find, as suggested, that circling the knee outward into empty space first rather than inward (which still allows them to access some structure and base) works best, but you can circle inward.

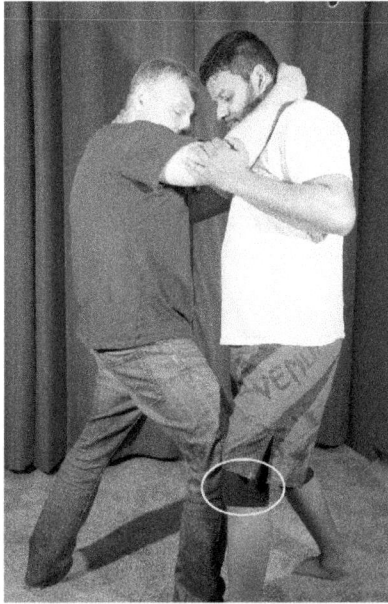

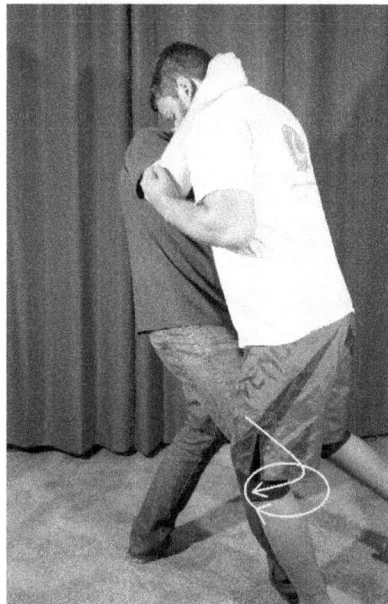

If you are going to circle inward you can still use your knee or hook with a foot.

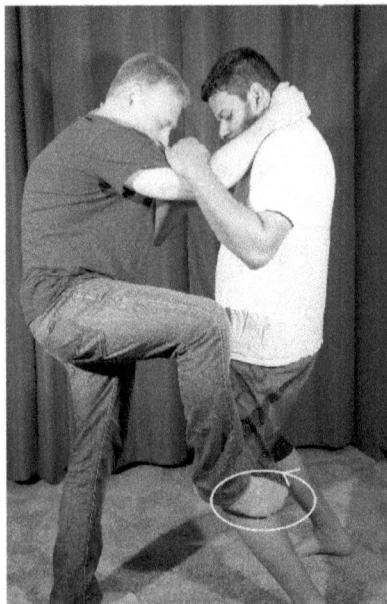

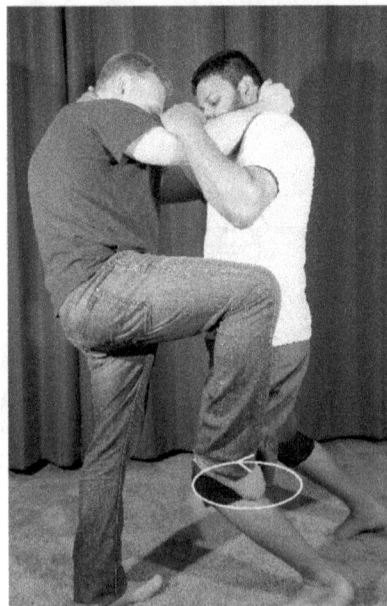

BE CAREFUL, GO SLOWLY AND DO NOT INJURE YOUR PARTNER. KNEES TAKE A LONG TIME TO HEAL.

You can combine this action with an attack into empty space on their upper body, best if it is in the opposite direction so a circular two-way action into empty space is created.

Play with this but, and I repeat because it is important, always be very cautious and take care of your partner when working with knees because they take a long time to heal when injured. Do not use force. If you are using force then you are not using empty space, which is the purpose here.

Circling the knee is an interesting use of moving a part of the Aggressor into empty space to break their structure.

Let's Sum Up

The lower structure of an Aggressor is also susceptible to being taken into empty space and using circles enhances the effect. It is always best to think about the whole structure of an Aggressor and remember we can attack all parts of it using empty space. In fact, you can attack both the upper and lower structure at the same time.

Destruction of Structure

Something I teach is a process called "Destruction of Structure," a drill I have adapted from one on a Scott Sonnon DVD.

Destruction of Structure can be described as using empty space in close quarters to progressively manipulate the Aggressor's structure in such a way that their balance is taken, never given back, and totally destroyed until they end up on the ground.

While it can stand as a separate seminar or topic, it fits exceptionally well into any discussion of empty space, use of Voids, and also works well following the discussion of the close quarters work we've had so far.

As you work this drill, I want you to focus on how empty space is used to accomplish our goals.

Destruction of Structure is something we always want to be seeking in self-defence. If we have broken their structure, then we are a step closer to surviving the assault. When their structure is broken and their balance compromised, most people seek to regain balance and structure. If we can shift their focus from injuring us to regaining balance, then our opportunities to survive go up. If we can take their focus away from injuring us as we end the threat, even better.

You will need to think back to the chapter of voids and how to access the Major and Minor Voids using empty space as well as how and what direction to take them.

Drill: Destruction of Structure

Part One

One partner is going to simply stand in a neutral stance with hands down at their sides. They are the meat puppet.

The other partner is going to gently push or pull on parts of the meat puppet's body until that part is moved about six inches.

The meat puppet doesn't resist the push or pull and once they have moved, they stay (hold) in that position without recovering.

The goal is to have the meat puppet lose their balance in as few pushes or pulls as you can.

At this stage, the partner pushing or pulling can move around the meat puppet looking for their next move, much like you would play pool.

If you can, try it before reading on. If not, no worries, you'll just have hints on how to make it work better.

Part Two

You may have done very well, or you may have found something kept going wrong. One common thing that people do in this drill, and in striking, is to make a great move to unbalance a partner and then in their next move put the person back into structure. We don't want that. See in the pictures below how that second move gives your partner back his structure.

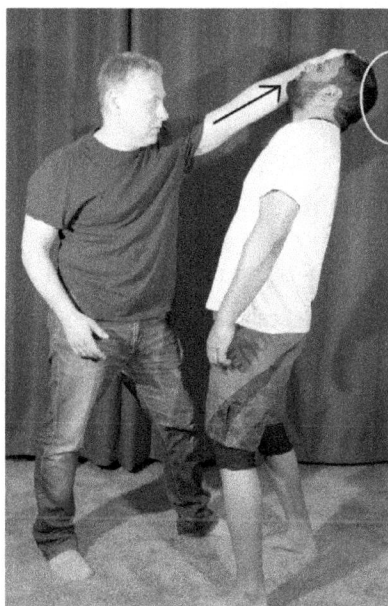

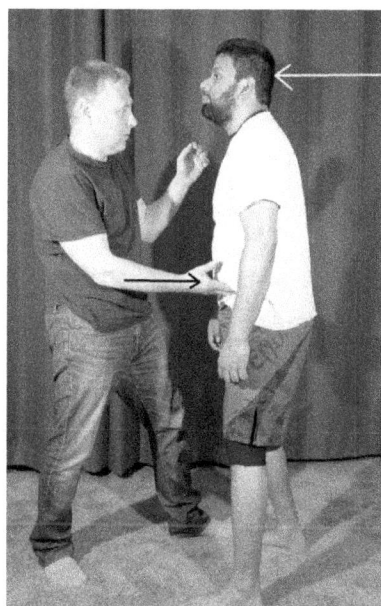

Don't give them back their structure.

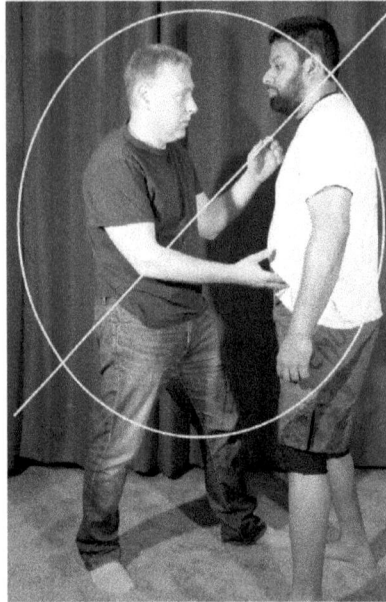

Begin to think of using empty space if you haven't already.

We haven't touched on manipulating the head yet, though will in much more detail later, but for this example, since they're not resisting, put your fingers on their forehead and press back into the empty space behind them six inches or so.

Now place your fingers on the small of the back and press forward into the empty space in front of them six inches. Two angles are shown below to illustrate that the press on the small of the back does not return the head to the balanced position.

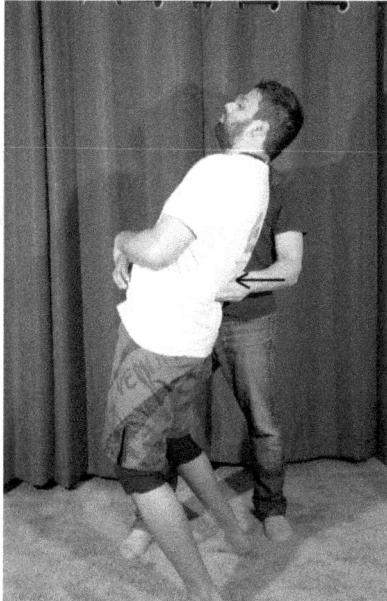

They should now be in poor balance tipping backward, so place your fingers on the top of their chest and push down six inches towards the rear Major Void.

They should easily fall.

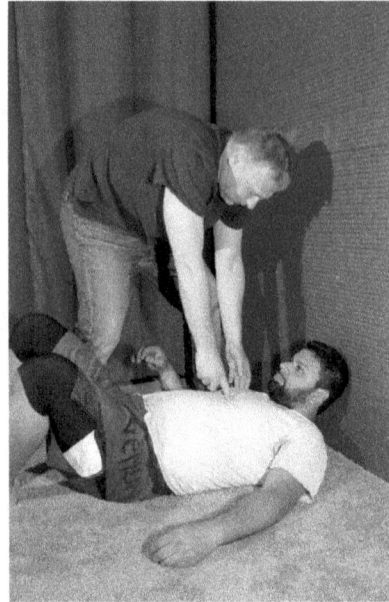

If we look back, we moved body parts into empty space taking the meat puppet out of structure until they were dangling over the empty space of a void and then one final touch and ... down they went.

Repeat the drill and try moving different parts first and in different ways but always into empty space.

Part Three

This time the meat puppet takes a fighting stance or guard position of their choice.

This time instead of pushing you will be striking SOFTLY AND GENTLY. Remember your meat puppet is not fighting back or resisting, so let's not take advantage of that to slap them around a little.

The goal is the same, you want your partner losing their balance and hopefully falling in as few strikes (punches, kicks, elbows, knees) as possible.

Run it through. Remember the hint from the first step where your strikes should TAKE their structure away from them and not GIVE IT BACK, as is shown in the pictures below.

You kicked their knee buckling them and taking them off balance with their upper body tipping backwards. Often the next strike is driven into the midsection but that restructures them. We do not want that.

Don't give them back their structure.

By now you should have thought about using your striking to take your partner's body parts into empty space, but if you didn't, then repeat the drill with moving them into empty space in mind.

Note the same opening kick gives you the same disruption of our partner's structure, only this time follow it with a strike that continues to spiral them into the rear Major Void.

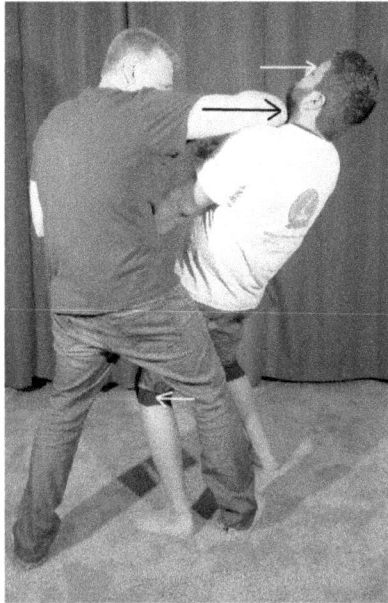

How did it go?

Some find when moving from the pushes and pulls into striking that they repeat the error of striking to take structure and in the next strike returning structure.

Every strike, every manipulation should take them deeper into your chosen void and nothing should be done to help them recover their position.

There is a little more that can be played with and learned from Destruction of Structure but for our purpose here, empty space, this is all you need to focus on.

Play with this until the flow of strikes always takes and keeps their structure.

Let's Sum Up

We know we can move and manipulate an Aggressor by taking them, or parts of them, into empty space. Now we are moving that into another level, because every time we take a part of them into empty space we continuously and increasingly break their structure/balance until it is destroyed.

Side note here, this isn't hard to catch on to. In some of Rory's Miller's seminars there is a drill where you get to deliver a specific number of strikes to your partner in a row to work on targets and flow. Every time I've done it my partner stops and asks why when they hit me the number of strikes I am still standing, but when I hit them, they always end up on the ground. I explain basically this chapter to them and within two turns they are doing it constantly. They had just never thought of using empty space that way before.

Head Manipulation

One of the best levers to work on the human body, and my very favourite, is the head. The old saying where the head goes the body follows is very true. Of course, what makes the head easy to manipulate is the proper use of empty space.

IMPORTANT NOTE: Before working on head manipulation make sure your partner doesn't have any neck injuries or issues (before and after please). Always, ALWAYS take care because when manipulating the head because you are directly affecting the neck. GO SLOWLY, be safe, be careful and take care of your partner.

The head is like a ball on a stick.

It has more strength to resist moving forward or backward than side to side, but even pressing directly to the side has some strength. Of course, this strength comes from pressing into their structure rather than using empty space.

Drill: Let's Play with the Head a Little

Once again, we do not want to go into their structure. If you press down into the neck you are engaging their structure.

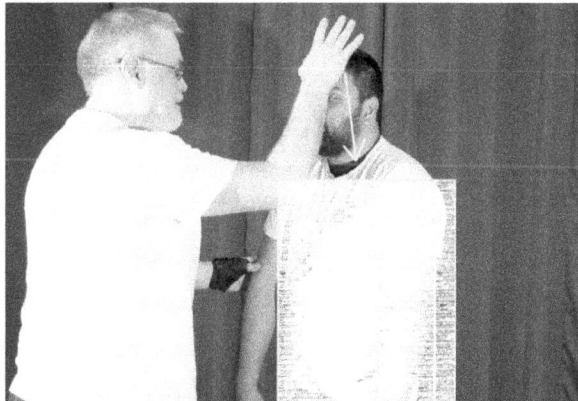

Grip your partner's chin in a C-clamp with your right hand, then slowly and gently press backward and rotate to the side (towards empty space) and see how well structured it is in those directions.

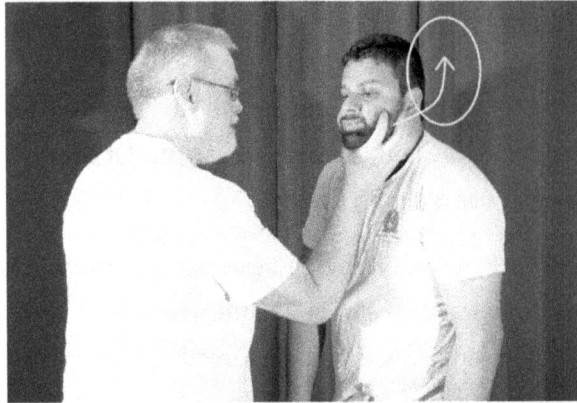

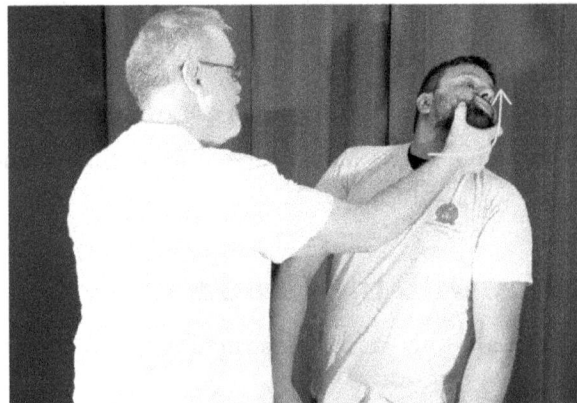

Think of all the empty space around the head, above it, to the side, all around.

Was it now easier to move the head?

I prefer to use the edge of my hand, wrist or forearm to shear along the head to manipulate it into empty space.

Often moving the head in a circle, much like the knee, accesses empty space quickly.

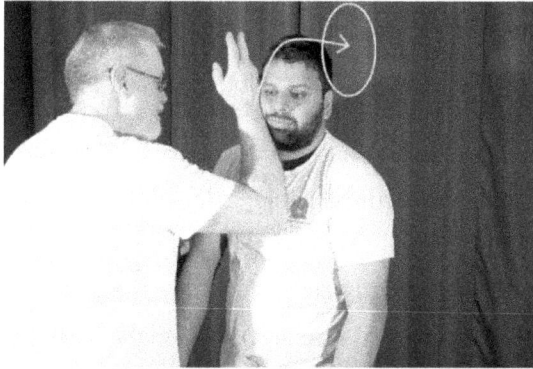

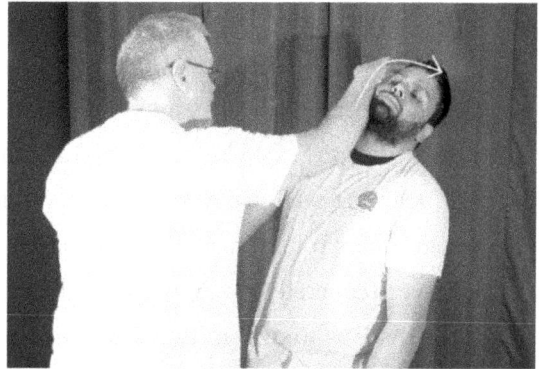

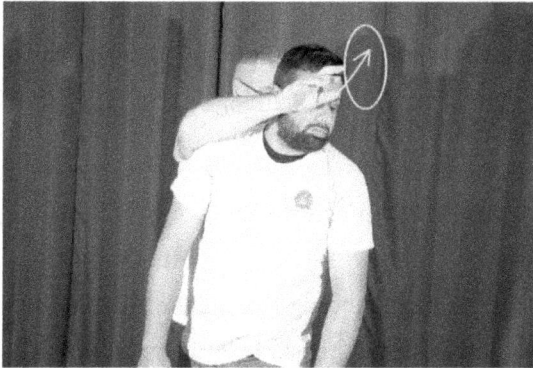

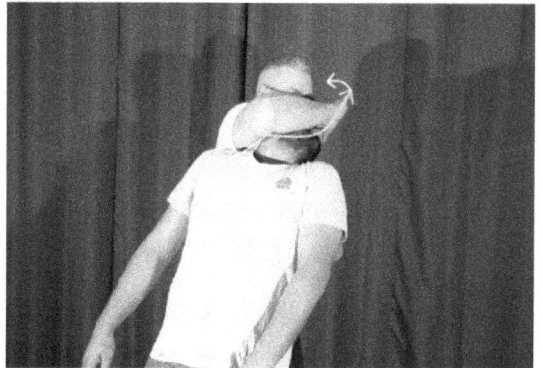

Once you get the head moving it is easy to continue along the destruction of structure progression.

Let's Sum Up

Head manipulation is an excellent skill set to have in self-defence and works best if you shear and roll through and into empty space. A final caution: always look after your partner's health and safety, particularly when working the head and neck. We need to practice it BUT we need to be able to practice it safely and that is where our next chapter comes in, as we look at the ancient art of Ball Rolling.

Ball Rolling Drill

One of the best drills for manipulating the head and smaller body parts, such as the elbow, is one I learned from Sensei David Mott: Ball Rolling. Ball Rolling has a long history in Chinese martial arts training where it was often a wooden ball on a round table. I have also seen clips of practitioners rolling various sizes of stone or concrete balls on various sized tables and different surfaces (concrete, stone, wood, and so on.) I just recently saw one where the person used a basketball, as we will in this drill. The increase and decrease in size and weight carry with it a requirement for different control and skills.

The book *Collected Writings of Old Chinese Boxing Masters* by Bradford Tyrey has this on Ball Rolling from the article on Wu Tu-Nan's "Method of Power and Striking According to the Body's Upper and Lower Seven Stars":

> "The ability of rolling is derived from the ancient practice rolling a wooden ball upon varied surfaces and in one one's own hands. Wooden ball methods are closely guarded secrets by many boxing sects, including that of the Righteous Red Fist clan in Nanjing. Master Wu demonstrated his skills to us on his small table in his room. The ball rolled back and forth, turning in circles, and spiraling, all movements guided by only his fingers. Though the entire hand and lower sections of the arm can be employed, it is only the finger tips that are specifically trained in this manner for nerve striking."

This quote is accompanied by a picture of a person rolling a wooden ball on a round table.

As the quote says, ball rolling used to be a closely guarded secret but now, in these more open days of information and the Internet, I have found clips and references (such as the book quoted) out there on this excellent training method, which have brought it out from behind the veil of secrecy.

In that part of the book, the ball rolling was highlighted for striking nerve points, but for our purpose it will be for the manipulation of the Aggressor's body parts; therefore, we will use not only fingers, but as the quote said, the entire hand (the edges) and sections of our forearm. We will also use our elbows.

You will need some props for this drill.

You need a table at least two by two feet.

Particularly for one part of this drill you will want the table sitting on a mat or pad, so the floor doesn't get damaged should there be a mishap.

You will need, in this order: a basketball, a bowling ball, a soft rubber ball about five inches in diameter, a tennis ball and a golf ball.

You can find cheap bowling balls at pawn shops or used sporting goods (it doesn't have to be top quality.) We simply want heavy, round and solid. A medicine ball or Taiji ball may also work.

The basketball and bowling ball represent the head.

The small five inch ball represents the shoulder, hips or knees.

The tennis and golf ball represent the elbows and wrists.

As you roll the balls in this drill take note of the fact you are moving into empty space to do it. You are using all the space around the balls to manipulate them.

Drill One: Ball Rolling

Part One: Basketball

Place the basketball on the table and place one of your forearms on it.

Bend your knees rather than bend over if you have to lower yourself to touch the ball so that your back remains vertical (or as vertical as possible given the height of the table.)

Begin to shear the basketball with your forearm, elbows, wrist and hand to move it around. Shearing is a cutting action that slices through the edges of an object.

Move your forearm along the ball but not directly into it, instead along it and into empty space.

Switch back and forth from inside forearm etc. to outside.

Switch back and forth from right arm to left.

Switch from forearm to wrist to edge of hand.

You need to see in this drill that all your moments are cutting along the ball and into empty space. This is essential and once you get this skill it makes the manipulation of head, limbs, torso etc.

much easier, as you are no longer ever going directly into and fighting their structure, but constantly using empty space to manipulate them.

I hope the number of pictures this section shows the subtle but simple movements and demonstrates just how important I think this ability is for fighting in empty space for self defence.

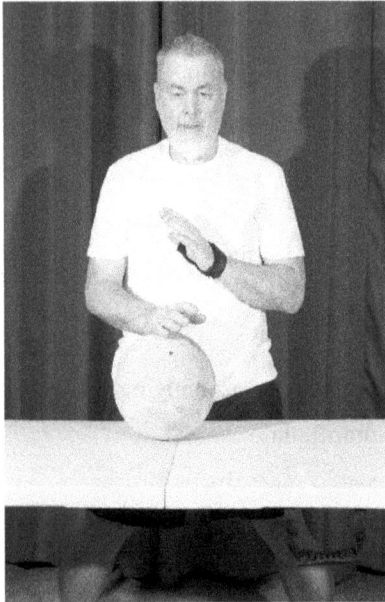

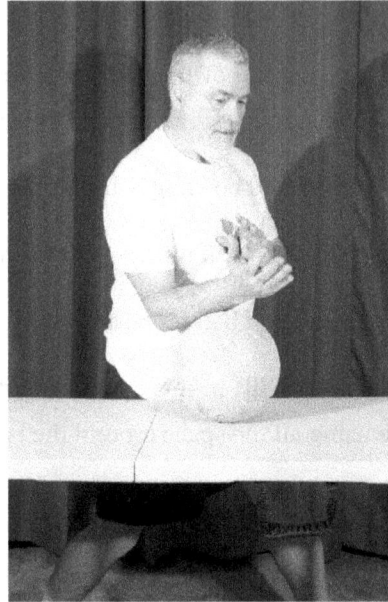

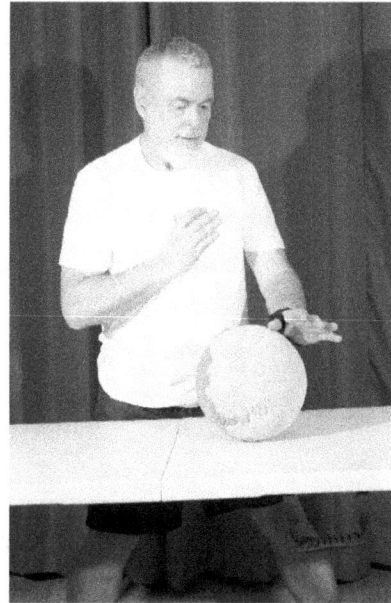

Once you are comfortable working the ball with your forearm, wrist and hand, make sure you also use your elbows. You can also focus on working with just your elbows, but always finish working switching between all contact areas.

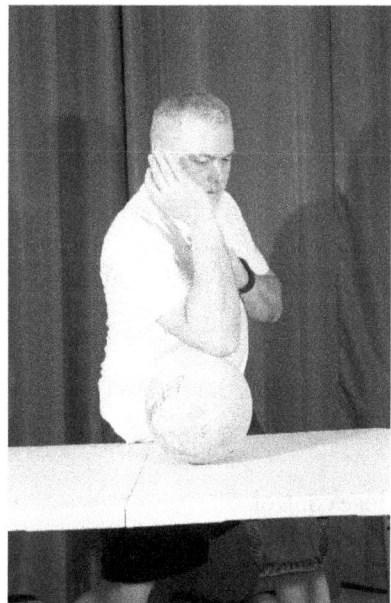

NEVER lose control of the ball and roll it all around the table within your reach.

Both the basketball and the bowling ball are representing the head in this tool for learning how to manipulate body parts into and through empty space.

Part Two: Bowling Ball

NOTE: Be careful, because if the bowling ball falls off the table it can injure your legs and feet and possibly the floor if you have not protected it. It is best to have something soft and safe for it to fall on should it fly off the table. And get yourself out of the way if it does.

Start just as with the basketball and begin to roll the bowling ball around with your forearms, elbows, wrists and hands.

Again, switch from the inside to outside of your forearms etc. and switch back and forth from right to left arm, changing control.

Never lose control.

You will find the bowling ball's weight makes it harder, but it increases your level of control.

Constantly take note of how you are running along the ball but not into it. Your movement is into empty space.

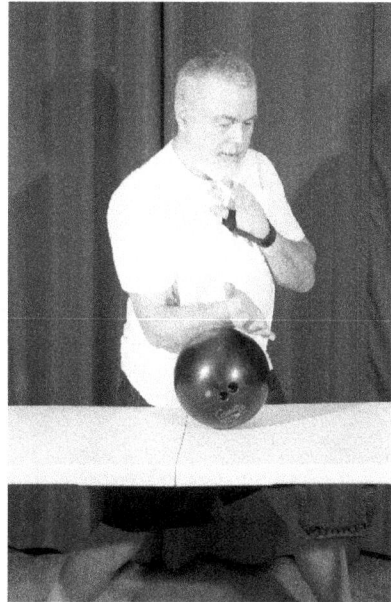

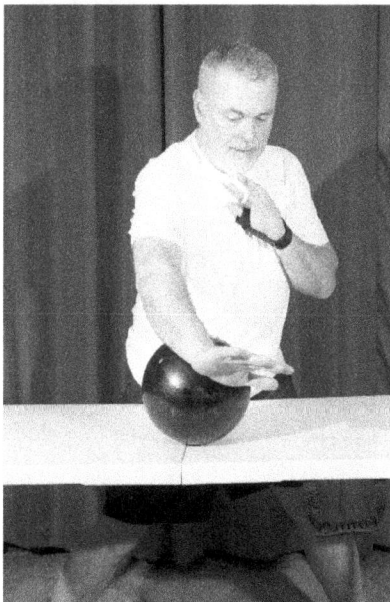

Once again shift to using your elbows to manipulate the bowling ball around using shearing into empty space.

Part Three: Small Rubber Ball About Five Inches in Diameter

You are going to do the same drill, but the ball is now smaller. Just as the weight of the bowling ball added a challenge so does the drop in size. This size represents shoulders and hips.

Keep in mind you cannot roll through the ball, so you are shearing along it into empty space to roll it.

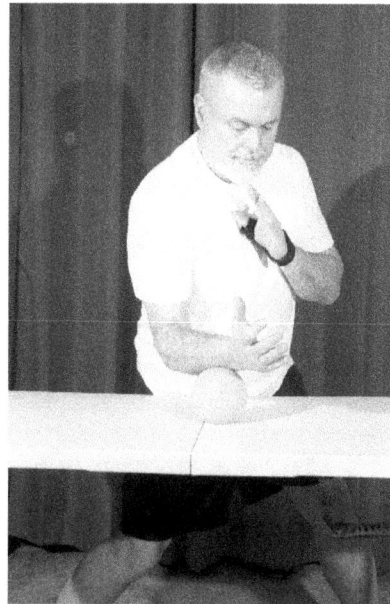
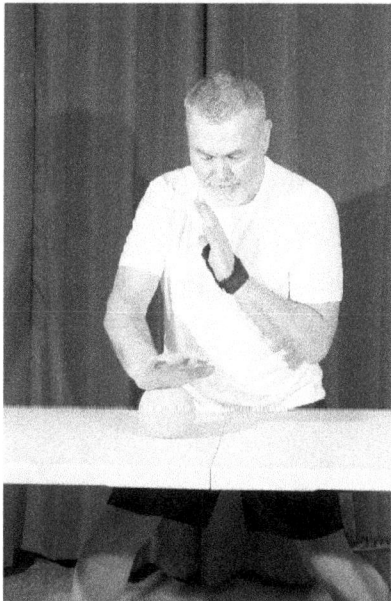

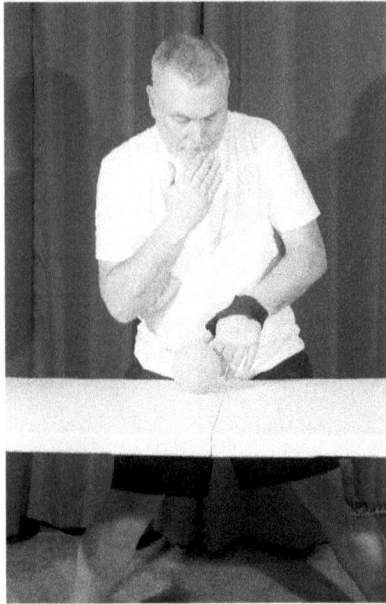

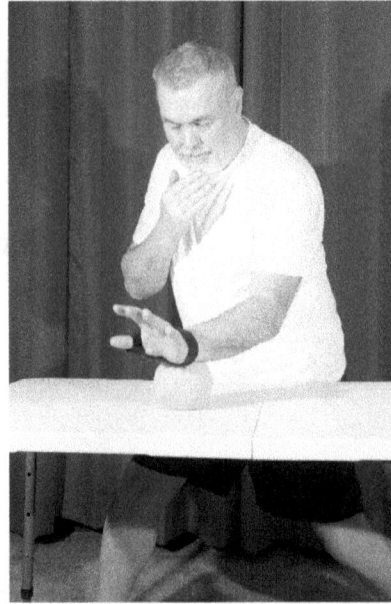

Once you have control using your forearm and ridge of your hand switch to the elbows. Of course, as the balls get smaller this control means seeing smaller and smaller angles of empty space to use.

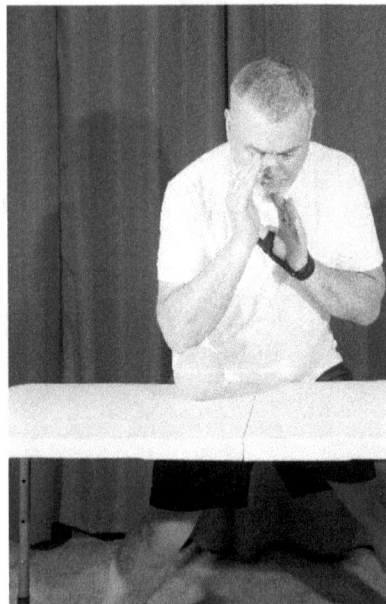

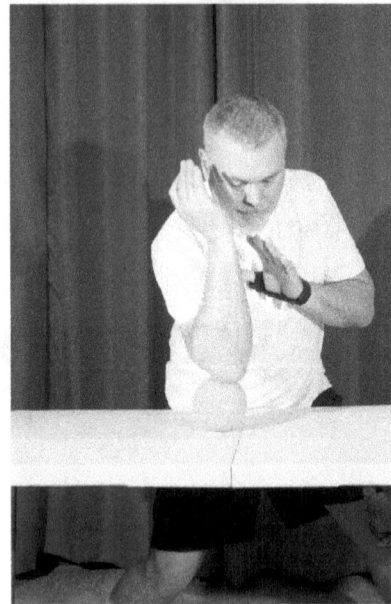

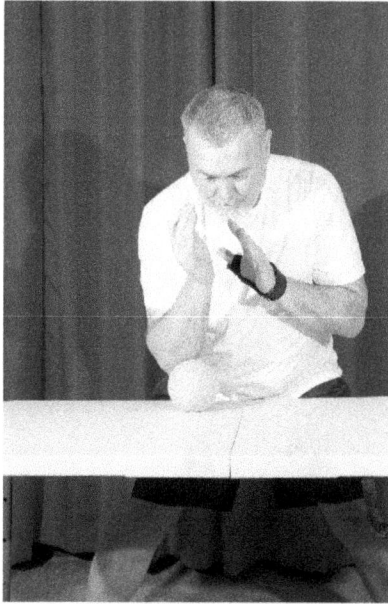

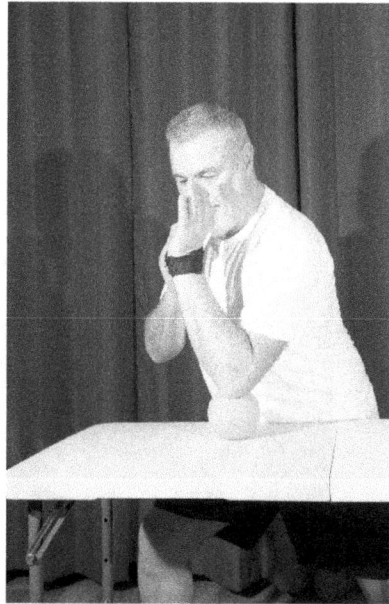

Depending on the size of the ball, and you are welcome to substitute different sizes between this and the basketball if you'd like, represent either the hip or the shoulder but really this drill teaches you to manipulate any body part into empty space.

Part Four: Tennis Ball

The ball has gotten even smaller and that increases the challenge of controlling it.

The smaller ball is about the same size as an elbow or knee which makes it an excellent representation to practice manipulating.

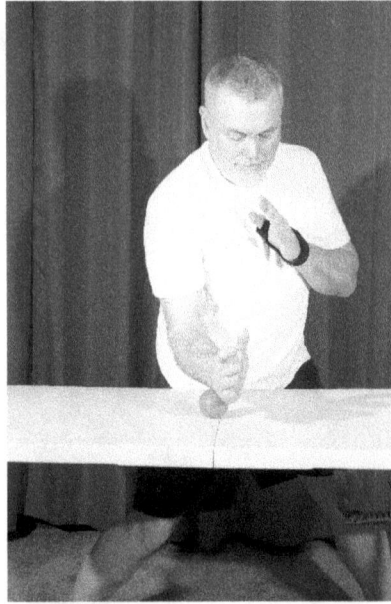

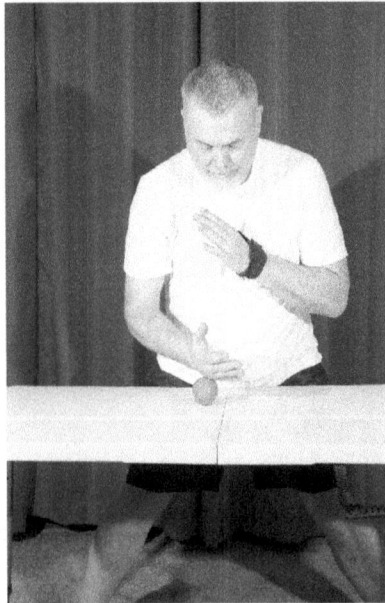

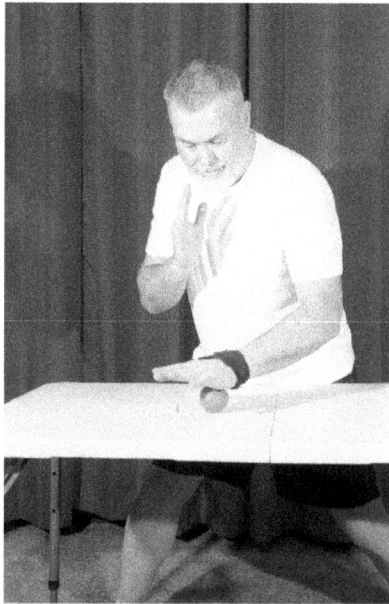

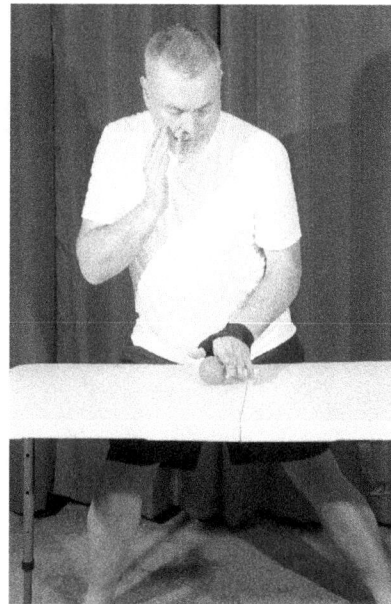

Once again switch to elbows.

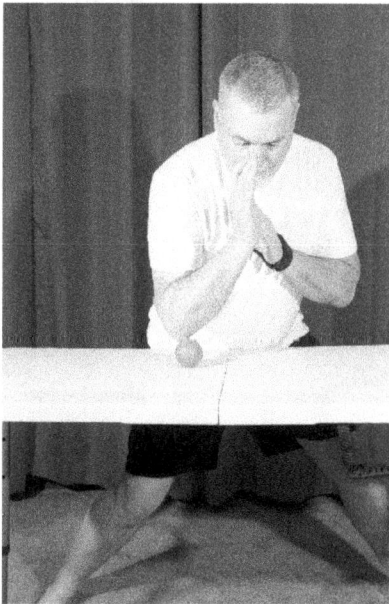

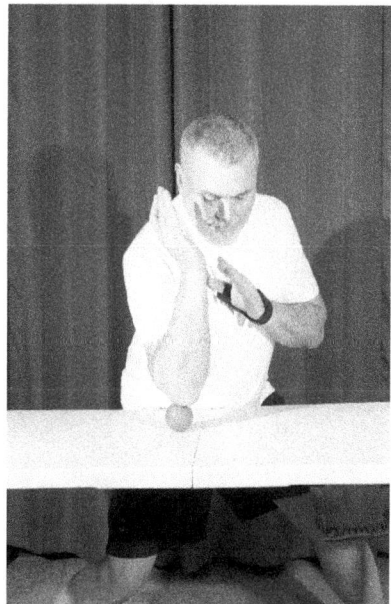

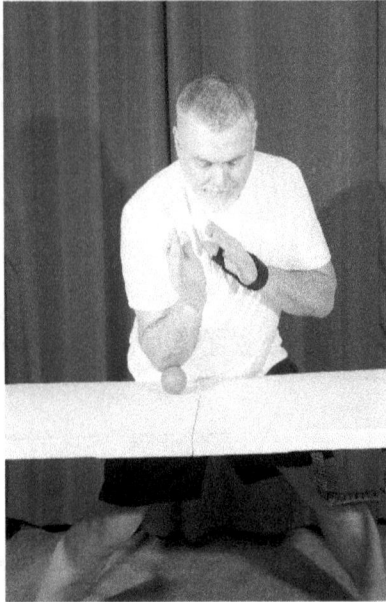

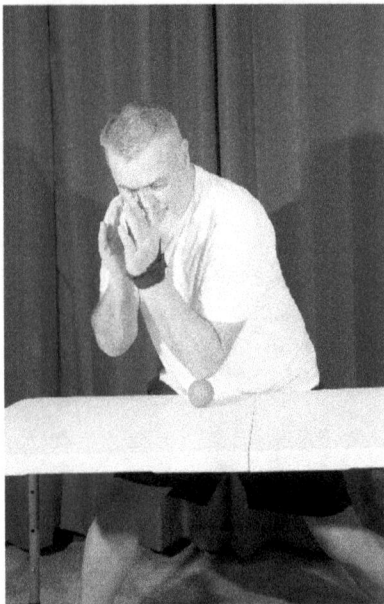

Remember once you have done hands and arms then elbows combine them, switching back and forth and from arm to arm.

Part Five: Golf Ball

The golf ball size is even smaller and works to refine your control and manipulation of both small and large body parts into empty space.

It also represents a point manipulation most often affected with the elbows.

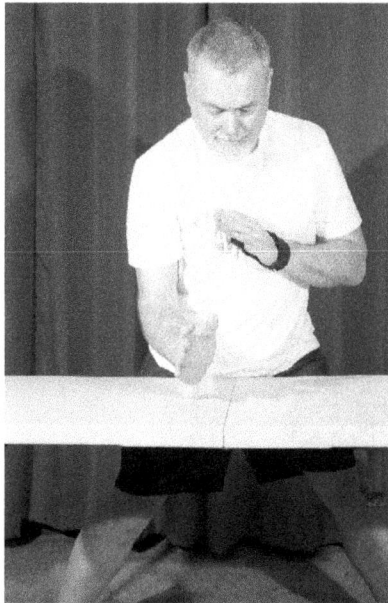

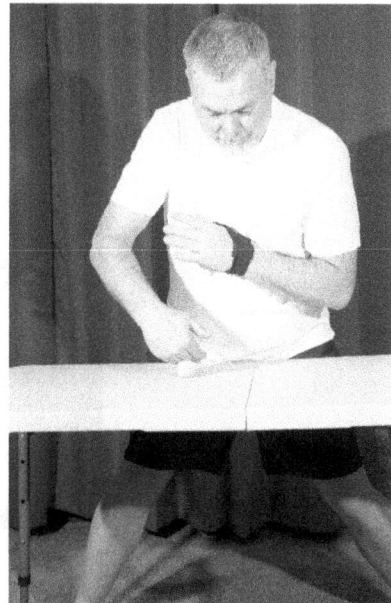

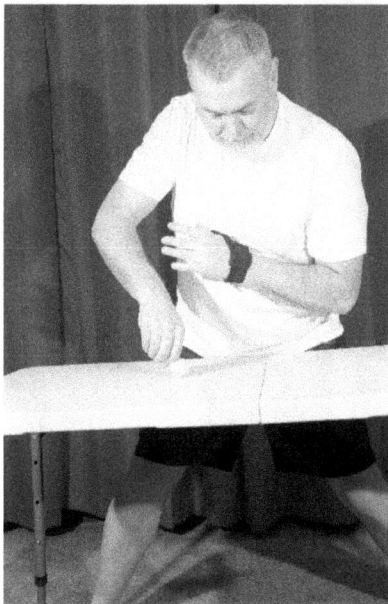

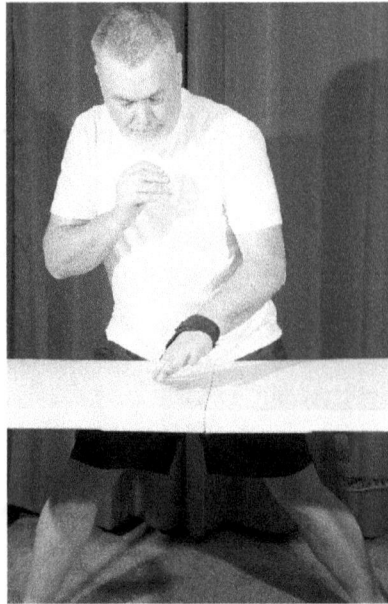

And, now once again, switch to using your elbows. This type of empty space shearing can be used to collapse a torso when done into the chest.

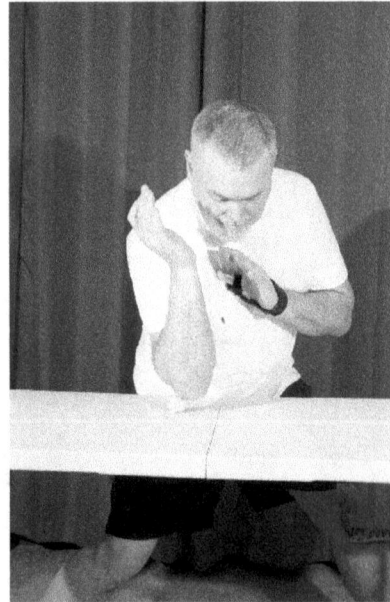

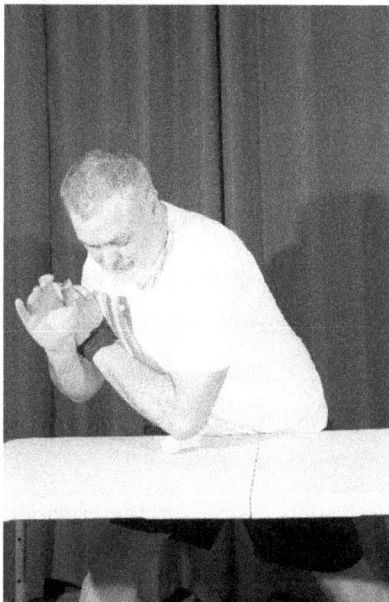

The Ball Drill is one of the best tools I have found to learn small manipulations into empty space to take control, particularly of the head and other body parts.

Drill Two: Play

Once you have rolled the ball, play a little. Take a close quarters position with your meat puppet partner and then slide your forearm up to their head and, being careful not to injure your partner, simply think of their head as the ball and begin to roll it.

- Take the outside of the lead hand position again and reach up your hand and wrist to their head and (CAREFULLY) begin ball rolling the head.
- Take the outside of the extended arm position again. Place your forearm on the back or front of their shoulder and begin ball rolling to roll their shoulder and down to destroy their structure or manipulate them into a shoulder lock.
- Take the outside of the extended arm position again. Place your forearm on the back of their elbow and begin ball rolling to roll their elbow pit over and down to enable an arm bar.
- Take that clinch position again and with the hand you've hooked their head, connect (eliminate the empty space), place your elbow to their chest and begin ball rolling with the elbow.

You can place your elbow to their chest, sides, back, thighs and ball roll with the elbow.

REMEMBER all ball rolling moves into empty space; therefore, you must roll the head, elbow, chest all into empty space to make the manipulation of the Aggressor work.

FINAL CAUTION: Always keep your partner's health and safety in mind when doing this type of manipulation. Make sure they have no injuries before you begin and make sure they have none when you finish.

Let's Sum Up

Ball Rolling is the safe way to practice manipulating the head from the previous chapter. We can practice rolling the ball without worrying about making an error and injuring our partner. It teaches us that by using empty space we can twist and roll the ball/head into submission. It also safely trains you to manipulate hips, knees, elbows, shoulders and other various body parts in the same manner using empty space. Working the Ball Drill is the best way to learn this particular aspect of using empty space to manipulate the Aggressor.

Merging the Jar of Marbles and Moving into Empty Space

We have covered using empty space to move.

We have covered owning the pocket of empty space you move into.

We have covered moving through empty space to strike.

We have covered using empty space to manipulate our partner.

We have covered eliminating empty space to connect to our partner.

We have covered using empty space to destroy our partner's structure.

We have covered eliminating empty space by filling the jar of marbles.

Now, before we move on we have to put it all together. In the chaos of an assault you need to do all these things out of habit. The last thing we need to do is remind ourselves that when we connect in close quarters and fill the jar of marbles we will be doing so as we strike, as we manipulate them, as we destroy their structure and as we use the empty space around them around the jar to move through.

NOTE: As we move on in this book I will be moving away from limiting you to specific things in the drills. I will be providing examples, but I recommend you play and discover other things to do before looking at them. Some of the upcoming chapters will be providing information on how things are done using empty space and it will then be up to you to explore the information further.

Drill One: Off the Lead Hand Strike

One of our first drills was our partner throwing a lead hand strike and we moved into the empty pocket beside them. Here, we go back to that movement.

When they throw the lead hand and we move into the empty space beside them it should mean we have also opened up empty space through which we can strike as we move. Once we are on the outside there should be a lot of empty space to work with from the top of their head to the bottom of their feet.

We do not have to just move and fill empty space while avoiding the strike; we can also strike through empty space AS we move into that space.

Once we have occupied the space at the side of the Aggressor, either by just avoiding and moving or by striking as we avoid, then we have a choice of where to go next and it may well depend on your training and preferences.

For the purpose of this drill I'll want you to work on possible follow ups, so you experience the use of empty space in a number of ways.

Once you've stepped into the empty space pocket at the side of a lead hand (you can also strike with the edge of your right arm as you do so), then you have three options for continuing:

1. Continue to strike through empty space using empty space to destroy their structure and put them down and out on the ground, or
2. Connect and manipulate using empty space to move them, destroying their structure and eventually placing them in position to use a take-down.
3. Combine striking and manipulation.

Remember to always step into the empty space, connect and fill the jar of marbles then move and manipulate them destroying their structure.

Work as many as you can. Explore and play.

Once you've given the drill a try, have a look at an example below.

In the example below, you move into that empty space beside the Aggressor and strike through empty space to the head (ball rolling) and to manipulate the lower limbs. The result will be to drop the Aggressor into the Rear Major Void.

Drill Two: Off the Looping Sucker Punch

We also looked at the looping sucker punch. Once again, we will move into that pocket of empty space and then decide to strike or grapple or a mixture of both as we use empty space.

Just as with the lead hand strike, work options off that Looping Sucker Punch Intercept.

Work as many as you can. Explore and play.

Once you have given the drill a try, have a look at the example below.

In the pictures below, you enter then there is empty space between your lead hand and the Aggressor's neck. With a rotation you can strike, which moves them enough to open up their knee to strike and continue to break their structure.

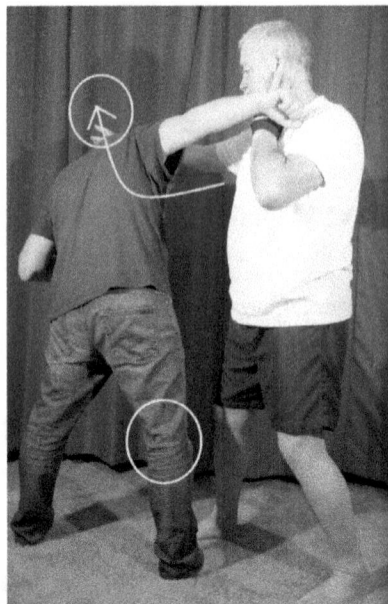

Your strikes or manipulations should always keep in mind what we learned from Destruction of Structure: never give back their balance and structure once we have taken it. Be sure your strikes and manipulations spiral them constantly to the ground. In the picture below the strike to his knee is used to prevent them from stepping forward as you pull them out over empty space of the Front Major Void.

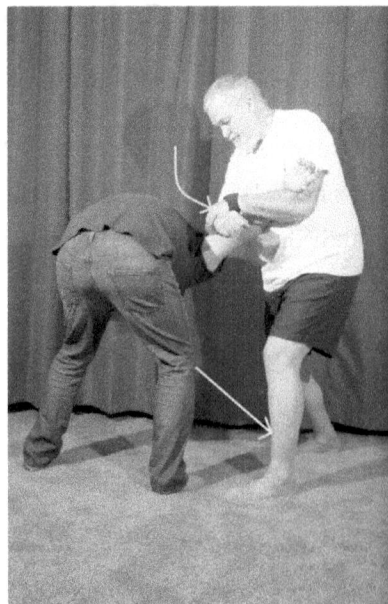

The strike to the knee prevents them from stepping forward to recover their base as you move their head out over empty space. As they are moved forward, their weight comes down on that leg pinning it, making it harder to move and easier to perform the arm bar take down into the Front Major Void.

Drill Three: Pinned to a Wall

We talked about having empty space even when the Aggressor is so close many would think there isn't any. Here is another example. The Aggressor has pinned you against a wall. While there is no empty space in front of you and no empty space behind you, there is an abundance to the sides along the wall. You merely have to enter it and use it by sliding along the wall.

Allow yourself to be pinned to the wall. Try to find and use the empty space along the wall.

Explore and play.

Once you have given it a try, have a look at the example below.

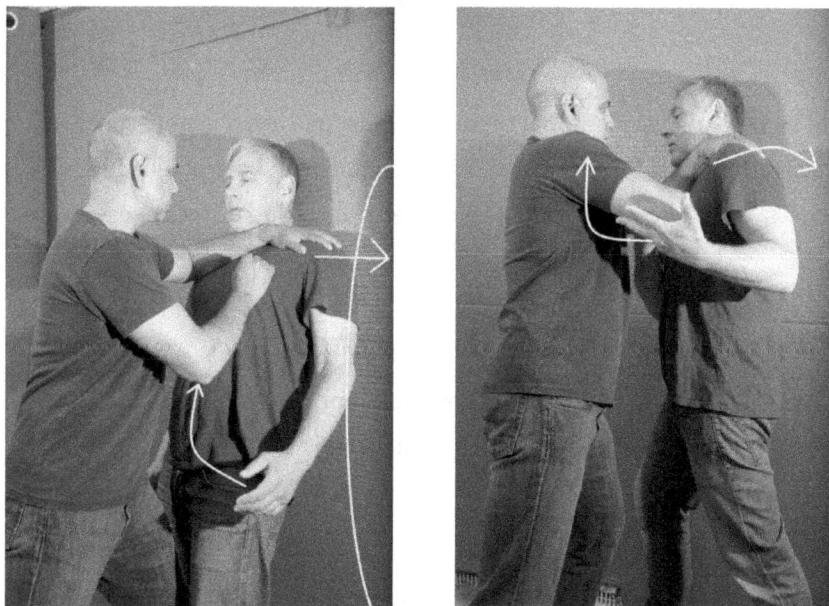

Once you slide along the wall it opens up even more empty space options. Keep in mind every action you take will have an element of using empty space. In the second picture above the Aggressor's elbow is pressed upward driving their shoulder into empty space and disconnecting it from their structure, weakening their pin.

The picture below shows that after sliding to get away from the pin you can move backwards to escape using empty space, but as the line in the picture indicates you give yourself more time to escape by continuing to manipulate the Aggressor's shoulder, pushing it up into empty space.

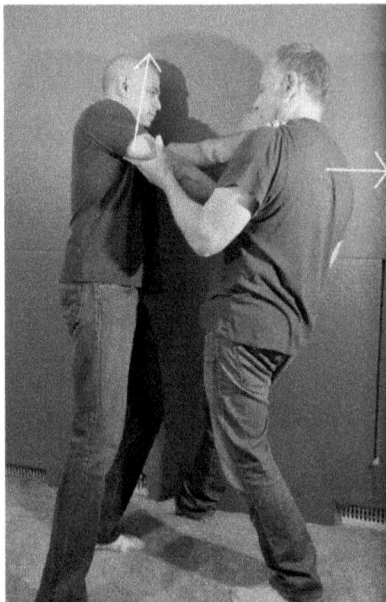

It should be becoming evident that there is not just one use of empty space. Every movement and contact can add a use of empty space. Every contact will have stacked uses of empty space. Just as principles are stacked/layered to increase efficiency and effectiveness so are the uses of empty space.

Drill Four: Putting it All Together

Note: The following examples each show different possibilities for putting it all together. The drill is for you to play and find your own sequences.

Example One

The Aggressor clinches with you and you can see the empty space between where the oozing of the honey into the jar of marbles can be used to take control. You also have a hand on the back of their neck and where you touch you want to eliminate empty space to connect completely (that Gecko thing.)

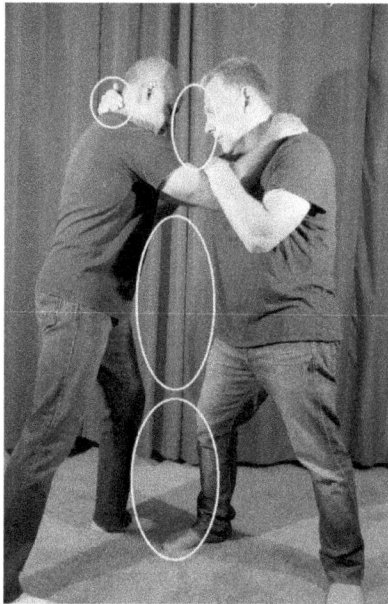

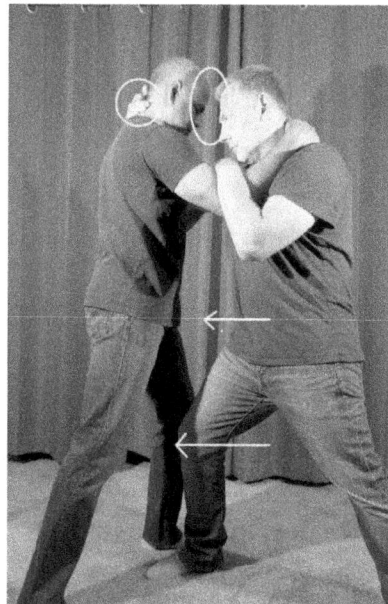

Notice the effect "connecting" has on their structure where the loose contact cannot do that to them.

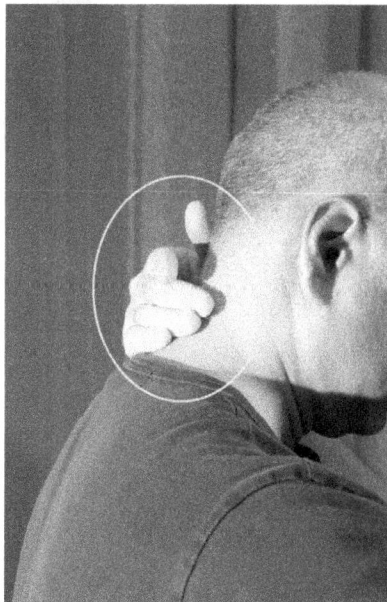

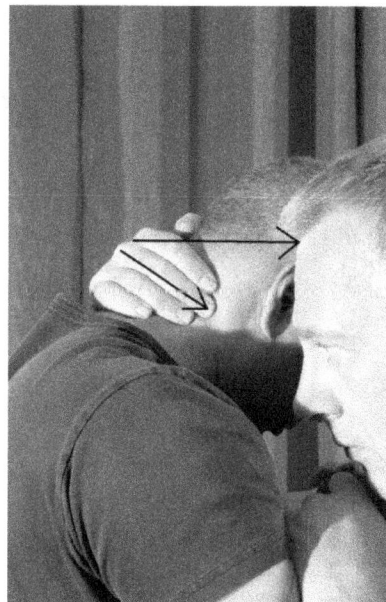

Even so close there is plenty of empty space to begin striking through. Simply solve the maze.

Example Two

Look in the picture below. Right from that connection, by rotating left and extending your right arm you deliver a forearm strike to the Aggressor to disrupt their structure (as well as do damage.) In the second picture, you will also see you have compressed your left arm to collapse the Aggressor's right arm and disrupt their structure.

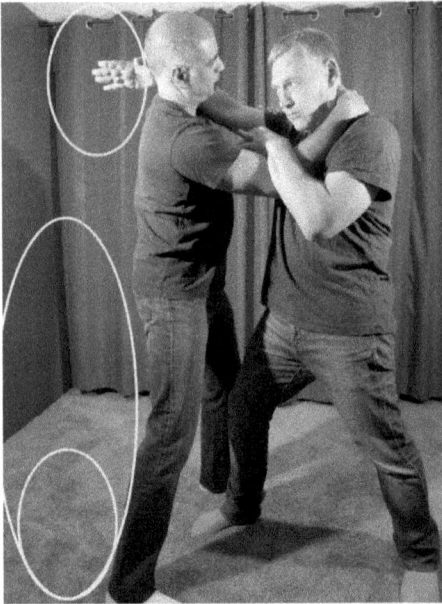

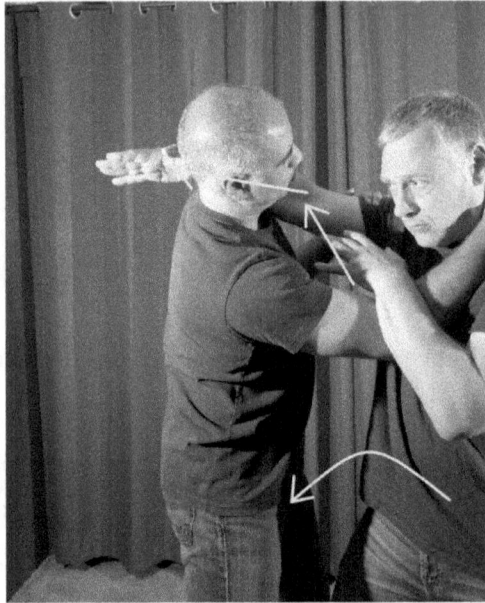

We must not forget the void and destruction of structure so that we can take advantage and see how to put them on the ground. Now that the Aggressor's structure has been disrupted you can follow the lines in the picture below to see the path through empty space and into the void.

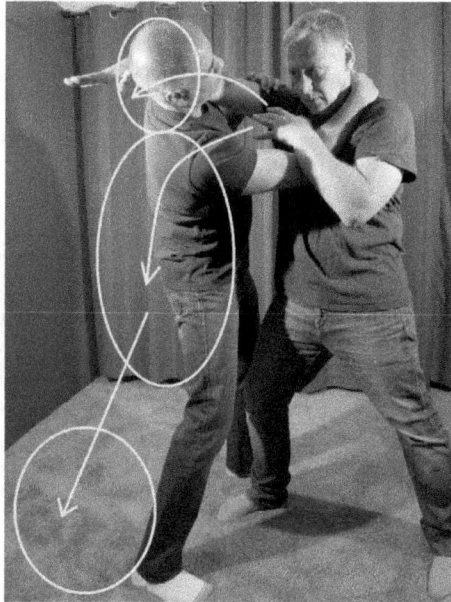

Example Three

As soon as you begin striking you can use empty space to manipulate the Aggressor. As you can see in the picture below, by rotating to your right you can bring the Aggressor's elbow across. By moving out of the way to open that space, you move to empty space, which means you are attacking through empty space and not into the Aggressor's structure (where trying to move the elbow across would fail.)

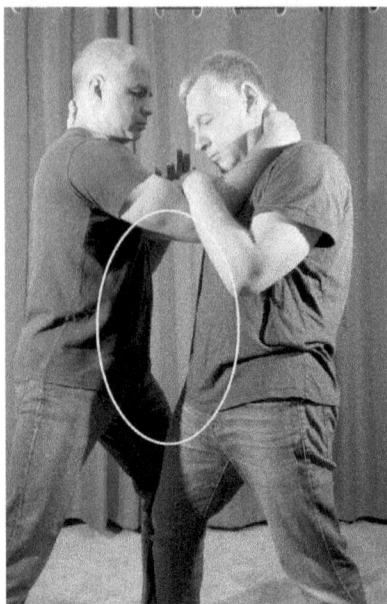

Take a close look at the picture above showing you have rotated completely to face empty space. If you do not rotate fully you can be trying to move the elbow across through their structure, which is hard to do. Moving it across into empty space is much easier.

There is not just one choice: strike or manipulate. Once the Aggressor's balance has been disrupted by a manipulation, it often opens up new empty space targets, such as the side of their neck in the pictures below.

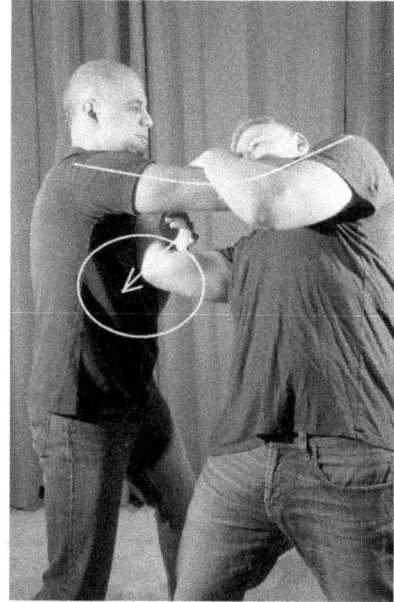

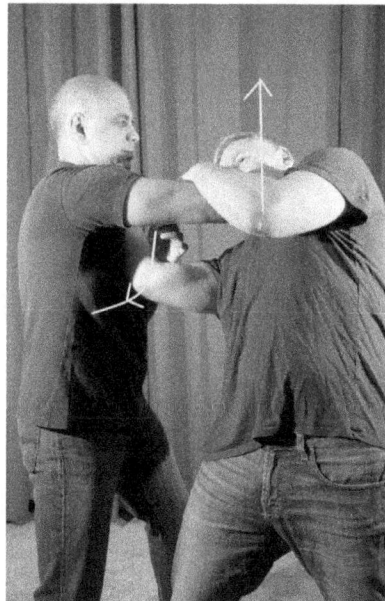

Example Four

You can use connecting and moving to empty space to initiate a throw.

In the picture below your left hand connected to the Aggressor's neck and your right to their hip. You use these connections to move the Aggressor, because you have bone slaved them to you; therefore, as you shift into empty space they go with you.

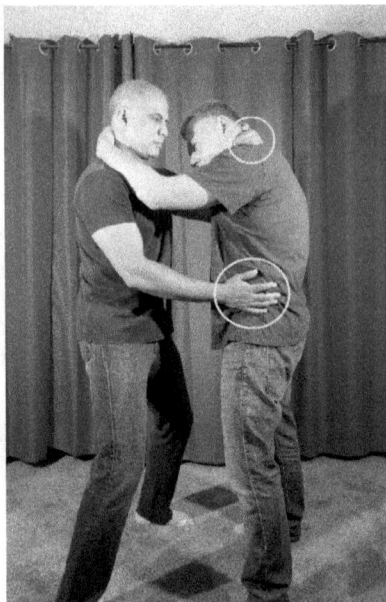

Note once again how connecting has disrupted their structure as shown in the close-up picture below.

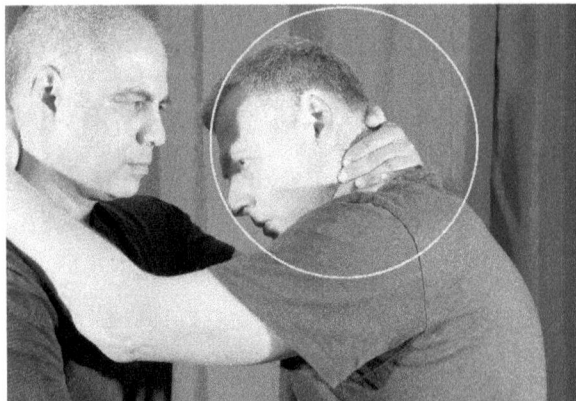

Shift your centre to your left and because of your connections the Aggressor will move, too. The movement will pin their right leg, allowing you to balance them on that leg as you then under hook their left leg to dump them into the Minor Void.

The "block" below shows the Aggressor's pinned leg and how you can use that structure (you created) to throw them by simply driving the head down and the leg up. Note you are not lifting them. Instead you are tipping them over the pinned leg – over the barrier and off the cliff into the Minor Void.

Example Five

As close as bad breath range might be there is, as stated, an abundance of empty space to be used. If you incorporate the use of shearing into empty space learned in the Ball Rolling drill, you can attack the Aggressor's structure by rolling their head and elbows.

Note in the pictures below how the Aggressor's head is just a bowling ball for you to roll around the table.

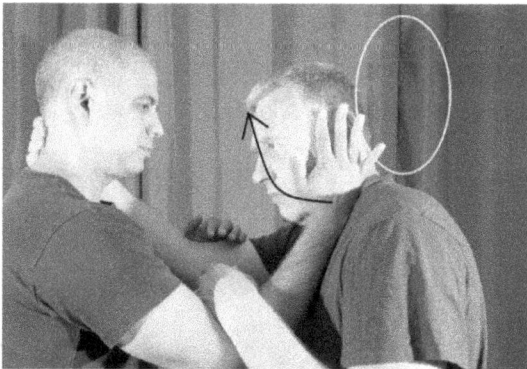

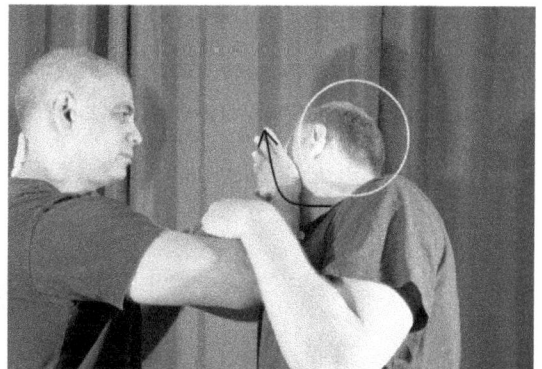

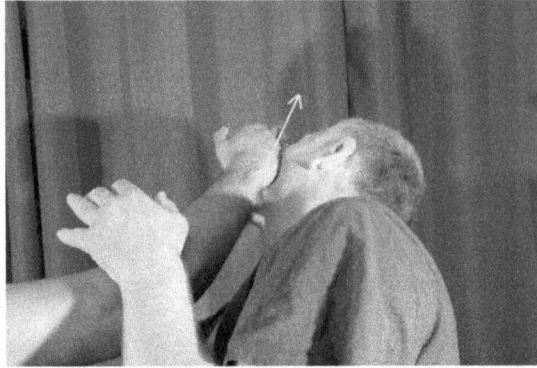

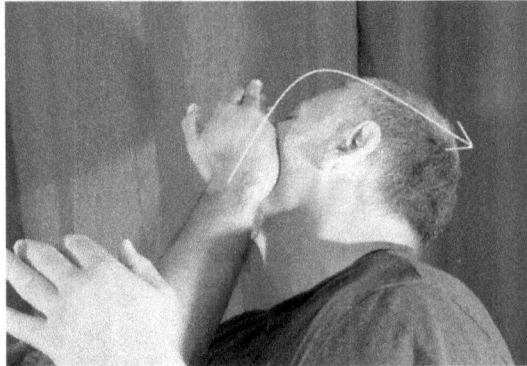

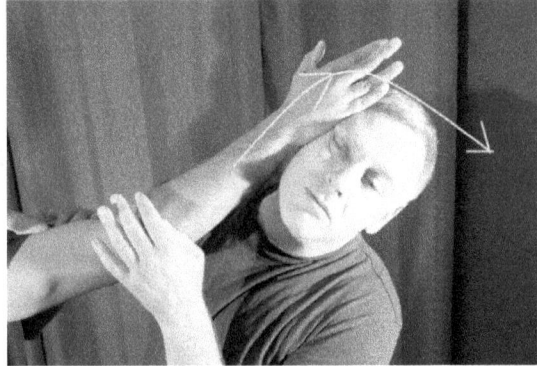

As an additional note, while the above pictures show us manipulating the head, they are showing the "kind and gentle" way. Every move above shearing into empty space can also be done with a ballistic movement (okay, we can also call it a strike).

In the pictures below, the same skill from the ball rolling is used in close quarters to manipulate the elbow and therefore the Aggressor's structure. And yes, these too could be done with a ballistic movement and possibly damage the joint. (So pay attention and do some reading on the plea of self defence to determine what level of damage is a reasonable response.)

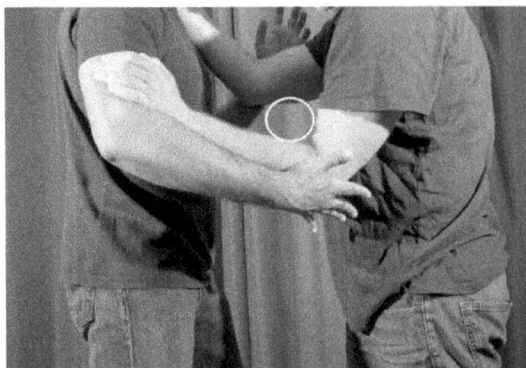

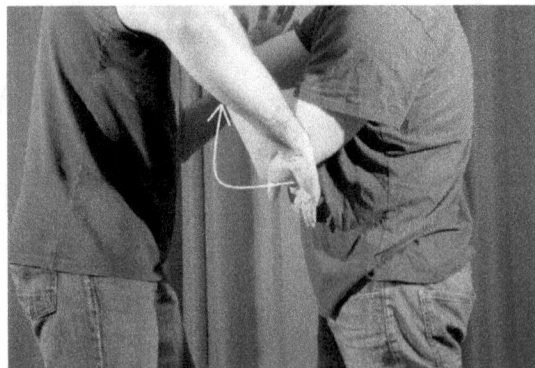

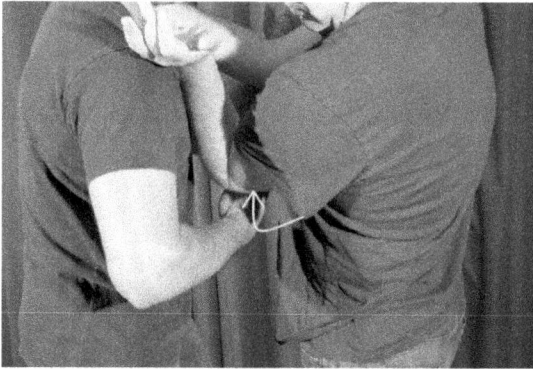

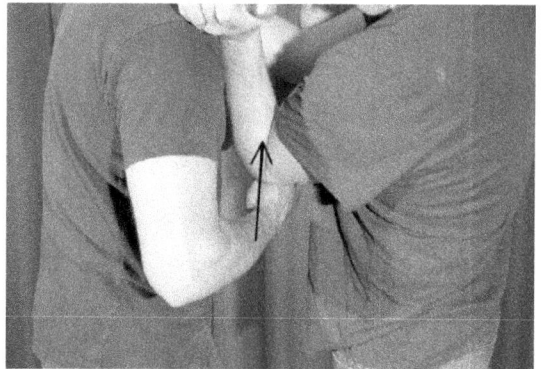

Example Six

The sequence of pictures below illustrates how your arm can thread through empty space. The first three pictures below look similar, but note how in the first picture your right hand is shooting upwards into empty space, allowing it to take the Aggressor's arm up and out of structure. In the second and third pictures (as indicated by the lines) the direction of your arm changes and begins to curve downward.

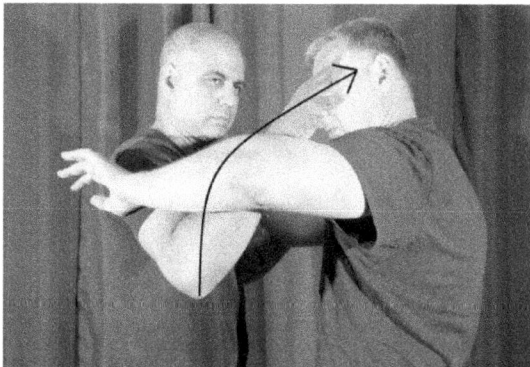

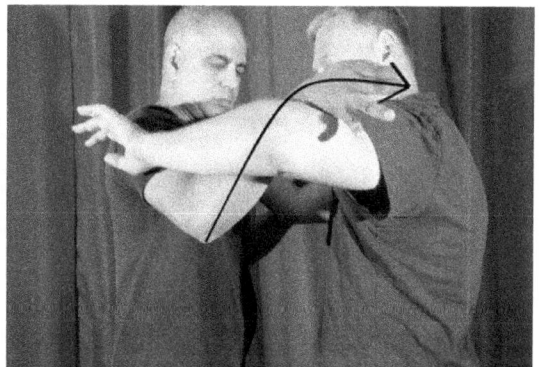

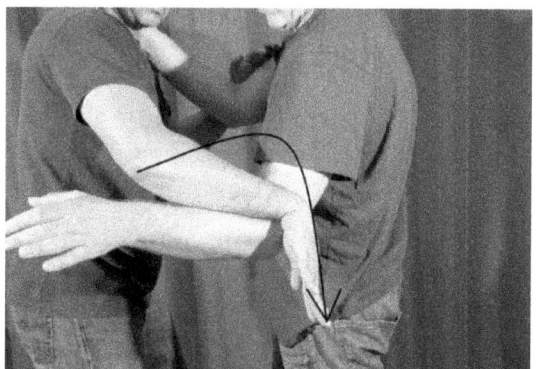

Now that you have rolled your arm over and downward you can rotate and take the Aggressor's elbow across in preparation to apply an arm bar. Note how the arm is threading (snaking) through empty space where it can flow without hitting resistance. Also note the contact of the arm is constantly shearing.

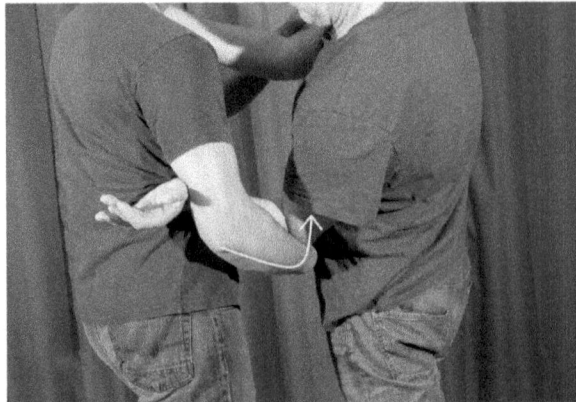

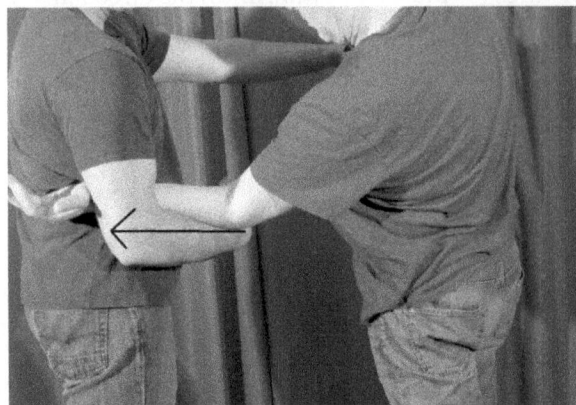

Now that the arm is trapped, step back into empty space and lift the elbow up into the empty space above to lock the arm (more details in Chapter Twenty on using empty space to apply locks.)

Example Seven

In the ball rolling drill, we also used the elbow to roll. Below you can see how you can incorporate this into striking in close quarters. Even though you are clinched with the Aggressor you can drop your body forward by either a drop step or emptying your front foot as you drive your elbow into their chest (a nasty little strike.) Strike and connect to their chest, then you can roll the elbow (as in ball rolling) which tends to have a "collapsing" effect.

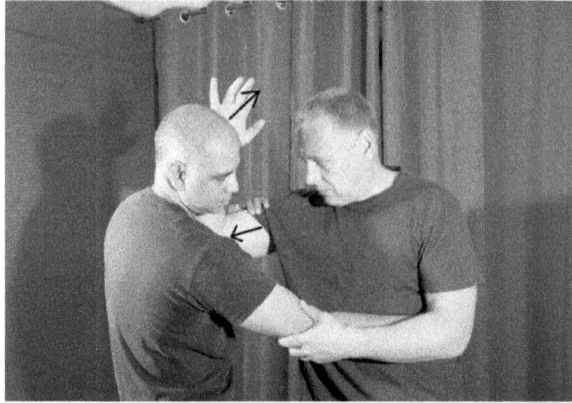

The elbow strike hits their chest and that contact allows you to roll as in rolling the golf ball which can have a collapsing effect. That collapse opens up empty space to the chin for a strike.

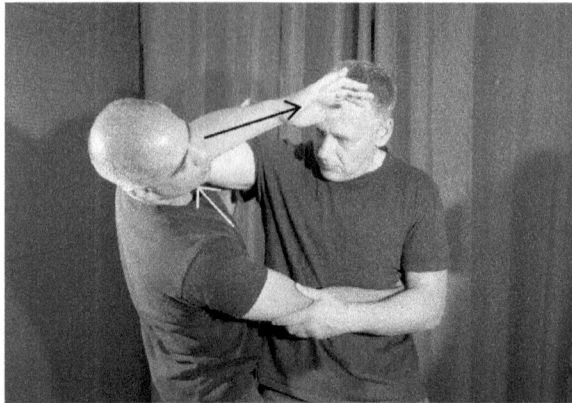

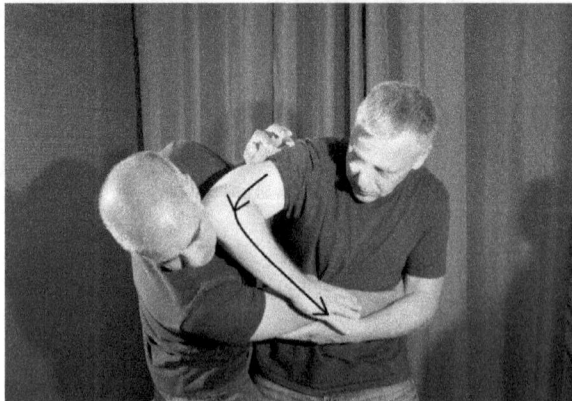

You can then roll the elbow again but add in a back of your forearm strike as you do. This also creates the opportunity to drop them back into a Void.

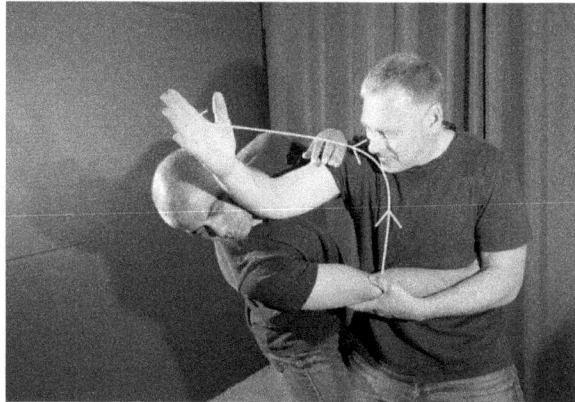

Example Eight

Connecting is used to manipulate the Aggressor and open, or open wider, areas of empty space for striking and body manipulation. In the picture below you have once again connected your hand to the back of their neck. By rotating to your right, your connection pulls the Aggressor into empty space. Not only are they off balance, but it opens up the side of their head for a strike to a very effective target: the ear.

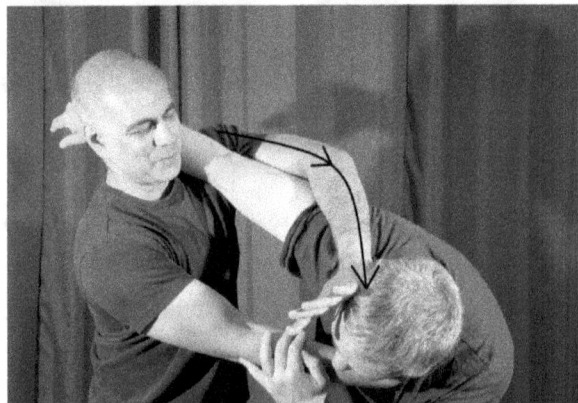

Example Nine

You do not need to separate body manipulation and striking. In the pictures below, you use that same connection to move the Aggressor and open up their chin to a strike. This time you do not separate the actions. Instead, you rotate to your right allowing your connection to pull the Aggressor over opening the target and as you are rotating you land a palm strike to their chin.

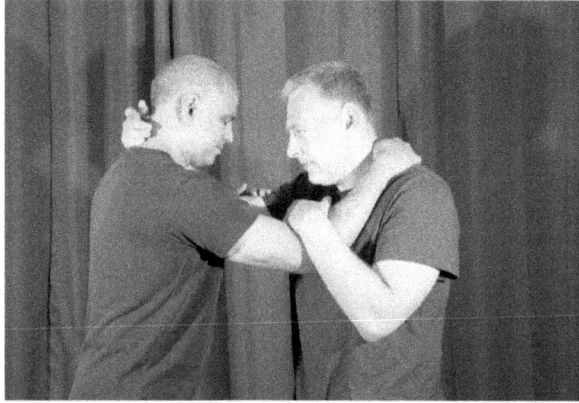

Once they are off balance remember to continue to move in a direction that will not return their balance putting them back in a structure they can fight from.

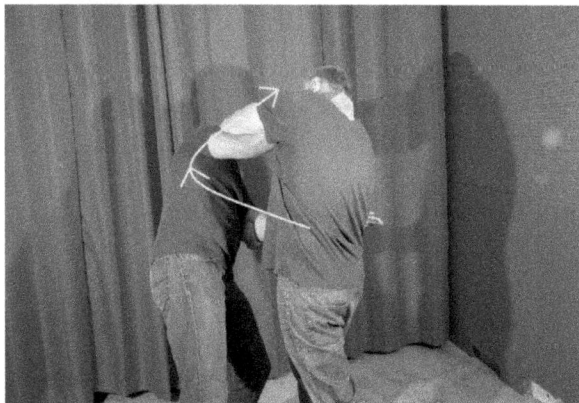

At this point I want you to go and be creative with your use of empty space. Play and have a little fun with it.

Let's Sum Up

We are moving on in the use of empty space and needed to pause here to put it all together, working on how moving into empty space, striking through empty space, eliminating empty space to connect and moving the Aggressor through empty space all fits together. Watch how the same body mechanics/movement can use multiple layers of empty space. Playing to learn is also highlighted here, and it's fun too.

Rushing Water

This very effective visualization for using empty space comes from a long-time training partner, Stan Tubinshlak.

When teaching, the hardest thing is to try and find something that resonates with the student. Not every thought or way I have tried to express using empty space in this book will resonate with everyone and that is simply because we are all individuals. It is also the reason I have more than one visualization to try. I don't know what will resonate with you. Hopefully one or more of them will.

The more you train using empty space, the more applications you can see using empty space. Often an idea can pop into your head when working on one aspect that opens up a whole new line of thought. This visualization came from Stan working on movement without a partner and he wanted to have the feeling of moving into empty space. The honey into the jar of marbles was too slow for what he was trying to feel, so he substituted water and began to think of rushing water.

As my long-time training partner, Rick Bottomley, will tell you I tend to take ideas from others and find way to apply them in self-defence. Well Rick B has a different term but this is a polite book. (Alright he says I bastardize his ideas – except he also reluctantly admits I also make them work very effectively). While Stan was using the visualization to move I had other thoughts....

Rushing water does not stop when it hits things. Instead, it simply folds around them into empty space, enveloping them. This concept brought us to play with some odd applications of the thought of rushing water and we found them creative, enjoyable and also effective. Of course, once you get the feel for it the visualization can be dropped.

Drill One: Rushing Water

Part One

Once again, I'm going to ask you to do something without the thought process or visualization that will be part of this drill so you can compare the two experiences.

I have not tried this with women so, if you are female, please feel free to adjust this drill to fit more comfortably with your anatomy.

One partner stands with arms a little apart ready to clinch. Their job is to remain firm and in structure, to be a wall.

The position you are going to be moving into is a bear hug clinch. There are various take-downs that can be performed from that position.

You are going to start from a short distance of ten to eighteen inches (just to moderate the possible force) and slam chest on chest into your partner as they try to stay in structure. This is the brute force on force approach to dominate.

Give it a try and start with a lower force so there are no injuries, but you can build up to where you are both comfortable.

You, of course, have to pause and reflect on how that went.

- Did you knock them off balance?
- How did it feel slamming into them? Solid, flimsy, etc.?
- How did they feel?

Think about it for a moment and commit it to memory.

If you are like most people, you felt like you ran into a brick wall. (We used Paul Hunter because running into Paul really is like running into a brick wall.)

Part Two

Before you adapt this to our movement I want you to think of water rushing down a river.

It flows unimpeded and without interruption.

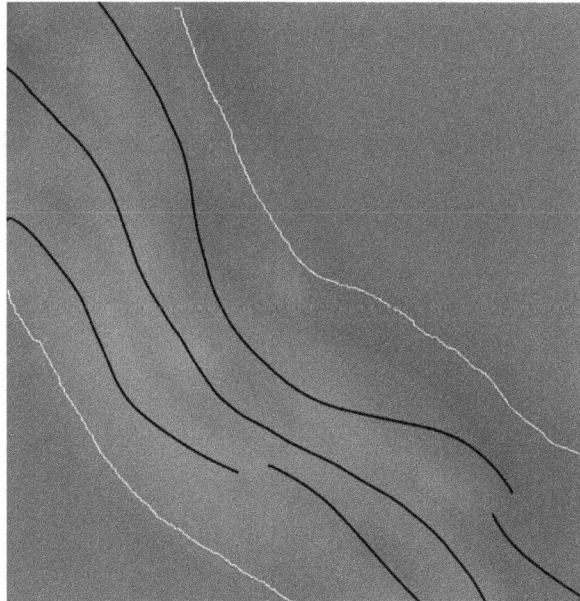

Now picture the same river only this time there is a boulder in the middle of it.

Picture how the water hits the boulder but does not stop instead it flows around it.

The water rushes by the boulder as it hits it.

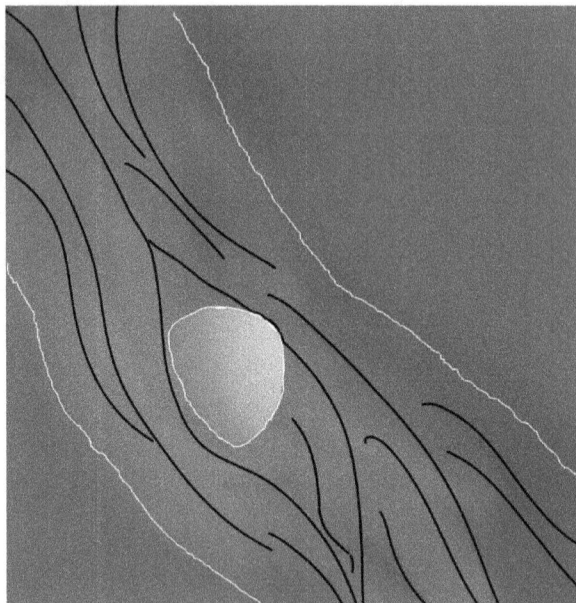

You are the river and the water, and your partner is the boulder.

Again, slam into your partner. Only, instead of thinking force on force think of being that rushing water flowing around the boulder as you contact your partner. Picture flowing around the boulder.

Start slow, then, again build up speed as the two of you are comfortable with it.

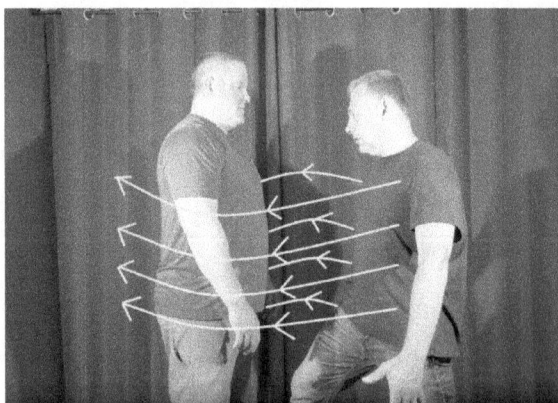

Ask yourself the questions again about this experience.

- Did you knock them off balance?
- How did it feel slamming into them? Solid, flimsy etc.?

- How did they feel this time?
- How did this experience compare to part one?

If you had the right thoughts in your mind it went very different. Those who have it done to them are often shocked because they were moved but felt nothing, no crash and bash just them moving backward.

When it was done to Paul he was totally surprised. He said "I was thinking, I don't feel anything but then why am I being moved backwards."

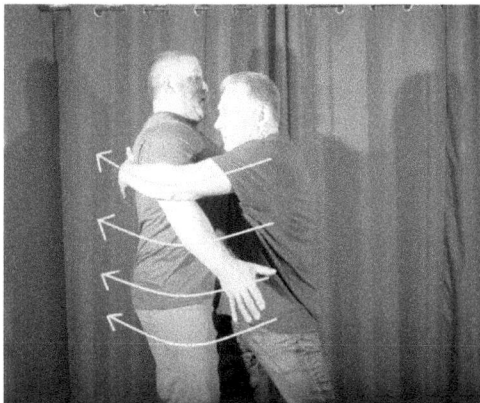

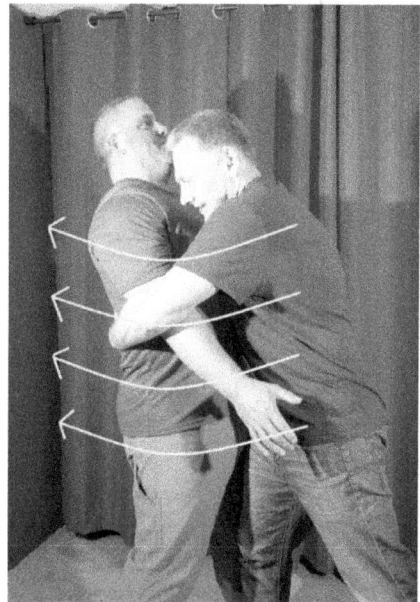

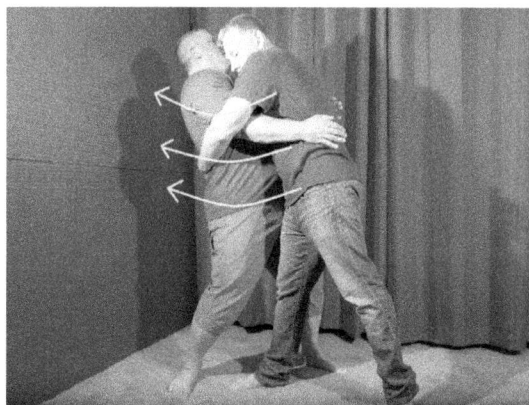

Note: We have previously thought of entering as honey seeping into the marble jar. One of the reasons I chose that visualization is to have not only the idea of completely filling the spaces but to have a sticky quality when you fill and contact. Here it is the closing and rushing past: we want to overwhelm them. (If you poured water into the jar of marbles it would also fill all the empty spaces, but in a faster way than the sticky honey.)

Drill Two: Rushing Water to Deflect

Part One

We're going to make a different use of the rushing water analog.

Empty space is something that can be used against us as well; therefore, our use of empty space has to be better than theirs.

This time the action is a low level single leg take-down.

Have it done on you without any visualization. (Illustrated in the pictures below.)

As we illustrate the single leg take-down I thought I would also highlight how empty space is used to make it work efficiently.

The shoot begins with targeting the empty space in front of the opponent.

You change levels to access that empty space and a small spot of empty space behind their leg you want to place your foot into.

You step one knee into the empty space in front of them and your other foot into the empty space behind their leg (to hook them). Your arms will pull and collapse their knees and your shoulder drives them over into the Rear Major Void putting them on the ground.

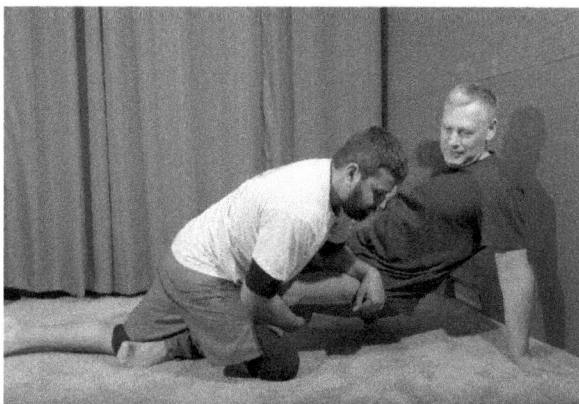

You, of course, have to pause and reflect on how that went.

- Did you get knocked off balance?
- How did it feel being slammed into? Solid, flimsy etc.?
- How did your partner feel about their take-down attempt?

Part Two

One defence for a shoot is a sprawl, which is really moving you into empty space away from the takedown. We are going to add to that with visualization.

This time as they come in for the single leg visualize yourself as that water rushing, only this time dropping down on top of them like a heavy waterfall driving them into empty space.

Note the driving of the Aggressor's head off into empty space, taking it off structure and preventing the Aggressor form accessing their back muscles.

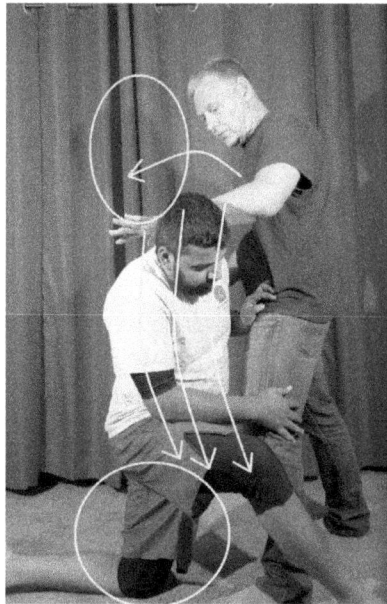

Once you have them off balance continue the visual of a waterfall only direct it, and them, into the empty space (Minor Void) at their side dropping them into it.

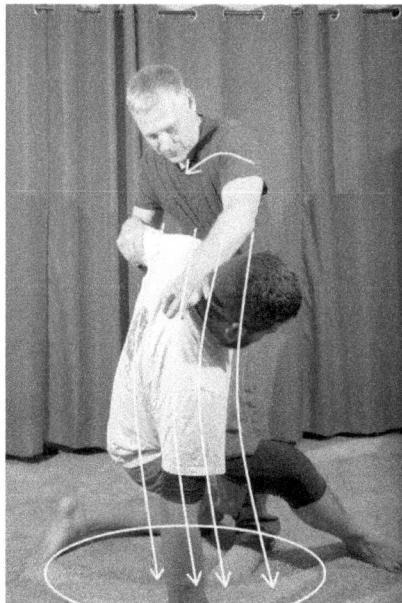

You, of course, have to pause and reflect on how that went.

- Did you get knocked off balance?
- How was it for your partner this time?

- How did it feel being slammed into them? Solid, flimsy etc.?

NOTE: Of course, this visualization of rushing water can also be used when you are doing the take down. As always, more skill can result in more success.

Let's Sum Up

What we have done is exercised our minds again to find another application of filling empty space. By using the thought of rushing water, we don't get entangled with slamming into the Aggressor's body (a maze line) but instead we rush past it to envelope it. Once you get used to this type of entry the visualization won't be needed. It is a tool, a set of training wheels.

Locks

By now you've got the idea of empty space and we've run through a number of drills where you explored the difference of not using empty space and using empty space. You should be able to tell now when you are, or are not, using empty space. Therefore, we'll keep in mind the visualizations, but we won't focus on them or have you first try things not using empty space any more (well until the first conditioning drill.) From this point on you should always be looking for and using empty space.

Locks, yes, empty space makes locks work wonderfully well, too.

Almost all locks work on the same basic principle of connecting to a point at the end of the lever you want, and a point just passed the joint you want to lock, then drawing a circle with those two points. I do mean draw a circle. A two-way action is good and certainly works, but a two way action forming a circle has more effect. Using empty space has even more.

I'll use a simple finger lock to show how the circling into empty space applies a lock. Note the taking of two points, circling those two points, and the fact the circle has to be done through empty space.

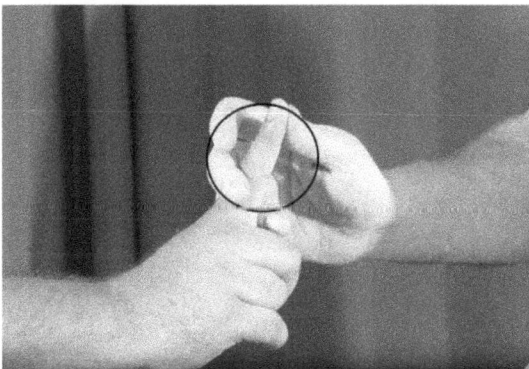

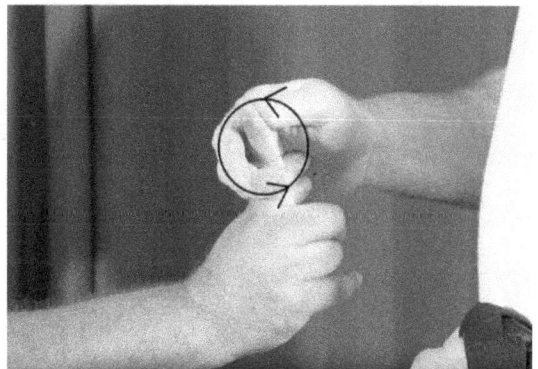

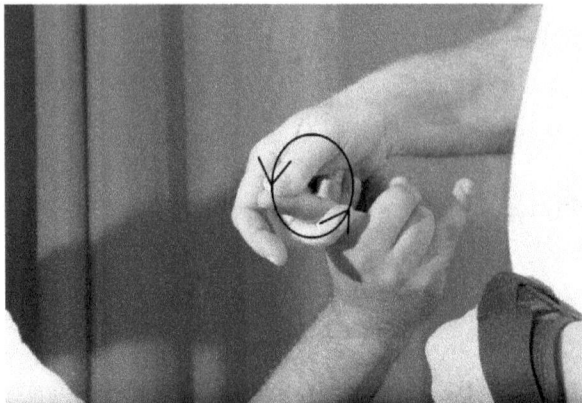

The wrist lock works off the same circling into empty space. Your fingers are placed at or just passed the inside of the wrist joint and your thumb is placed on the expressive finger's back knuckle. Rotate your fingers and thumb in a circle to apply the lock. But if you simply bend the hand towards the arm, some people with strong wrists can resist. However, if you circle so that their fingers go to the empty space beside their wrist, then resistance most often disappears.

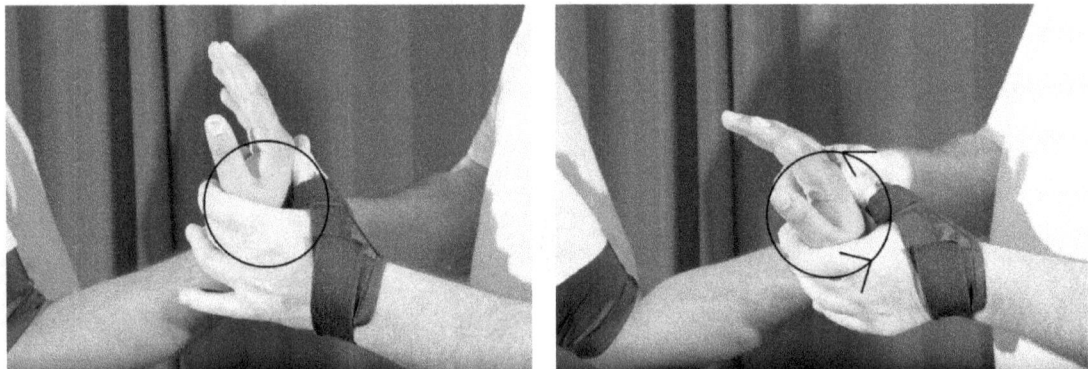

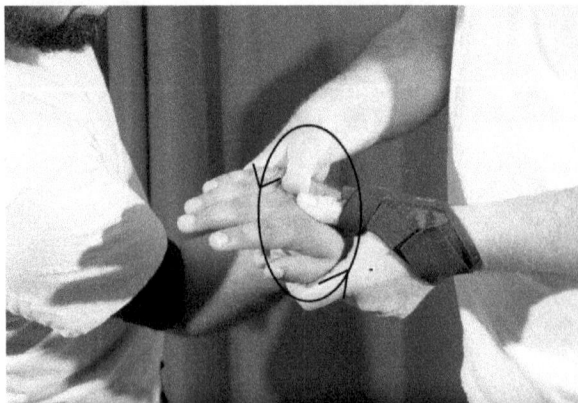

184

An arm bar is a simple lock. Connect to the forearm of the Aggressor down by the wrist and connect your other arm (or body part) just below their elbow. Once again, draw a circle, driving their elbow up and hand down. If the hand is taken down into empty space and the elbow is raised up into empty space it works exceptionally well. Stepping out into empty space taking the arm along with you to elongate it out over empty space also adds to the effectiveness.

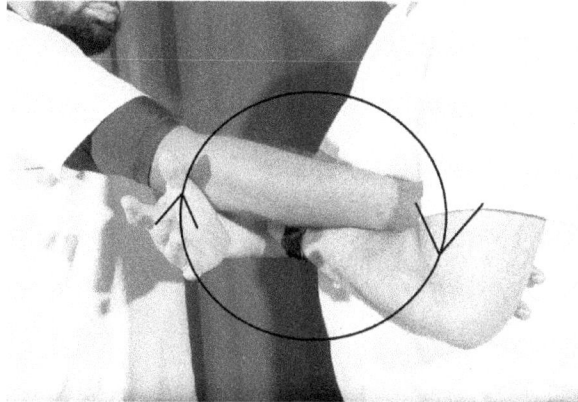

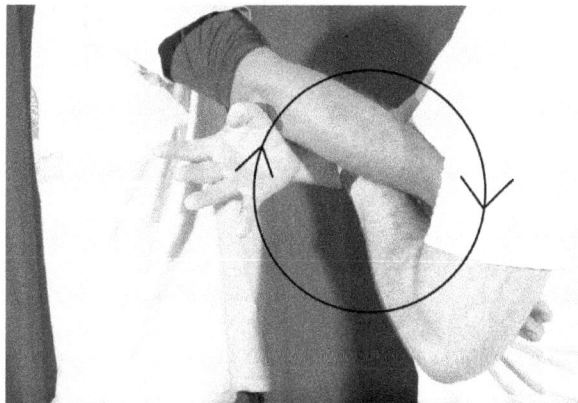

This isn't a book about locks, so I am not going to detail a lot; however, always look to where you take the limbs to gain the lock. Where is the arm taken in a Kimura (figure 4 lock) and where it is taken first often to get in position to apply the lock?

A Come Along

Let's look at the compound use of empty space in applying a come along, because the best locks lock more than the joint being focused on.

You need to control and escort a person out.

Approach on their front left side (from empty space) and grip their left wrist with your left hand.

Use the back of your right wrist to strike the front of their elbow joint (elbow pit) driving it back into empty space to bend their arm.

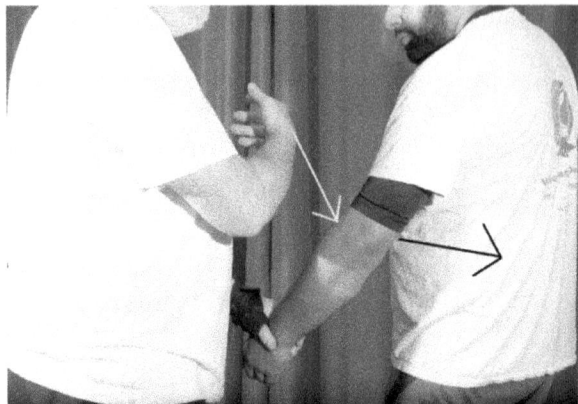

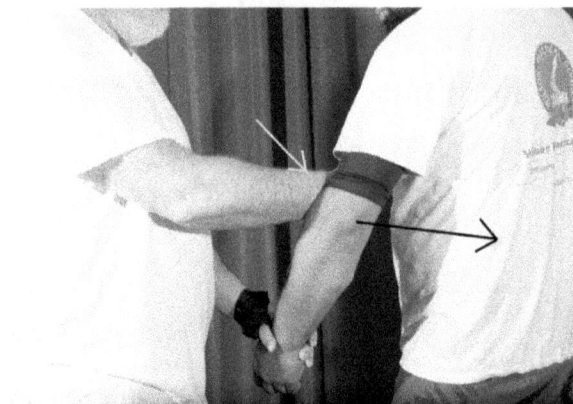

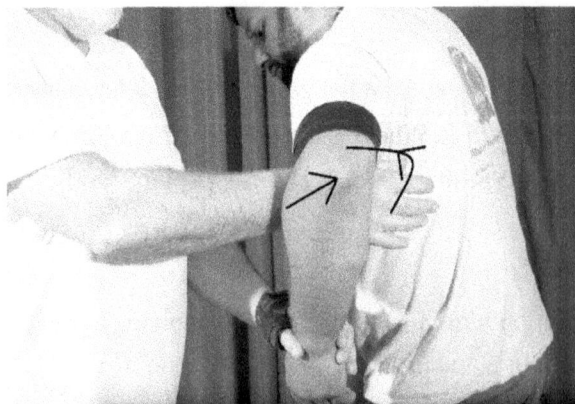

Slip your right hand around the elbow à la ball rolling, continuing to slip around their elbow joint coming through empty space up over the triceps and hooking onto their arm right at the elbow joint.

This rolling off the back of the wrist strike to slip up around to control their arm is just the type of maneuver and manipulation the Ball Rolling Drill was meant to enhance.

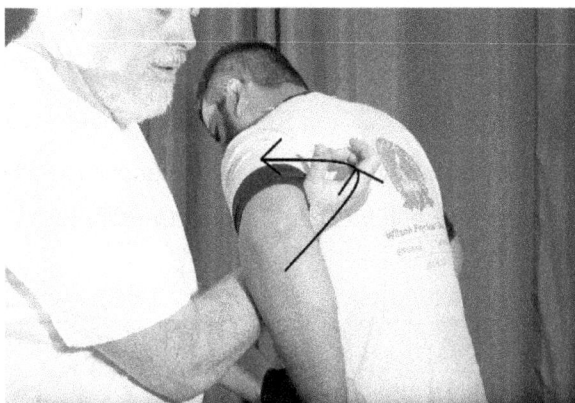

In the next picture note how you begin to move through empty space to get to their back.

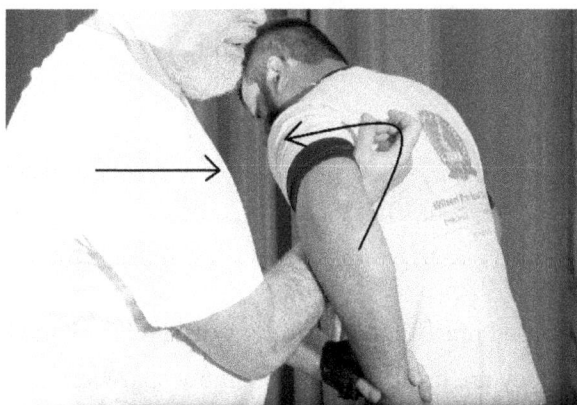

As you are rolling your wrist around the elbow, you slip through empty space behind them. Your left hand lets go of their wrist to come up and hook under their chin, with the back of your left wrist to pull their head to their left (through empty space) twisting their head to the left à la ball rolling.

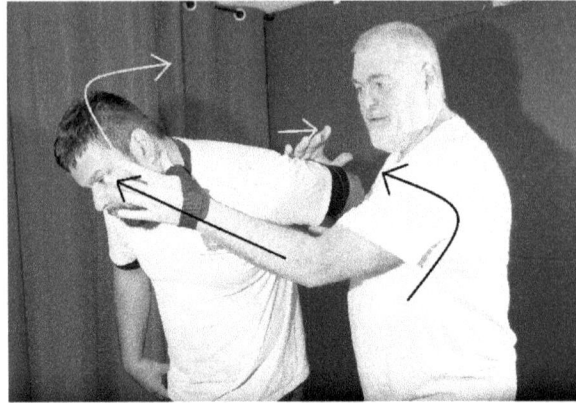

Finish by moving their chin through empty space to control their head as you finish your move through empty space to move behind them locking the arm into the control position to escort them out.

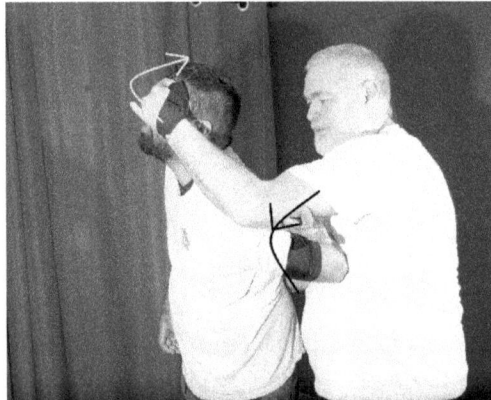

Aikido

While many reality-based practitioners express a dislike for Aikido because they see the attacks in Aikido as unreal, they are brilliant at using empty space and locks. I like Aikido and see the attacks they use as simply representations of lines of force.

Let's have a look at an Aikido technique, *Jodan Tsuki Hiji Kime Osae*, and use a shoulder lock for a takedown. The main difference between what is shown below and the formal Aikido technique is the entry, but after that the locking used is the same.

The Aggressor drives a left lead hand strike at your head.

Fill the empty space to the right of them rotating to your left and as you do, your left hand slips through empty space to position inside their arm ready to take control. You can see in the picture below the nice spot of empty space on the ground picked out for them to hit.

Now rotate to your left, bringing your right arm along the back of their shoulder, just off the joint on their upper arm. As you do so, your left arm will remain bent and raised to attach to the inside of their forearm. This rotation will bring them out over the Front Major Void.

Now that they are out over the Major Void you can use the arm bar control of their shoulder to drive them into it.

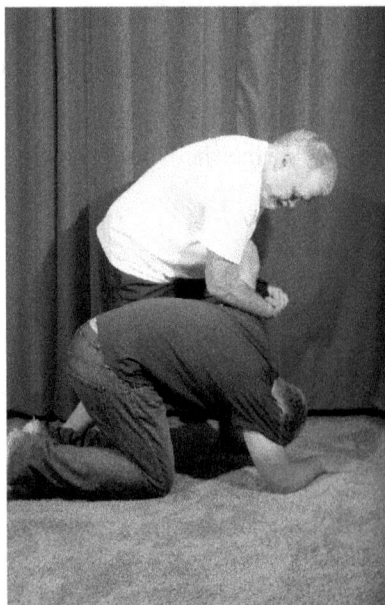

The picture above uses the Clamp from *Watch Out for the Pointy End*.

Drill One: Play

At this point simply grab a partner and play with applying locks, looking for how you use empty space.

One point I want to make on locks. Trying to grab a limb and apply a lock can be very difficult, particularly in a real situation where the other person is not a cooperating partner. You would think then locks are hard to get, but not so. If you move properly through empty space, you often find the Aggressor offers you the gift of a limb and the opportunity to apply a lock.

I like thinking of locks as gifts because it is exceptionally rude to try and grab a gift before it is offered, but it is also rude to turn one down.

Let's Sum Up

Locks are a manipulation of a limb or body part (head for neck cranks). Anytime you manipulate the Aggressor you will use empty space to do so; locks are no different. Most martial arts contain some locks, so take a moment to look at something from your style or system and look see if the use of empty space is already there or how you can add it and if adding empty space made it better. The best locks are ones that create a chain of locking joints, something we will see in the next chapter.

Hand Rocking

I have added this eclectic use of empty space, or rather the elimination of empty space, right after locking because it can be used to control an arm and manipulate the Aggressor so that you can get into a position to put a lock on them. It can also be used to get behind them, control them or have them in position to handcuff. In fact, it was with my Peace Officer friends that the main use for this came to mind. It is very useful to anyone whose duty is to control someone, law enforcement, security, doorman (bouncers), and so on.

Hand Rocking can be very useful for Law Enforcement officers (LEOs) when they have a passive person who is actively resisting the officer's attempts to put them under arrest. The passive but active resistance person can be the hardest to deal with.

A cooperative person simply turns around and allows themselves to be cuffed. The aggressive resistant person is also easier to deal with because they are trying to damage the officer and the use of force is clearly justified to most that see it.

The passive active resistant person is not trying to harm the officer, but they are actively avoiding cooperating by refusing to give control of their arms to the officer and refusing to turn around. What makes this difficult is the fact that to observers they are not fighting the officer, so they mistakenly think the person is not resisting. Most people are unaware of how difficult it is to get control over a person who is not aggressively trying to do something to you, but is totally resisting and uncooperative.

Hand Rocking is a way of closing out empty space at the Aggressor's wrist that creates a chain of locks from the wrist to the shoulder. It can be very useful not only with the passive active resisting person, but also in any lock where control of the arm is gain by connecting to the wrist or hand.

Your hand is in the C-clamp position and placed on the wrist of your partner. Your thumb and fingers must each be on a "bony side" not fleshy. You then "rock" your hand up or down to close the empty space out between your thumb and their wrist and your fingers and their wrist.

NOTE: You are NOT squeezing, simply rock your hand.

The purpose of rocking the hand is to do it in the direction that locks the elbow and the shoulder. This makes it hard for the person to turn in the direction of that arm and makes it easy for you to take control of that arm.

While Hand Rocking can be applied at any time, let's look at taking control of the Aggressor's arm from the front to either move them or take their back.

Example One

The Law Enforcement Officer (LEO) comes up to a person and they refuse to turn around to be cuffed. Their arms are at their side and they refuse to present them.

I am going to continue to use the term Aggressor even for the passive active resisting person because they are illegally resisting arrest even though not aggressively at this point, but as far as the officer is concerned at any moment that may change.

NOTE: For those unfamiliar with law enforcement work when you do not cooperate with an arrest you are resisting, no matter how many times you may shout "I am not resisting." Preventing the officer from placing you in handcuffs is resisting. It is not aggressively resisting but it is resisting.

Start slightly to the Aggressor's right side. Place your right hand in a C-clamp position on top of the Aggressor's right wrist: palm down and thumb to the rear side of the Aggressor's wrist bone. Your left hand will be high on the shoulder and visible. This is the distraction to take the attention away from the real purpose of your right hand. Plus, your hand is up should the Aggressor go from passive resistance to aggressive (setting your own maze line.)

NOTE: You must position your hand so that your thumb is on the outside bone of the wrist and your fingers are on the inside bone. The only way to totally eliminate empty space in this connection by Hand Rocking is if you connect to bone. It will not have the proper effect if your thumb is on the inside of the wrist (i.e. close to where you would take a pulse) and your fingers are on the opposite side, as there is no way to close right to the bone.

Here is where things get different. Do not squeeze to grab, but instead simply rock your hand, thumb going up and fingers going down, to take all the empty space out between your thumb and fingers and the Aggressor's wrist.

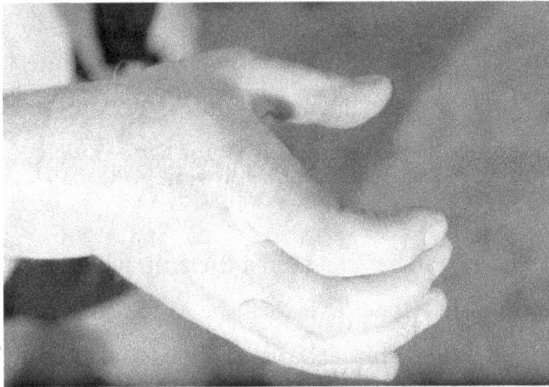

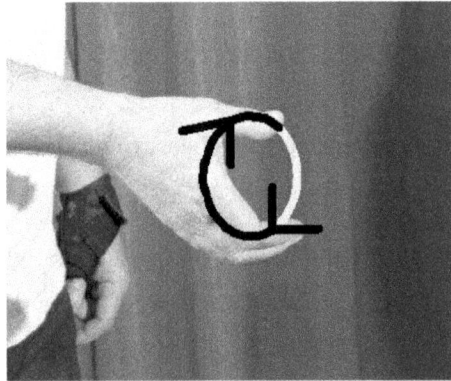

The next pictures are to give the idea of how Hand Rocking takes the empty space out between your hand (the C-clamp) and their wrist. The filled-in circle below represents their wrist.

Note the empty space indicated by the small ovals beside the circle in the picture below. These are the empty spaces that will be removed by rocking the hand.

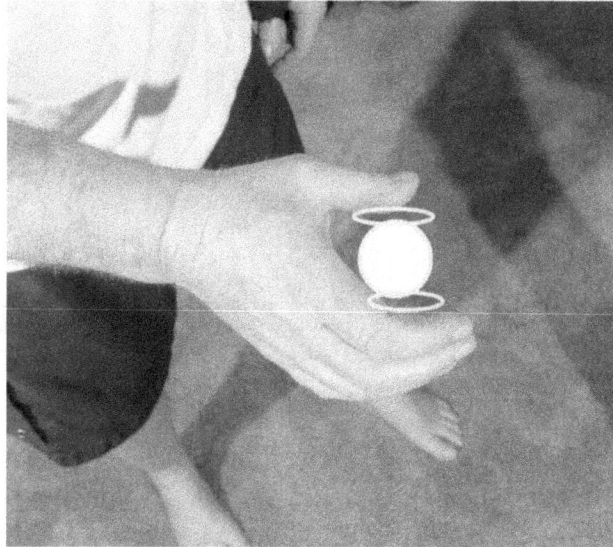

Note in the picture below that rocking the hand moved your thumb and fingers so that the empty space pockets are now gone. This is vital for Hand Rocking to work.

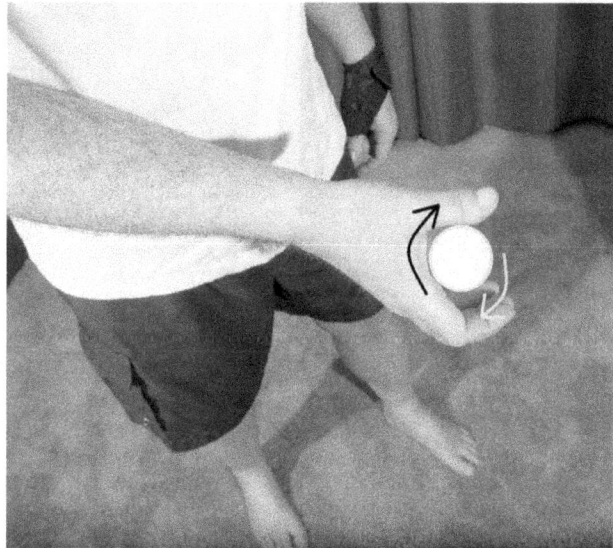

Make sure your hand is positioned when placing on their wrist as shown below.

Now you rock your hand as shown below and rotate right as you step towards the back of the Aggressor with your left foot. The Aggressor's arm is moved out in front of you to empty space by your rotation.

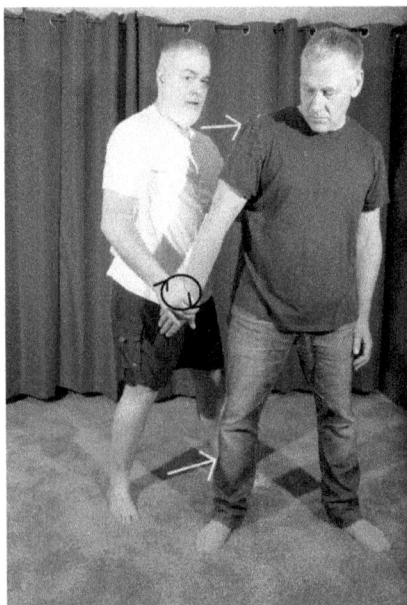

Let's take a closer look at the hand-rocking: the rocking of the hand is going to set up a chain of locked joints. When the rocking locks the wrist, their elbow will lock out as shown in the second picture below.

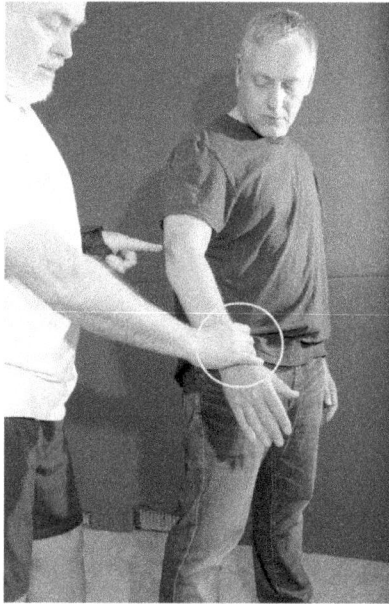

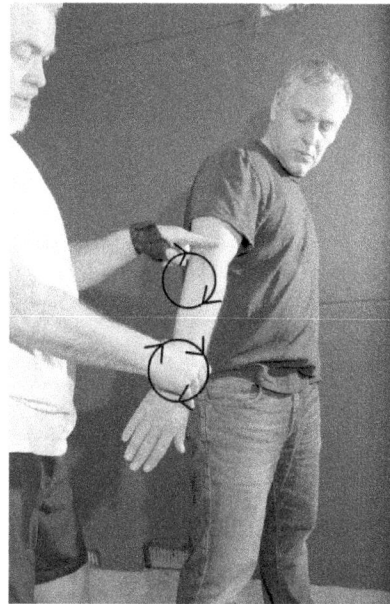

As the elbow locks their shoulder will rise up and away disconnecting (not dislocating) it from the strength of the back locking it out of place.

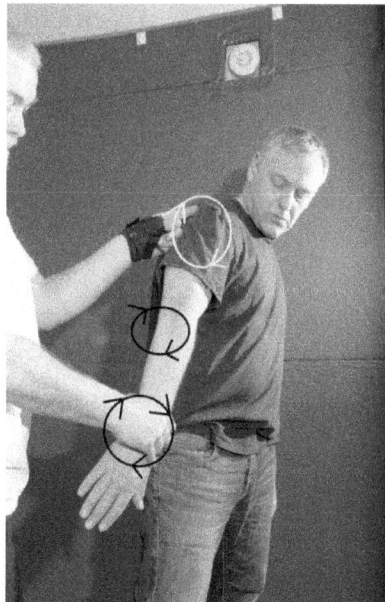

With the arm in this position it locks their arm like a stick the Aggressor cannot rotate to their right which allows you to step behind. Once behind them you can proceed to control and cuff.

Example Two

One move taught to LEOs to take an Aggressor to the ground is the arm bar. I have had reports that they can find it hard to apply out of the classroom setting. I believe an understanding of empty space and how to use it will enable the LEOs to take people down when they are resisting. I believe the difficulty they are having is due to trying to press the Aggressors down through their structure.

Hand Rocking can assist in applying the arm bar take down, because it creates the elbow lock. If the LEOs then use empty space the take down should happen much easier.

Start in that same side position.

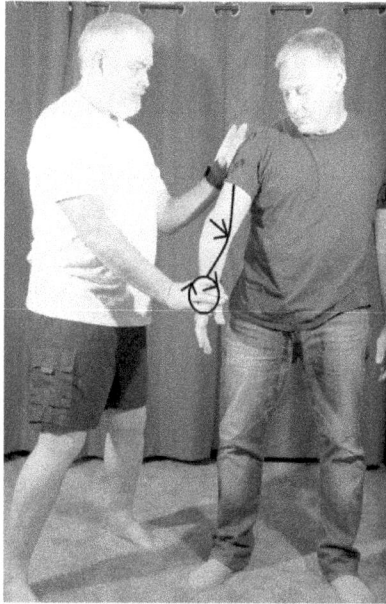

Hand Rocking is used, but this time not to step behind but to begin to lock the elbow. Note the picture below that as you rock your hand, you also move the Aggressor's arm out into empty space away from their body and shift your forearm to the back of their elbow.

Now step back and around into empty space and direct them to the ground, to that big void out in front of them, and not back into their structure. As per the section on locking you can use the circle into empty space to cause and control their descent to the ground.

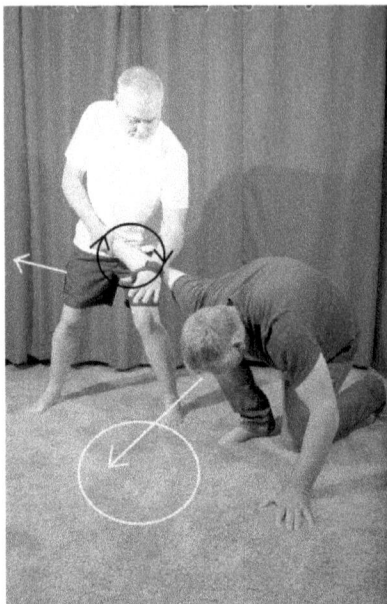

If you do not step, you do not open the empty space to move them over and put them down. By not moving you can end up pressing down on the arm into their structure. That will make the arm bar take down either very hard to pull off or fail all together. Simply continue moving to open empty space as you apply the arm bar until they are all the way to the ground.

Example Three

If you cannot approach from the side you can also use Hand Rocking from the front to enable an arm drag to allow you to move behind the Aggressor.

Start is in front of the Aggressor. While it can be done with either hand it works best with the outside hand; therefore, in this example, you place your right hand in a C-clamp position on top of the Aggressor's right wrist, palm down and thumb to the front side of their wrist bone. Your left hand will be mid-chest and visible. This is the distraction to take the attention away from the real purpose of your right hand and it sets your own maze line should things escalate.

NOTE: Again, you must position your hand so that your thumb is on the bone of the thumb side of their wrist and your fingers are on the opposite side's bone. The only way to totally eliminate empty space in this connection by Hand Rocking is if you connect to bone. It will not have the proper effect if your thumb is on the fleshy or flat part of the wrist (i.e. close to where you would take a pulse) and your fingers are on the opposite side, as there is no way to close right to the bone. I know I've said this before but it is vital so I'm saying it again.

You now rock your hand with the thumb going down and fingers going up.

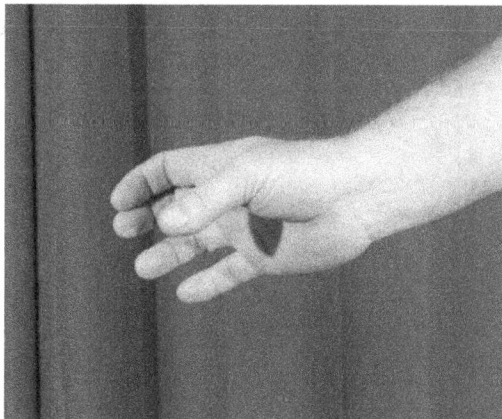

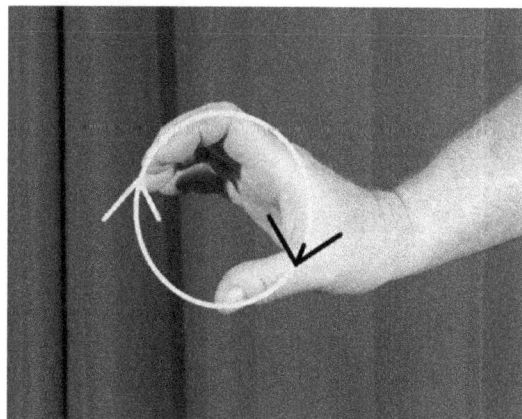

This will lock the elbow in place allowing you to use your left hand to grip the back of the elbow for an arm drag. The best way to use empty space is to NOT think of moving their arm but think of it as a hold to pull you through empty space behind the Aggressor.

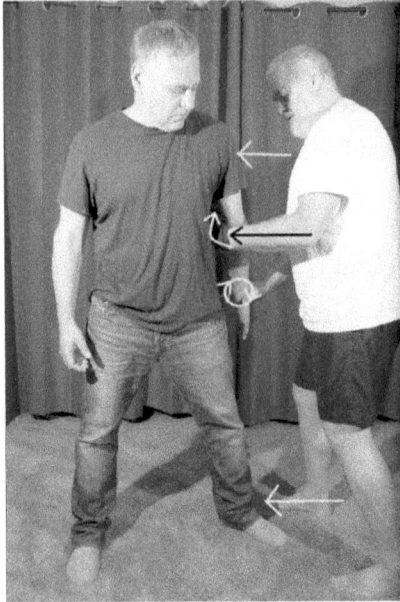

Let's take a detailed look at what hand rocking is doing when applied this way.

When you rock your thumb down and fingers up it brings the elbow forward into a locked position.

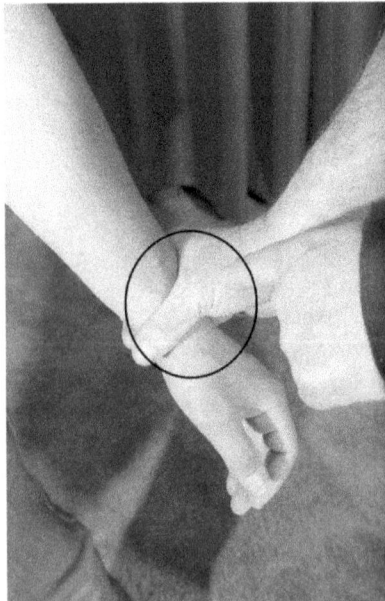

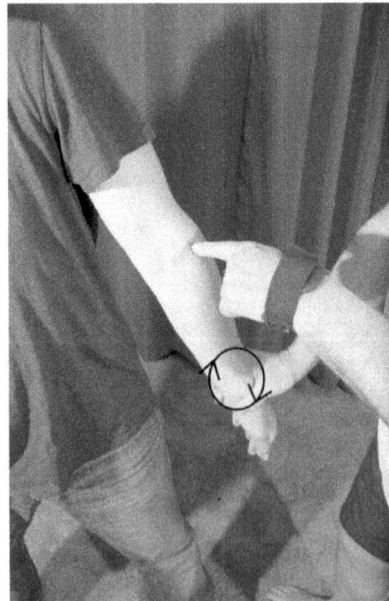

Because the elbow is now in a locked position you can easily hook it with your left hand and then pull yourself behind them using an arm drag.

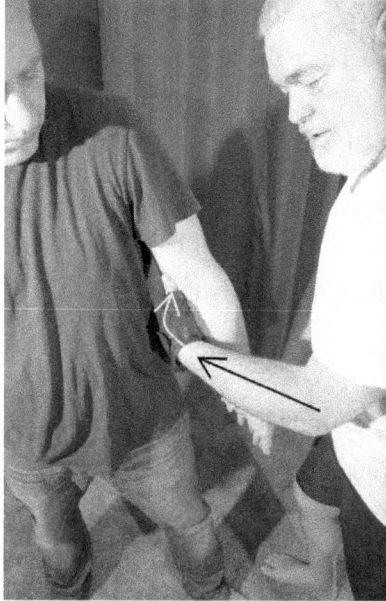

Once behind, you can proceed with the techniques to cuff or take down the Aggressor.

Note how the locking out of the elbow allows you to grab it for the arm drag.

SAFETY NOTE: Remember to release the wrist when you do the arm drag or it becomes a very nasty arm bar (or worse – arm break.)

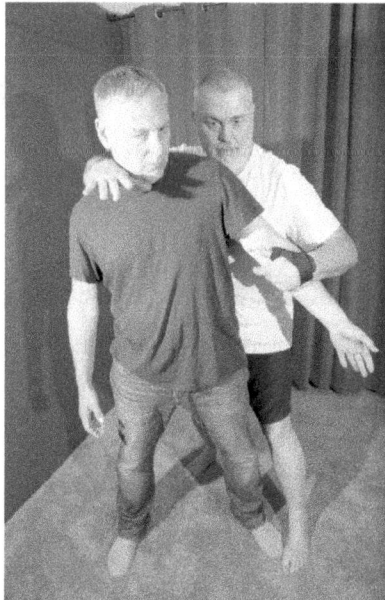

NOTE: In the examples one, two and three an alternative is to use the locked arm like a pole to drive the shoulder up to off balance the Aggressor and move them by driving the shoulder farther up.

Example Four

Another common position to actively resist being cuffed is for the Aggressor to cross their arms in front of them and hold them tight to their body.

For this example, their right arm is over their left.

Place the C-clamp (with your right hand) position over the Aggressor's right wrist with your thumb on the downward side.

Note: Again, for safety you set your own maze line, just in case the Aggressor wants to move from passive resistance to aggressive.

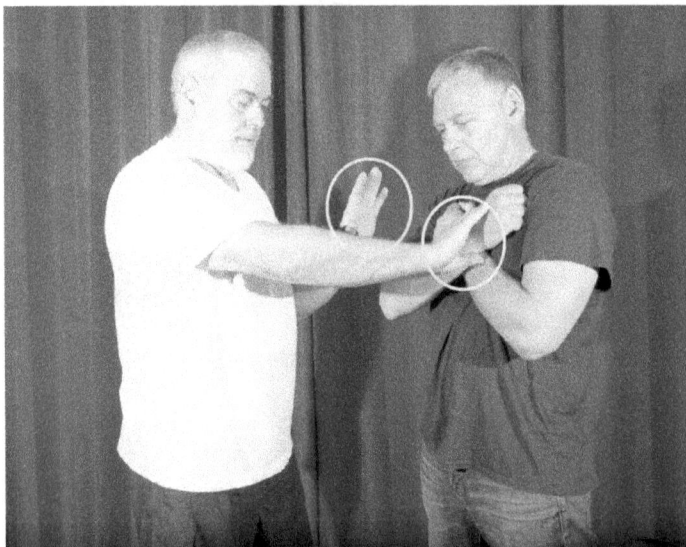

Rock your hand thumb up and fingers down closing off any empty space with their fingers rocking downward and their thumb rocking upward.

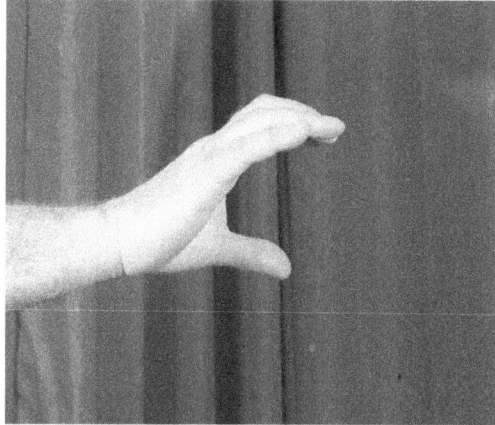

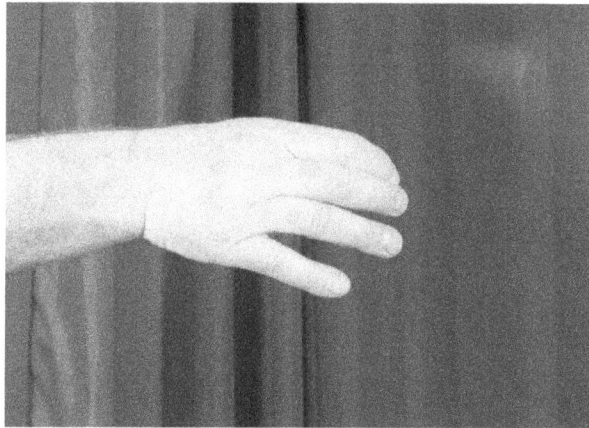

Once again, you can rotate to your right, then slide to their left and slip through empty space behind the Aggressor, because the Aggressor cannot rotate to their right to stop your movement while you have the Hand Rock on their wrist.

Note the drawn circles in the picture below to see how the hand rocking circle at the wrist creates a circle locking the elbow and raising the shoulder.

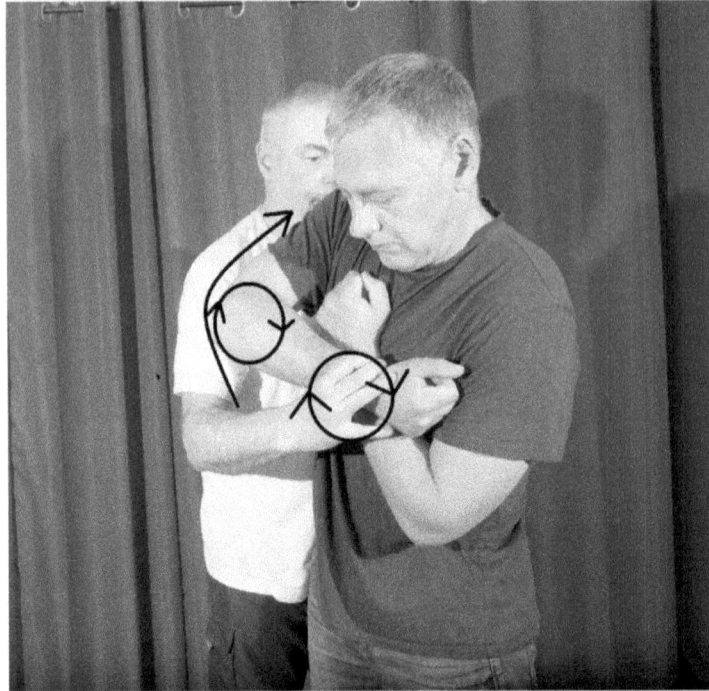

Hand Rocking is not a long-term solution. It is a momentary action to gain control and manipulate the Aggressor to allow your next action.

Hand Rocking can be used anytime you get a hold of the wrist. It is not grabbing; therefore, there is no squeezing or tensing involved. It is a simple rocking of the hand and often prevents (for a moment) the Aggressor from twisting and escaping, because of how it manipulates and locks the arm's joints in a chain.

Take a moment here to go back to the Locking chapter and add in Hand Rocking where applicable as you apply the locks in that chapter.

Let's Sum Up

Hand Rocking is using filling of empty space to create a chain of locking joints in the arm allowing you to manipulate the Aggressor into positions so that you can take control of them. You will note it also is used in conjunction with moving yourself through empty space and moving the arm you have Hand Rocked out into empty space. Empty Space is not a singularity, it is an exponential principle in it usage. And, again, Hand Rocking is a momentary action not a long-term solution.

Empty Space on the Ground

I am not going to get into striking on the ground in this book because it will be part of my upcoming book *From the Ground Up* dealing with counter assault from the ground. And before the naysayers jump in yes, yes you can strike from the ground and powerfully. Is it the best position? No, but it can most certainly be done, if you know how.

What I want to focus on here is the use of empty space on the ground to move yourself and to manipulate the Aggressor. Brazilian Jiu-Jitsu (BJJ) is a perfect style to study and look at if you want to see wonderful use of empty space. Absolutely, other ground systems use it, but BJJ is the one I look at.

Empty space is used so that you do not have to directly engage the Aggressor's size and strength. Helio Gracie was a smaller man who had to overcome his opponent's size and strength all the time, so it is no mystery as to why we find empty space a constant principle used in BJJ.

Again, just as with the locks, I am not going to go into numerous examples because once I show you a few techniques on the ground to illustrate using empty space I want you to look at your ground work or reference material on ground work to see and apply empty space on the ground.

Before we begin, anytime you are using empty space you need to figure out where it is. When standing, empty space exists in the directions where the Aggressor does not have a brace. The ground is no different. The first place we look for empty space is where the Aggressor doesn't have a brace: where they are not connected to the ground. The second place we look is at the holes in between the Aggressor's connections to the ground.

The Common Headlock or Scarf Hold Escape

Position: You are on your back. Your partner is at your right side, on their right side with their right arm wrapped over your head and neck.

Being flat on your back is not good in this position, so you want to shift onto your side. It is important in this use of empty space that you do not try to move the Aggressor, but rather move yourself into the spot of empty space right behind you. Pull yourself out from under like pulling the rug out from under someone or the old trick of pulling the table cloth out from under a bunch of dishes.

Note: You can also place your left forearm as a maze line to block them from applying pressure (but be careful of a head and arm choke).

Every movement into empty space opens up other avenues of empty space. Note how the shift below from the first picture to the second creates another opportunity of empty space to shift into.

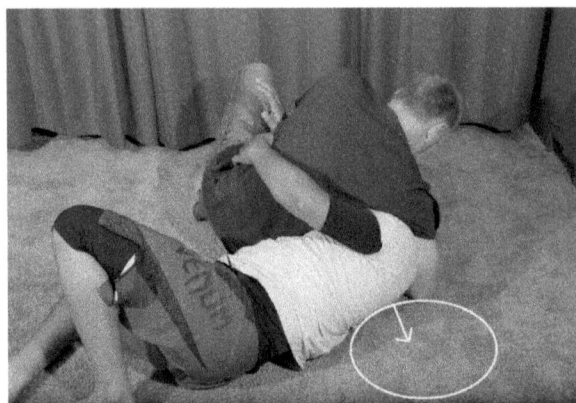

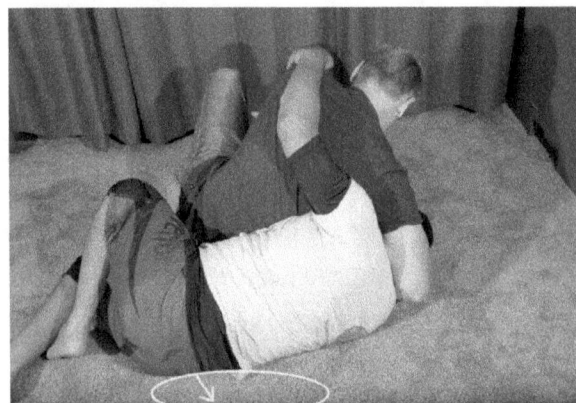

Now that you are safer on your side you can still use the empty space behind you to rotate your hips and go to your knees.

You will slide your right knee through empty space out away from your partner along the mat and as you slide twist (also through empty space) onto your knees.

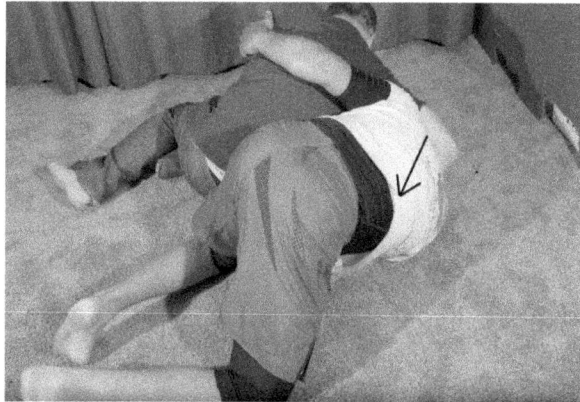

Once you move enough your head will be pulling your partner's right arm up into empty space making enough room for you to slide it out and get back to your feet.

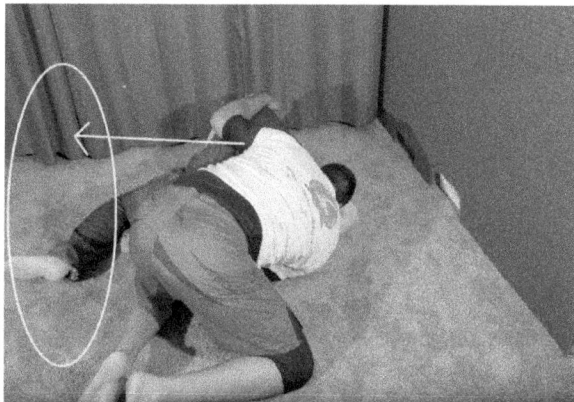

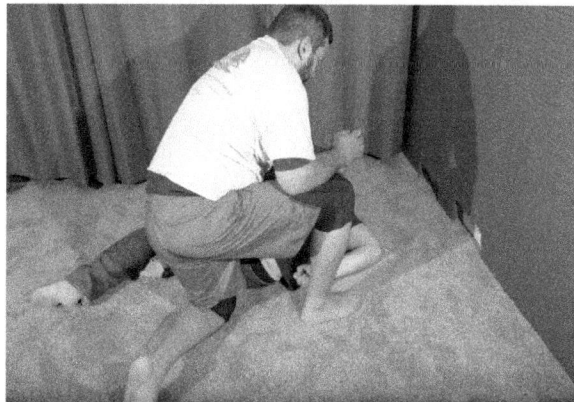

You'll note all these actions are done moving through empty space. (At this point you should not be surprised.)

The Common Conversion from Being at the Bottom of the Mount

Position: You are on your back with your partner in mount position.

You frame, or set a brace (a maze line), with your forearms and elbow so that the Aggressor cannot follow and adjust as you move (called shrimping in ground work) your hip up into empty space allowing you to pull your leg into empty space and wrap around your partner then you repeat to free the opposite side.

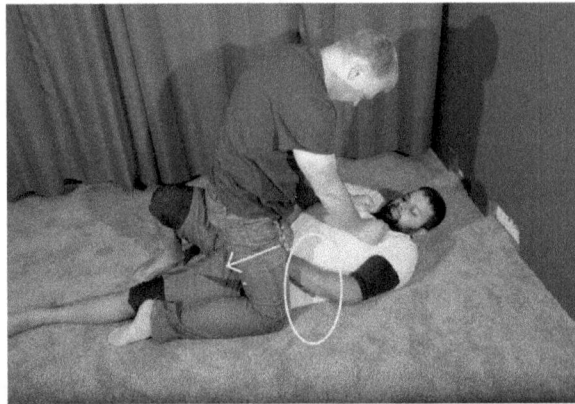

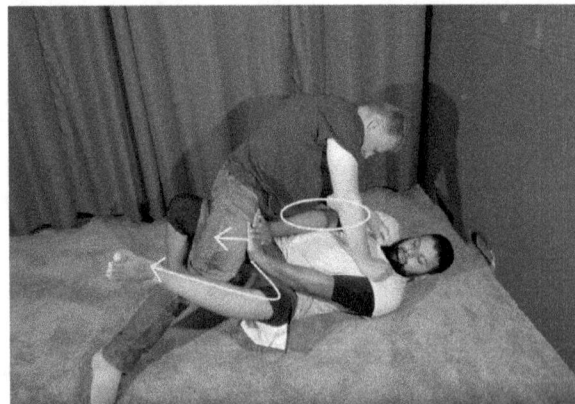

From here you have created empty space to move/shrimp your right hip up and free from underneath the Aggressor.

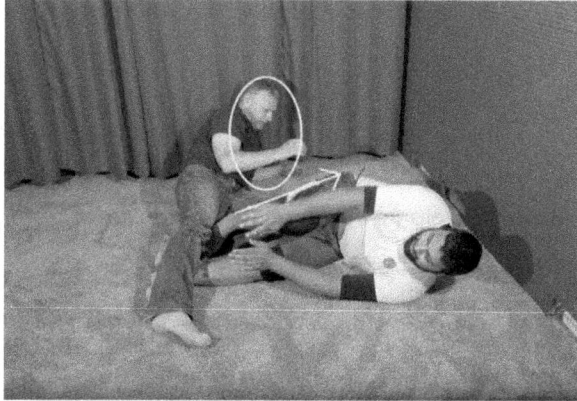

Don't forget possible strikes. Your movement has opened a path from his face to your foot, so use it. (Counter assault is not a mixed martial arts match; therefore, as long as you can legally justify your actions you can kick the Aggressor in the head while he is on the ground.)

While that was a very basic move, I like basic moves because the principles are easy to highlight in them. Framing or setting a brace is creating your own maze line, just as in one of our first drills, so that you partner cannot follow your movement. You are closing off that empty space to them.

Escaping the Back

Another escape that uses blocking empty space and moving into empty space is the shrug out of an assault on the ground from the rear.

A number of things are being done here (in the pictures below). You move yourself to create and use empty space, much as was done on the head and arm take down, and then block empty space so you, and only you, can use it. The pictures below will give a couple of viewpoints so you can see what is being used in this example. In counter assault the goal is always to get back to my feet from the ground.

Your left hand comes up to work for wrist control to prevent a choke. Shrug or slip yourself down as you slide your right leg out straight, which will open up space under the Aggressor's right leg. This allows you to drop your elbow on his leg forcing it down into that space and releasing his hook. Your shrug or slide adds power to you elbow drop.

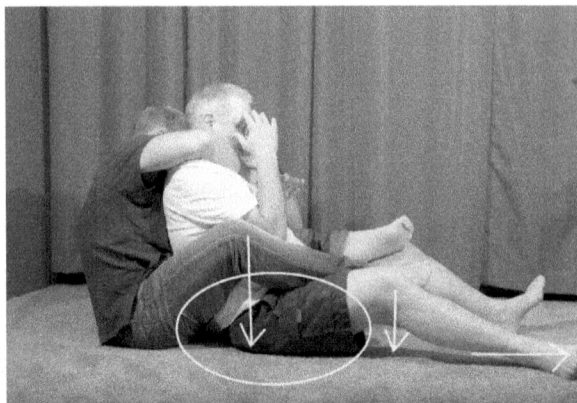

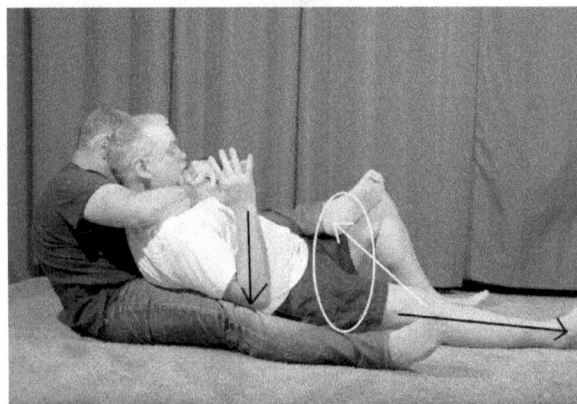

Now that he has lost his hook. Bend your right knee to prevent him getting it back (setting a maze line) and rotate to your left up and over his other hook to break free.

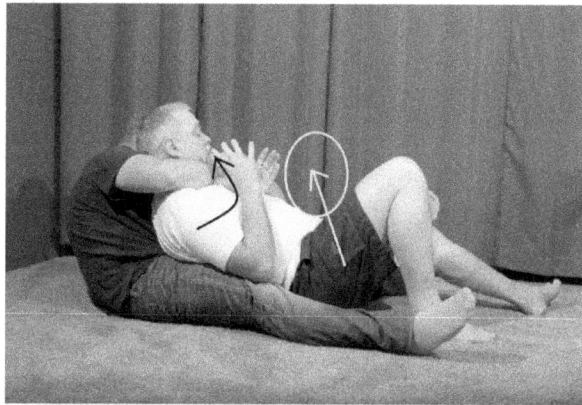

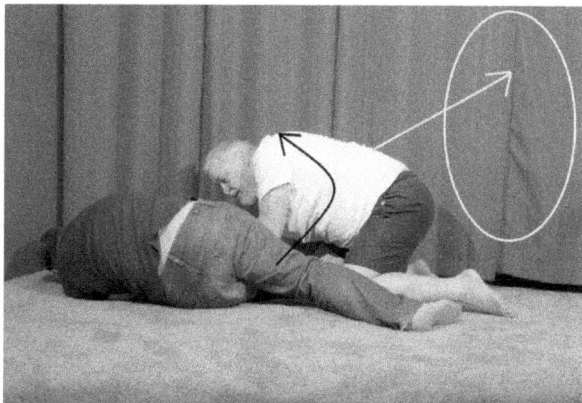

Now get back to your feet.

Below is a look at the other side. This is working on wrist control to prevent the choke, so as you roll to your left, use that to take his arm into empty space.

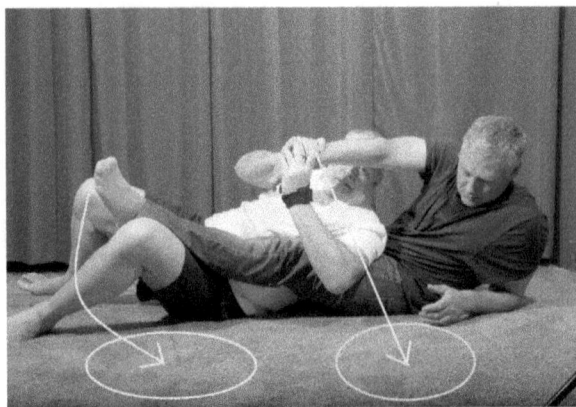

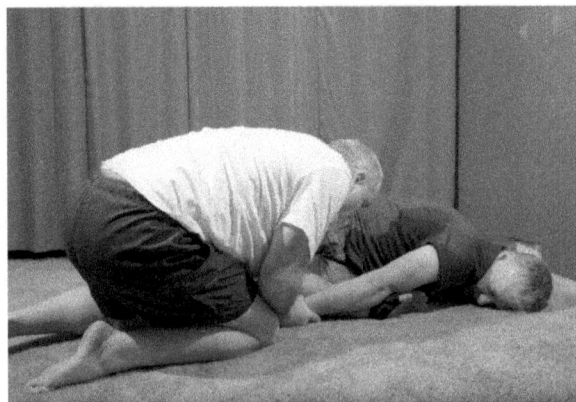

If you look at all good escapes you will see they first establish where the connections are: seeing the lines of the maze. Then they focus on where those lines are not, where the empty space is: the path out of the maze. Sometimes we have to move to create the empty space we need just as we did in the head and arm take-down.

The examples here are not earth shattering. They are simple and intentionally so, because I don't want the simplicity of empty space being obscured by needless complexity. However, you should now see that every technique, be it simple or complex, either uses or would be improved by using empty space.

Recommended Reading

I highly recommend picking up a good BJJ book (and there are many), from solid basics in *Brazilian Jiu-Jitsu: Theory and Technique* by Renzo and Royler Gracie, Eddie Bravo's *Jiu-Jitsu Unleashed* to *Mastering the Rubber Guard* and *Mastering the Twister* all have moving through empty space. If you look at the closing in and elimination of space used in those positions, you can see filling the jar of marbles. I also like series of books on the Guard by Joe Moreira and Ed Beneville. These are all great books to see empty space and my favourite book is *Jiu-Jitsu University* by Saulo Ribereiro with Kevin Howell. I could go on, because any good BJJ book is a great book to see empty space.

Let's Sum Up

On the ground you have a maze to solve. It is a basic problem. You note where they are connected to the ground because you want to move through where they are not. You want to note where they are connected to you, because you do not want to move into that connection. You note the holes between their connection to the ground and their connections to you. You want to see the path through the empty space, so that you can set up your own maze lines (framing) to block them from cutting you off. Just because you are on the ground doesn't mean there is no empty space.

This is not a Duel

We have today what I call a dueling mentality. What I mean by that is our idea of conflict and confrontation is squaring off with an opponent.

It was not always like this.

On a battlefield, it wasn't like we see in the adventure movies where the hero seeks out the big bad in the middle, the sides separate and then the two then fight face to face as all others hold back. The truth was you could be attacked from all sides, which is why troops in a strong formation were successful. They limited those more effective assaults.

We are even jaded by old westerns where the good guy and the bad guy meet out in the street to see who the fastest draw was. Billy the Kid did not die in such a gun fight. Sherriff Pat Garrett waited in Billy's hotel room in the dark and shot him as he entered.

What happened to bring in this face to face mentality?

As time moved on and conflict moved off the battlefield there was a shift. Conflicts transformed, and the concept of dueling came into being, where it was one on one and face to face. Rules were created and enforced.

This concept of dueling and rules continued into most combat sports. Boxers face off one on one and face to face. Wrestlers do too, as do Judoka, BJJ, Fencers, and MMA.

The concept of facing your opponent head-on has been built into us through this dueling mentality. Attacking from behind is seen by some as unfair.

The old concept of stepping outside compared to the violent predator that blindsides you. One is seen as honourable and the other evil, yet in violence and self-defence your survival is the goal and how you do it (as long as it is within the bounds of our legal system) is irrelevant.

We also find that the dueling mentality places us in a box and confines us.

Here is a simple drill that often (not always) shows the current thought process.

Have two participants face off, and EACH TAKING A TURN TO MOVE one partner moves to angle off on the other.

After one partner has moved the other can readjust. And if you try the drill before reading this you will find that they often readjust by moving back into that face-off equal position.

Once we engage is there really any need to be facing your Aggressor?

Once we engage is there any benefit to being head-on face-to-face?

No, I am not saying give them your back.

The first option is to readjust by getting an angle on your partner. Therefore, when your partner moves instead of moving back to equilibrium, move so you have an angle and a better strategic position.

In this case, you are in a better strategic position, but the dueling mentality still shows because we tend to then face into our partner's core and structure. This means when we move we will most often move straight into their structure, and then we are in a force-on-force fight.

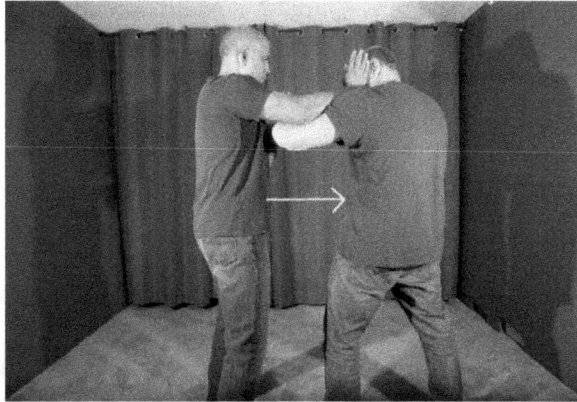

This isn't terrible but think back to our very first drill, the obstacle drill. When we focused on the obstacles we moved towards them, sometimes even bumping into them. My good friend and training partner, Rick Bottomley, worked in Africa many years ago and when driving through the grasslands they saw a crashed SUV. It had gone off the road and hit a tree. In fact, it hit the only tree, and I mean the ONLY tree visible on the entire plain for miles.

You might wonder how that could happen. I would say it is because when going off the road they saw the tree and, in order not to hit it, they focused on it and, hit it.

When my buddy and KPC Self Defense owner, Randy King was learning to snow board he was taught when boarding through trees to never look at the trees and to always look between them. This focus on the empty space between the trees prevented the type of collision Rick Bottomley saw in Africa. See, empty space can be used in many ways.

Let's apply that avoid the collision thought process to engaging the Aggressor and this dueling mentality of facing them head on. If we face them head on where will our focus be and therefore where will our next move be?

Right, directly into them. Right into their structure and strength. Exactly what we do not want to do.

Instead, once we engage there is no reason to be face-to-face and all the drills we have done can now be shifted and redone with us always taking a position that faces empty space. Once again, just like the obstacle drill, if we focus on where empty space is we will use it, but if we focus on the obstacle, the Aggressor, we will go head to head with them.

Think back to dealing with that looping sucker punch. In the end, we wanted to enter empty space but also finish the move facing empty space, so it could immediately be used in our next action.

This is not to imply we don't take note of the Aggressor and their position, but just as we note the lines of a maze and their position, they are used to lead us to empty space and not into them.

So instead of facing their structure, we can face empty space and then our next move is far more likely to be into empty space.

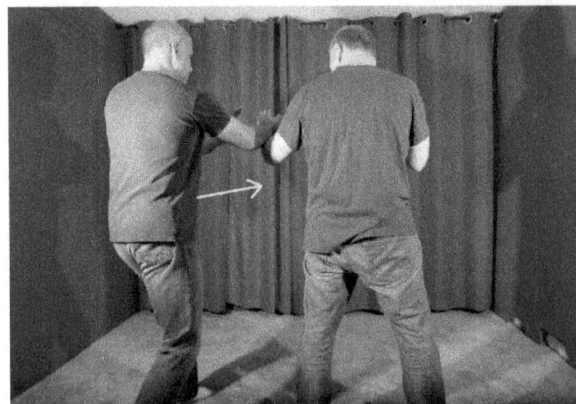

Once we are facing empty space then that is going to be the obvious way to move next.

When you are working on a technique think over for a moment how it might be enhanced if your entry did not end with you facing directly towards the Aggressor. Pause after your entry to see how you can change it to leave the dueling mentality behind and face empty space. See how that will enhance your next action against the Aggressor.

This same thought process applies to bad breath range. We are conditioned to clinch face to face when there can be advantages to shifting to face empty space.

Let's Sum Up

Every time you move you want to be well structured and in a strong strategic position. Face-to-face is an equal position, so don't make it your default setting. Change to always ending facing some empty space. But please don't give your back to the bad guy either. You want to be accepting the gifts, not giving them.

Ending Empty Space

We've covered moving into empty space and manipulating the Aggressor into empty space, but one aspect of getting them moving through empty space is to suddenly draw a maze line across their path, abruptly ending their movement.

This can be likened to the old clothesline technique in football, illegal due to the damage it can cause.

Or you can see this ending of empty space in Aikido moves.

You simply manipulate the Aggressor so they are moving, or moved, towards or through empty space, then place a part of you across their path, ending empty space.

Example One: Interrupt with a Strike

The Aggressor throws a front kick and you move into the pocket of empty space on the outside, much like we did for the lead hand, because they are both straight lines of incoming force. (You are not as deep because the leg is a longer weapon than the arm.) Once at the side, you can do a number of things. In this example, you can see there is a path from their face to your hand. We can cut off the Aggressor's movement through empty space by striking ala the football clothesline.

Before you look at the pictures, imagine a driven front kick expecting to hit a target but then hitting, nothing... empty space. This will cause the Aggressor to drop forward into that empty space, and that is where you meet and end that movement.

Example Two: Interrupt with Body Manipulation

This use of empty space is also consistent with changing directions in my book on knife defence, *Watch Out For The Pointy End*. When you are taking the Aggressor one way and either need to change direction or they begin to regain some control, you immediately reverse directions, cutting off their movement into empty space.

As the knife is brought from the hidden spot by their hip, begin to rotate to your right (through empty space) and pick up contact connecting with the weapon hand to lead, as we saw in an earlier chapter. In most cases (nothing is always guaranteed in knife defence) when they try to stab you it is not the "poke" used in some knife defence clips but rather a very committed stab, regardless of how fast they try to pull back and repeat. Continue to rotate until you are fully facing empty space.

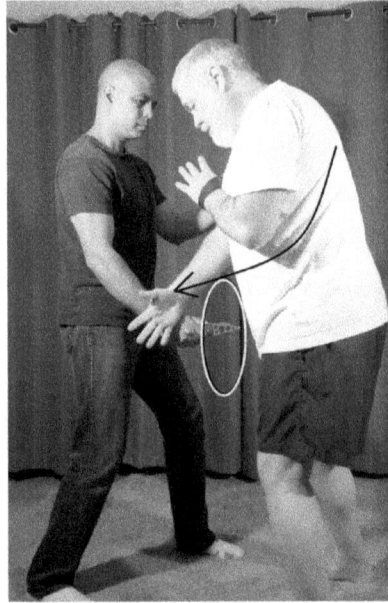

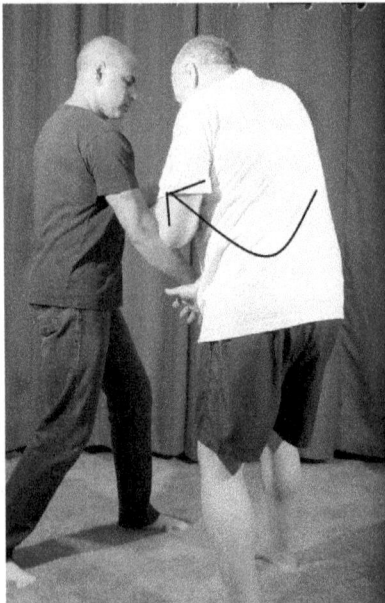

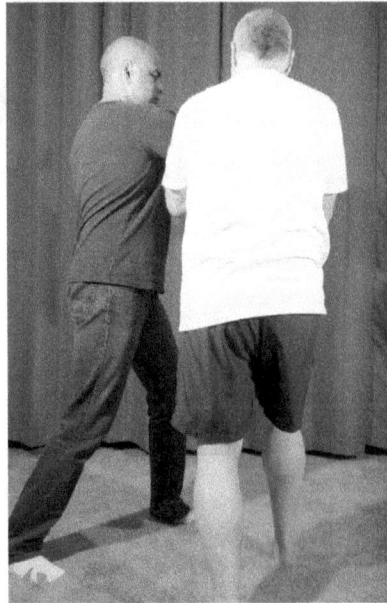

Let's use the magic of photography in the dojo to observe what happens from the other side. Pick up and lead until you are fully facing empty space, but perhaps they are squirmy or you see another body coming from behind. You want to reverse the directions, so use the fact that as you are leading them into empty space their stab is moving quickly, and rotate back the opposite way. This abruptly ends their movement and the result is often ripping them off their stance and to the ground.

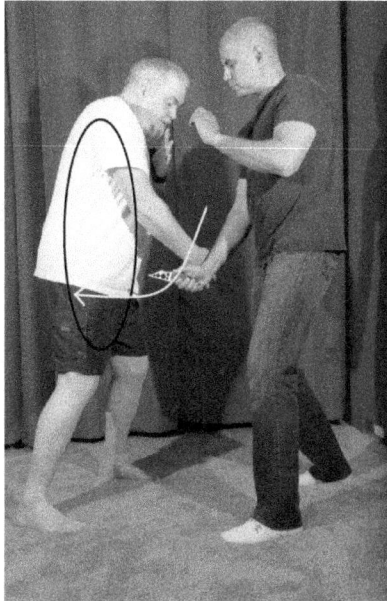

Let's flip back over to the other side to see the end result. Recognize the elbow takedown from an earlier chapter?

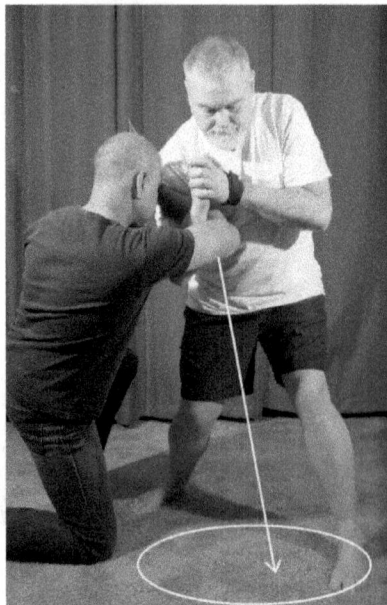

Let's Sum Up

Ending empty space is all about getting the Aggressor moving into one empty space and then cutting it off or reversing it before they can recover and counter your move. It can be done with a strike as in the first example or a body manipulation as in the second example.

Striking into Empty Space

In the chapter on Destruction of Structure we were always striking to destroy structure by striking towards empty space and we are going to illustrate that further here.

While I prefer to affect structure and balance with strikes, I would be remiss not to mention that you may choose to strike into a person's structure, their base, because it can have the effect of increasing the impact. This is because the force has no place to dissipate; their body has to absorb it all.

That is a choice, but, as stated, I prefer to have both the damage of the strike and the effect of destroying their structure by choosing to strike through their body into empty space. Perhaps the damage is slightly less than striking into their structure but the added value of disrupting their structure and taking their balance is well worth it. My opinion.

At a basic level we've seen in destruction of structure that striking into empty space will move the body-part struck into empty space, allowing us to manipulate them and break down their structure.

We can now take striking into empty space to a different place coming off of the "This is not a Duel" segment.

If we give up the constant impulse to be face to face, then we should always be angled in such a way we are facing empty space. If we strike the Aggressor either from that place or going to that place, then we go through the body into empty space, striking it in very different angles and lines of force than is generally done.

These odd lines of force can have a torqueing effect on the Aggressor and that torque can unbalance them, creating a wave of force that twists the Aggressor.

Recall the chapter of Voids and the stick or line being drawn between the legs of the Aggressor, with the perpendicular line at the midpoint. We can strike along that perpendicular line. This is the direction our force can be driven along to propel or drive the Aggressor backwards, because a forceful attack along that line will go into empty space where the Aggressor has nothing to stop it from traveling.

Example One

The looping sucker punch again (right hand). Step into our empty space intercepting, throwing fingers over the striking arm as we did in the Chapter on Entering and Attacking Empty Space (your right hand could also drive a heel palm into their chin.) Then, paying attention to that 90 degree line, drop your right elbow into their chest, breaking their balance and often bringing on a crumpling effect (remember though, no guarantees.)

Example Two

Use the position after side stepping a lead hand strike. Use that 90 degree line for a forearm strike and drive them back once again into the Rear Major Void. (This is a similar move that we saw in the Chapter on Ending Empty Space.)

The strikes in this Chapter are directed to Empty Space with the purpose of driving the Aggressor into a void and putting them down to the ground.

Let's Sum Up

In this short section, we take the "this is not a duel" thought process farther, showing we can strike as we rotate to face empty space. We also showed when we are facing empty space, we open unique angles of assault that hopefully come not only as a surprise to the Aggressor (it is often the strike or angle of a strike that you have not seen before that gets you) but also torques them into empty space, destroying their structure.

Examples

In this chapter, we are going to look at a number of techniques as examples of how empty space is used to enhance and increase the effectiveness of techniques or to make them work at all. It is vital that you focus on how using empty space makes the techniques work or work more efficiently and effectively, rather than the techniques themselves.

The techniques are only relevant as vehicles to show the uses of empty space and how it can relate to all approaches to self-defence.

Once you've read this chapter look at your own training and, if it consists of techniques, where empty space is used or where should it be used.

Up Rear Knee

You take a Muay Thai clinch, only use the empty space in front of their head to pull them horizontally forward to disrupt their structure. Note the connection of your hands to the back of their neck.

Drawing them horizontally forward uses the empty space in front of them to open empty space between your rear knee and their body allowing the strike to happen.

NOTE: Keep pulling their head down as the knee strikes so they are not straightened back up into structure.

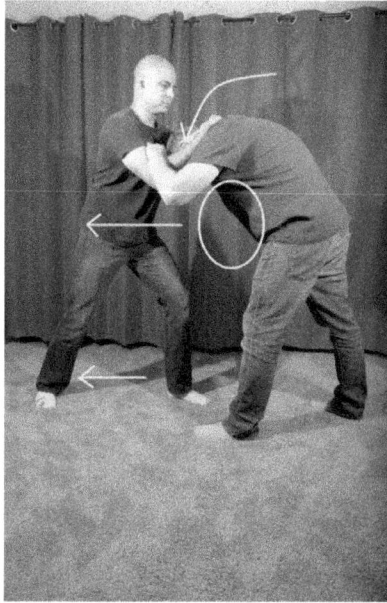

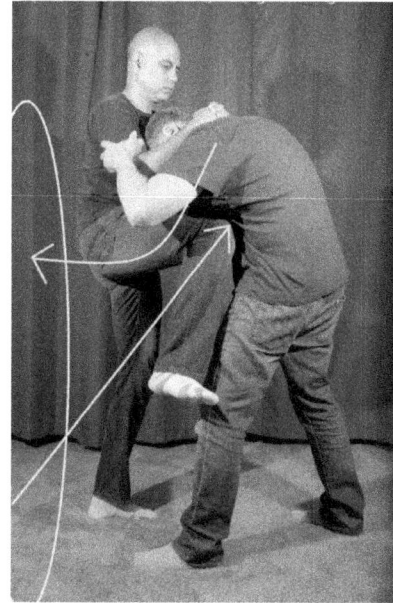

Now that the knee strike has bent them over you can use the head drag take down.

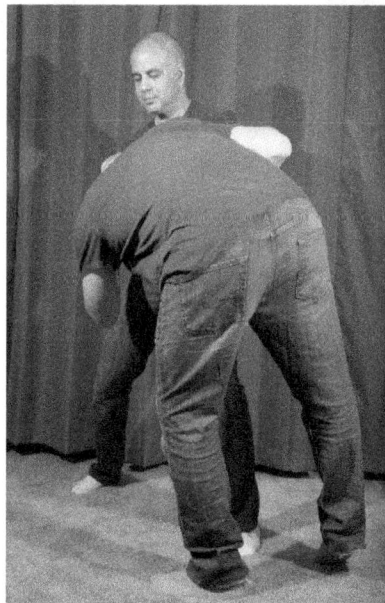

Lateral Leg Drop

This take down uses empty space and a Minor Void by means of a sacrifice throw.

You are clinched with the Aggressor with your left hand controlling their right elbow and your right arm hooked behind their head.

You begin to rotate to your left, pulling their right arm horizontal out into empty space allowing you to duck under through the empty space you've created to clinch around their body.

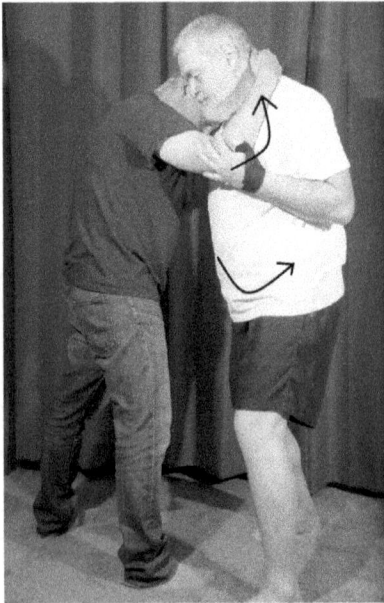

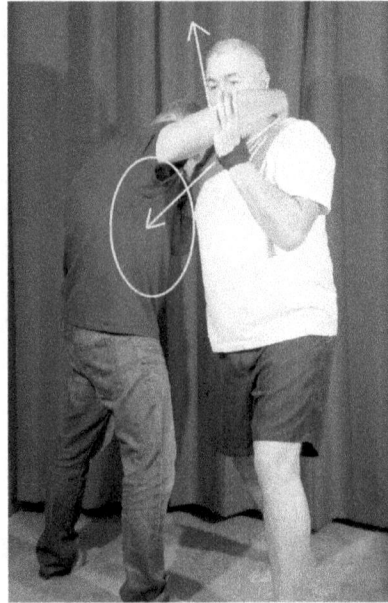

You shoot your left leg in behind their legs through the empty space, drop your body to the empty space beneath you and roll them to your left into empty space to take them down.

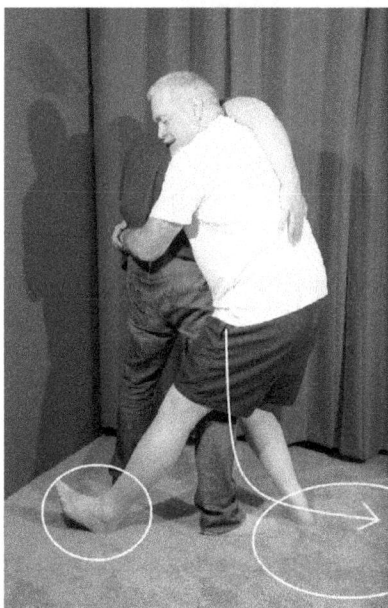

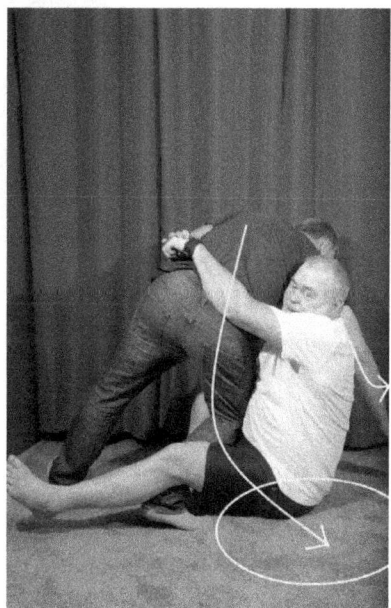

Over and Under Arm Drag

The Aggressor clinches with you. You have your left arm over theirs, hooking their elbow.

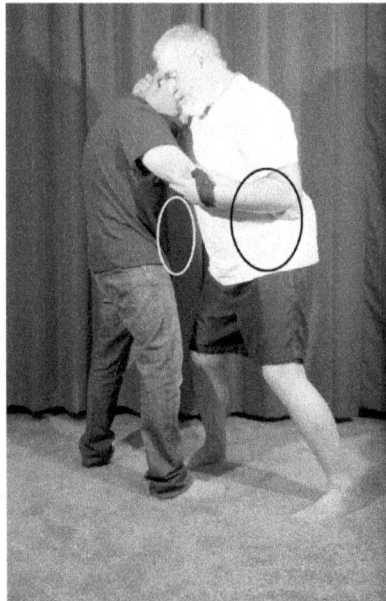

You want to sweep their arm across your body through that open space, but to do that you set them up to help you. Drop your right hand, rotate to your left to drive your arms across, moving their arm to your left into empty space. Because you are moving their arm their tendency is to resist and try to fight the movement which makes it much easier to abruptly reverse direction rotating to your right to sweep their arm across your body. Remember to move your torso out of the way to make the empty space for their arm to move through.

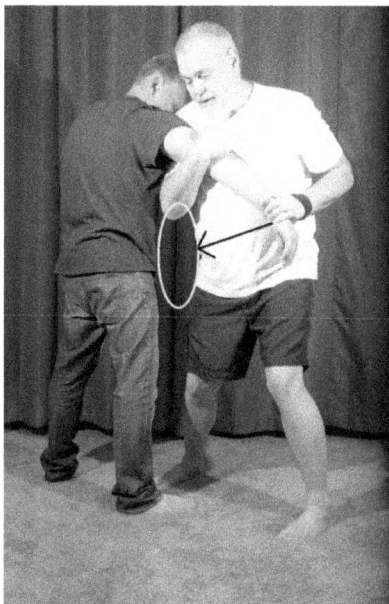
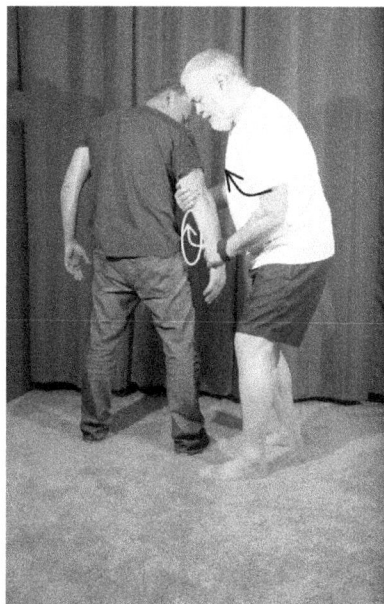
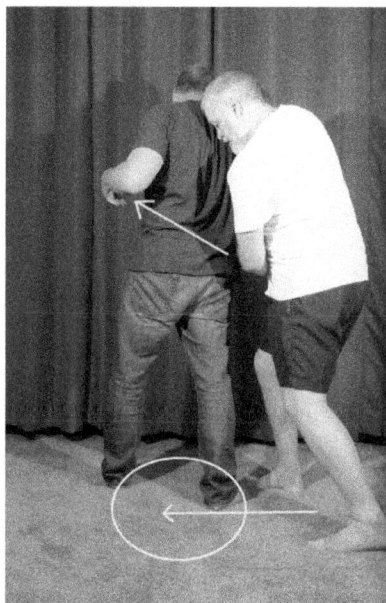

This now opens the space behind them allowing you to move through empty space to take their back and control their head.

Elbow Roll Take Down

Use the entering and attacking empty space against that looping (right) sucker punch.

You are going to make use of empty space with your step to open up the Major Void in front of the Aggressor. As you do, hook and shear to roll over their elbow with your right hand (ala ball rolling.) With your left hand, pin their arm to you.

With their arm pined to your shoulder, pull their elbow down into empty space (locking the arm). This is all done with the rotation to your right as you perform this circle with your arms.

As they begin to fall, step back with your right leg to make more empty space for them to fall into. Continue to apply the arm bar to encourage them to go down.

Knee Drop Throw

The Aggressor throws a right haymaker and you slip into the pocket of empty space rotating to face empty space, but this time you allow your right hand to strike their face as you do. This technique uses gravity and empty space for a sacrifice throw. You want to put your left foot back into the indicated empty space behind you and then drop both of you towards the larger piece of empty space to your left.

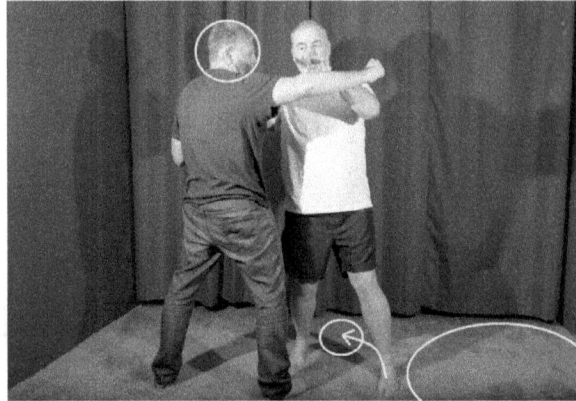

Take a step back with your left foot into the empty space behind you, drawing their right arm horizontally forward into the empty space in front of them. Your right hand adds encouragement by applying a shear ala ball rolling to move their head towards the desired empty space.

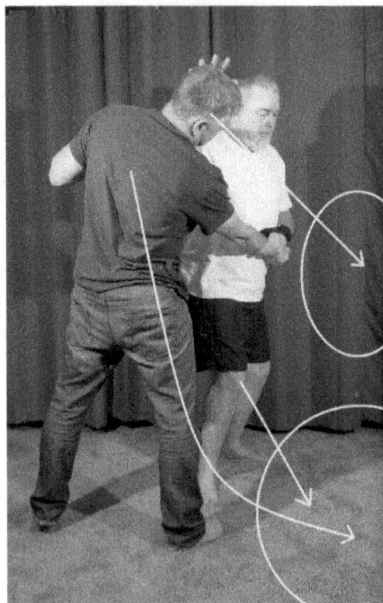

Drop your right knee into empty space as you rotate to your left. Drop your left hand into empty space, pulling their arm across and rotating them. At the same time, continue to rotate your right hand rolling their head toward empty space to take them further out over the cliff of the Minor Void and then drop your body into empty space to allow gravity to bring both of you to the ground.

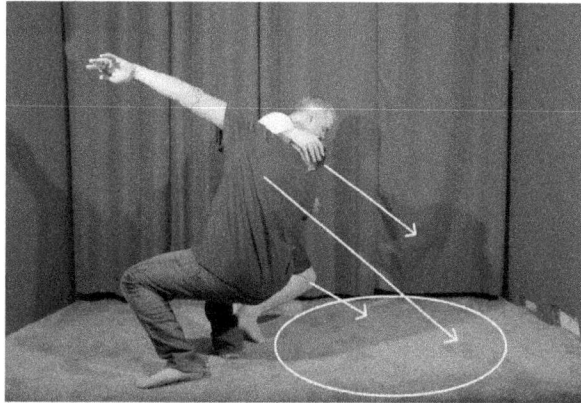

Elbow Lock Shoulder Take Down

If you recall in the Locking Chapter we used an Aikido technique, *Jodan Tsuki Hiji Kime Osae*. The movements below are inspired by that technique and although they may look different, if you look closely you will see the principles and movements used are the same.

To be clear, I have altered the application from the formal Aikido one to fit more with what we have already done in this book and to do it off an assault. Understand it is the use of empty space I want you to get out of this example.

The Aggressor grabs you by your right lapel with their left hand with their right hand cocked and ready to fly.

In the picture below, I have outlined where you will move through empty space. You can see the line showing how you rotate left into the empty space behind you which will allow your right hand to move along the line of empty space to their head and use your left hand to trap and draw their left arm back along the line into empty space.

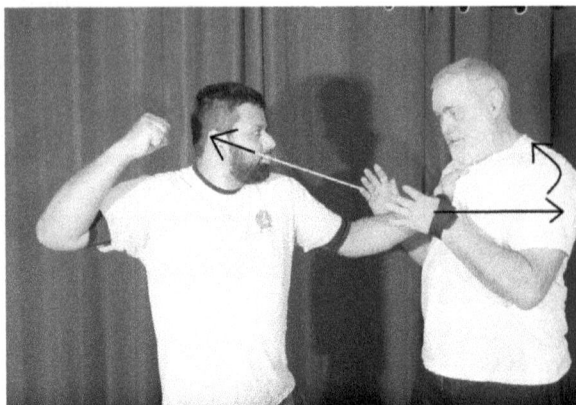

While they can push or pull you by grabbing you, they cannot stop you from rotating to your left and thus moving outside the arm grabbing you and away from the potential strike.

As you rotate, follow the lines set out a moment ago: your right hand swings up and around through empty space to strike, clipping and shearing through the jaw of the Aggressor's head back into empty space and your left hand connects and pins their left hand.

You now use your elbow as you did in ball rolling to roll their elbow over using empty space to extend the arm and bend them over by applying pressure to the back of the elbow (a lock) and continue to apply the lock extending them out over empty space to put them on the ground. Note the contact in the second picture below (circled) showing the ball (elbow) you are rolling. (Note: In the formal Aikido movement they use a shearing of their right forearm instead of the elbow rolling, but it is the same use of empty space.)

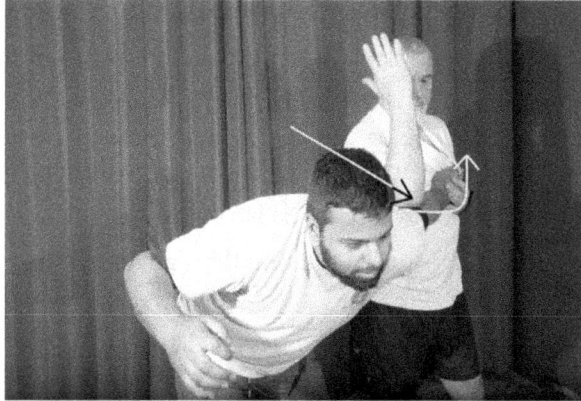

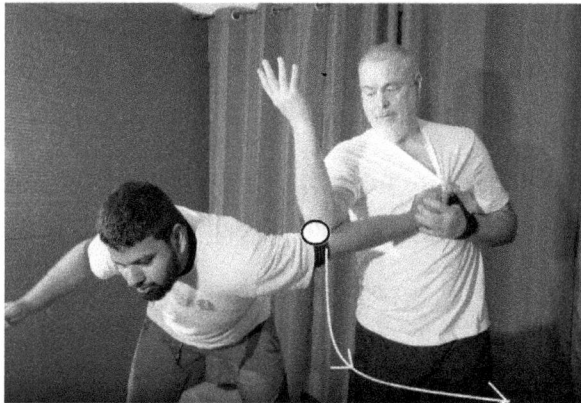

You can now step back and rotate into empty space driving them down into the Front Major Void.

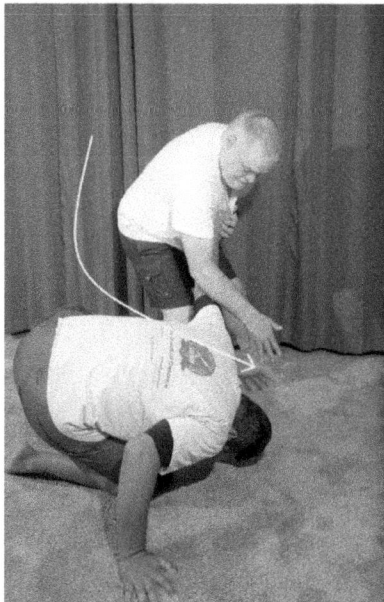

Because this movement is done through empty space it can be done even while they are using that grab to pull or push you. Both a pull or push add momentum that can be transformed into the rotation you intend to use.

While a lot is happening at the same time, but it is all done through large muscle movement, and the strategic placement of your arm and hands means it is not a complex movement, though it may sound complex. Really, it is only a rotation through empty space and a step back into empty space.

Wrist Weave Take Down 1

This may be more for my LEO and Security buddies, but the wrist weave take down is often taught without pointing out where empty space needs to be used. That leads to the officer either having to overpower the Aggressor or failing to control and put them on the ground.

The wrist weave is obtained two ways. The first is deliberately, which we'll cover here. (The second is the next example.) Begin behind and to the right side of the Aggressor.

Reverse the grip on your right hand to palm up and thread your left arm through empty space UNDER their arm. Then thread it through empty space over their forearm to place it under your right forearm. Keep your left hand in a fist with the thumb up.

I am going to use larger pictures here as the details may be hard to see in smaller ones.

Use the connecting to eliminate empty space and cinch their arm in between your forearm bones.

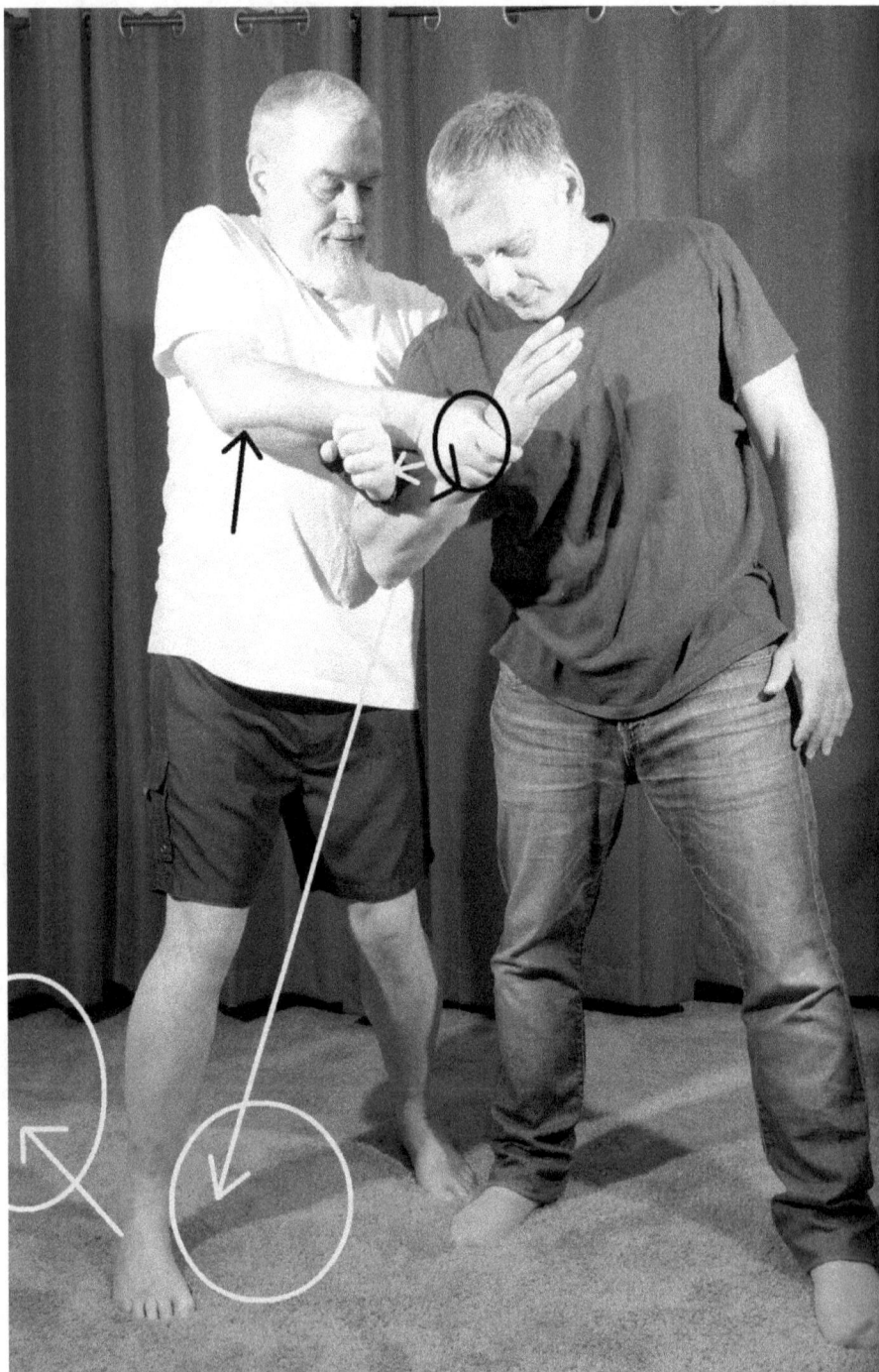

At this point, people try to put the Aggressor down by pressing straight down, and some instructors say to just punch down at this point. However, that is into their structure and unless you are a lot stronger than the Aggressor it has a high chance of failing.

Now here is the part I see sometimes left out: take a step out with your right foot, into empty space. (Even the instructors saying punch down here actually step out with their right foot.) This movement takes the Aggressor's arm out over empty space, and now you can drop your mass onto their arm and put them down into empty space in a similar manner to the elbow take down.

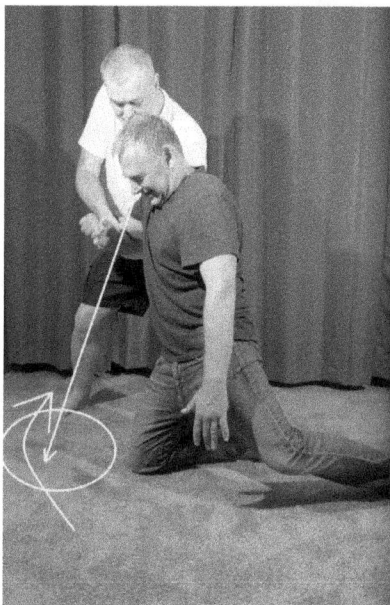

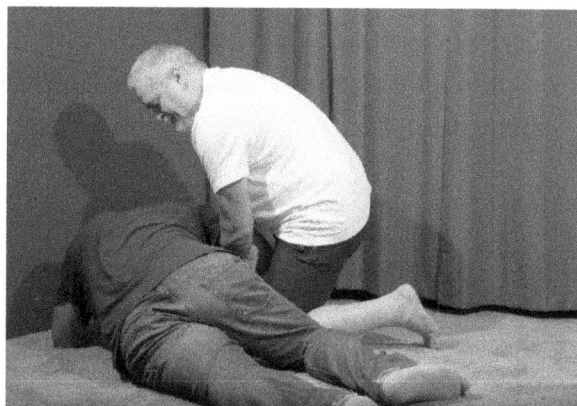

Wrist Weave Take Down 2

The second way the wrist weave is obtained is when the Aggressor bends their arm to prevent you from getting the arm bar take down.

Again, for this example I am going to use larger pictures so you can see the arm threading through empty space.

This time you thread your left arm through empty space inside their forearm to grab on top your wrist.

Once again, you are going to abruptly reverse the direction you have the Aggressor moving by rotating 180 degrees to take advantage of the Major Void behind the Aggressor. You do this by rotating to your left through empty space taking their arm back and out over that rear Major Void.

Continue to rotate, which moves the spot noted above behind them, and then drop your mass on their arm to put them to the ground.

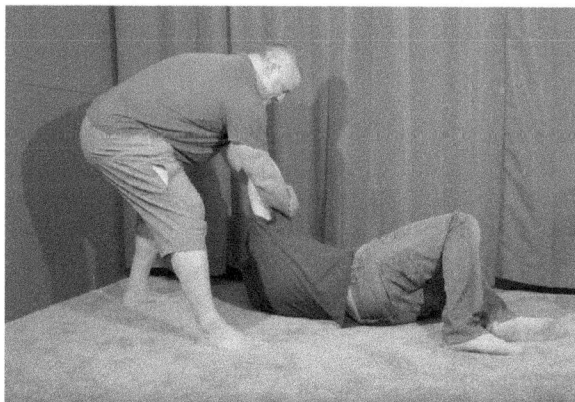

Let's Sum Up

What we have done here is walked-through a number of well-known techniques and shown how they either work because empty space is used or are enhanced by the use of empty space. Look at them and then take a look at your own system or style for where empty space is used or could be used. Always remember that the techniques shown here are merely delivery devices to drive home the use of empty space.

So Many People

I wrote at the start that every drill I create no mater how odd they may seem will be related to self defence. This simple drill may not look like self defence but in many assaults today there is more than one Aggressor and learning read, see and predict where empty space will be to evade and escape through a group is a good use of empty space for self defence.

This drill will only work if you have enough partners and space, but if you do then it can be a lot of fun and full of learning.

Pick a ratio of people 1 to 6 or 1 to 10, depending on the size of your group and the space you have.

Part One

Let's say you have 11 people for the 1 to 10 ratio.

10 people begin to walk in a consistent circle counter clockwise. Make sure you are spread out enough for people to walk between you.

Start walking slowly.

The 11th person begins to walk clockwise and has to work through the crowd of people coming towards them using the empty space to slip through.

The group stays on a consistent path.

The person going against the flow of the crowd gets to move around.

I have a small space so the ratio in the pictures is just 1:3 but it gives you the idea for the drills.

Look at the lines and the movement constantly to and through empty space.

There are also lines indicating where I was predicting the movement of the others, something you need to practice as you walk through the world.

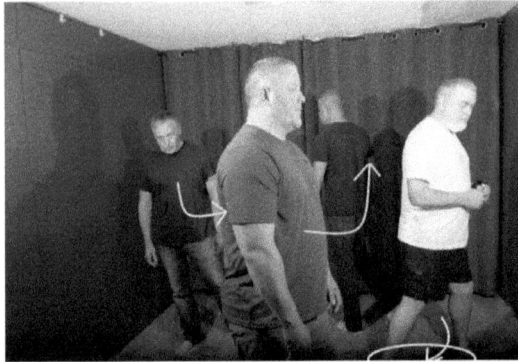
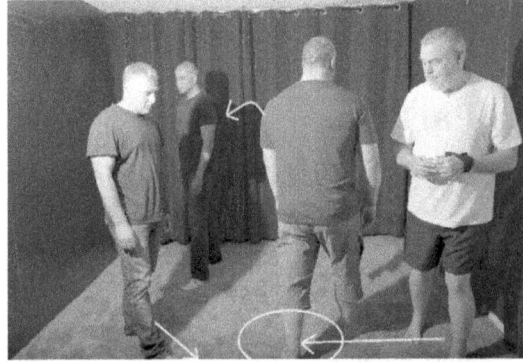
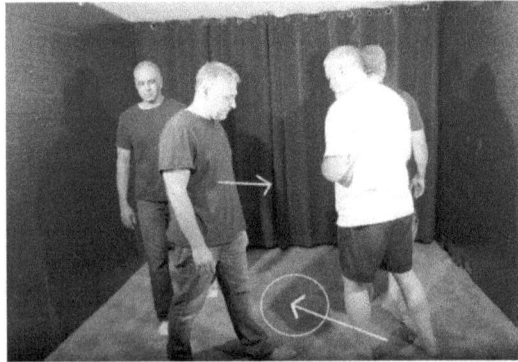

Part Two

The crowd picks an inconsistent but set path while walking the circle. For example, they could choose to move left then right then left etc. and they continue that pattern as they walk in the counter clockwise direction on the circle.

The person going against the flow now has to work through a more difficult maze.

This adds more movement to read and predict where the empty space to walk through will be.

Part Three

A little more difficult and now the crowd also has to be more aware, because they must leave space between themselves for someone to move through.

This time each member of the crowd gets to walk counter clockwise in a circle, but with random changes in their left and right progress. Remember they now have to watch the rest of the crowd so they keep as much space between them for a person to slip through as they can, but that won't always happen so everyone has to accept it.

They are NOT actively blocking the path of the person going against the flow.

Once again, we have added a further complexity to reading and predicting where the empty space to walk through will be.

Part Four

Add another person or two also moving against the flow and they all have to watch out for each other as well.

Part Five

Adjust the speed but keep it safe, no clonking of heads.

Let's Sum Up

I am placing this here near the end for a couple of reasons. First, this is very similar to the very first drill (The Obstacle Drill) so I liked how it ties back to the beginning. Second, as I mentioned because so many assaults today have multiple this drill helps train the reading, seeing and particularly the predicting of empty space to allow you escape a group of Aggressors.

A Helpful Hint

This helpful hint is to prepare you for the drills in the next chapter.

I find with people new to empty space, they often go directly into force and into the Aggressor's structure and cannot initially see that spot is surrounded by empty space.

This is a demonstration I found seems to bring things into clarity for people. Open one hand, and with the other hand place the tip of your index finger in the middle of the open hand's palm.

Hold your open palm up and point your index finger directly into the centre of your palm.

It should be clear you cannot move your finger directly through your palm, yet this is the same as moving into structure, and that is what we often do or have been trained to do.

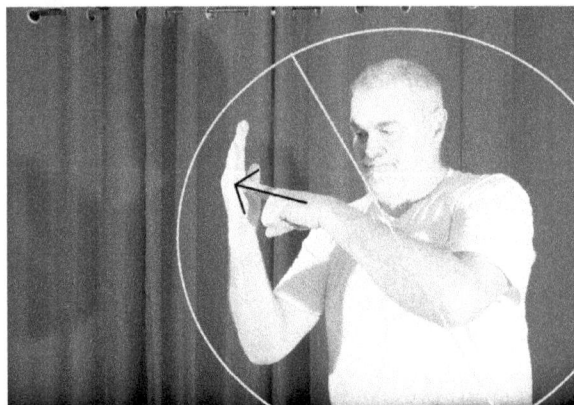

It is easy to move your finger back away from your palm, or down or to one side, or up or to the other side. These are all easy because they are into empty space.

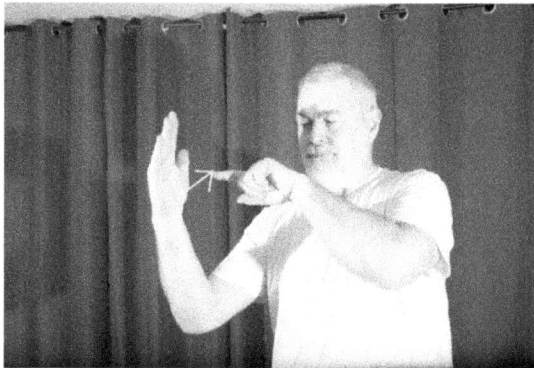

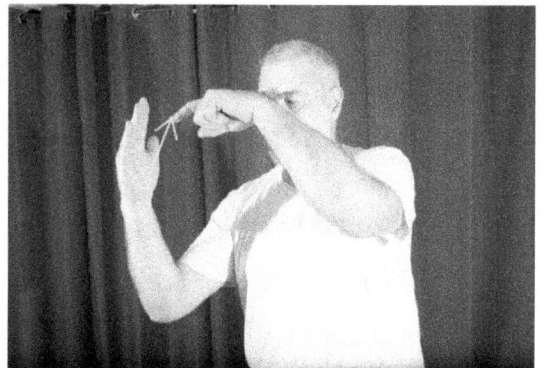

It is also easy to rotate your finger on the palm to move around in empty space.

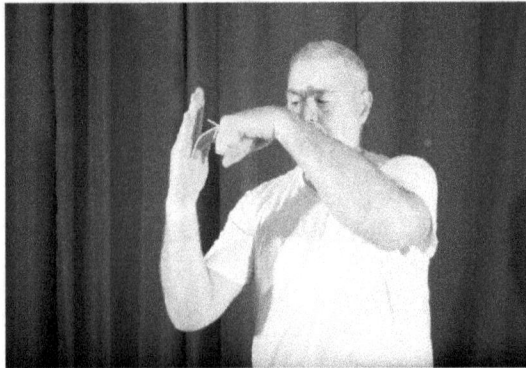

Let's Sum Up

I know this may seem obvious, but my teaching experience has shown me going from the concept to action is not always as simple as one might think and this demonstration has helped. You want to keep these movements in mind as you perform the drills in the Operant Conditioning chapter. You are your finger; the Aggressor is your palm. Do not move directly into the Aggressor. Instead, look at all the other ways to move into empty space.

Operant Conditioning

It might be helpful for you to slip to the end of the book and read Addendum One on the Three Progressive Zones of Training (Learning, Conditioning and Testing) before continuing.

So far in this book we have been in the Learning Zone, where you are thinking and working through drills to explore something very new to you. We will now evolve into the Conditioning Zone.

A Shift in Gears

My long-time training buddy and Taiji instructor, Rick Bottomley has said: "Many people want to be taught but only a few want to learn."

What that means is many people want to be told what to do, and that's fine. However, conditioning empty space is not the same as conditioning a specific response. It is not the same, because I cannot tell you how you are going to be attacked, what the circumstances will be, or where the empty space you will need to use will be. I cannot tell you what to do in all situations using empty space. If you truly want to be able to use empty space in the middle of chaos then you need to condition your brain to see it, to use it, and that cannot be done through techniques and being told what to do. It has to be something you learn and internalize.

I expect you to play and try the drills. However, because of my experience teaching I know some people still need some guidance, a few examples. While I included few sequences either illustrating what to do or showing how some problems are solved, the real learning will come through your own play and your own solutions, and these drills can help to begin that process.

Note: In these drills you will be moving slowly, allowing you time to solve the problems. (See Addendum One for more reasons.) The only reason to speed up is to win, but this is not a competition. Do not do it or you take yourself, and your partner, out of the purpose of the drills.

Drill One: Solve the Problem

Responding to a chaotic violent assault is problem solving. The difficulty is that you are not given any time to think over and ponder the situation. It is problem solving in an instant, not easy. Therefore, the level of problem solving you need has to be built-in deep into a tactical habit. We want the Aggressive action (the assault) to be our cue and the immediate use of empty space to be our habit.

To build this tactical habit we begin by giving you the time needed to problem solve.

In this drill your partner is going to put you into a bad place, and you are going to explore how to use empty space to get out of trouble and survive the assault.

They get one move to put you in a bad place and you have to let them completely take that move (go slow for safety.) Then you must fix the problem and you must use empty space to do it. Your solution should be done in two moves (three tops.)

STEP ONE: Find the empty space, find at least three different ways to move into empty space

You are in a bad place.

In this drill take a moment to not only test out where there is no empty space and where there is but what it gets you. TALK IT OUT LOUD. Think back to previous drills where you pressed or pulled on your partner to see if you were going into or against their structure. Feel where the empty space is. Think back to the Helpful Hint Chapter.

BUT talk it out. I mean it, verbalize it.

Look to where you CANNOT go and press there as you verbally say: "I push on you here there is resistance, no empty space."

Then look ALL AROUND THOSE SPOTS and see the empty space. Test those and verbally say: "I push here, no resistance so there is empty space, but if I move there I give you my back."

AND it is important for your partner to be part of the conversation.

Maybe you push on them and felt resistance, and say "can't go there," but they felt they really couldn't fight that push. They must SAY SO: "Hey try pushing a little farther there I felt myself go."

Once you feel where empty space is then find at least three different ways you can move into empty space and take a look at where they put you. Pick the one that puts you in the best place. That is where you want to move.

You do not want to move directly into the strike.

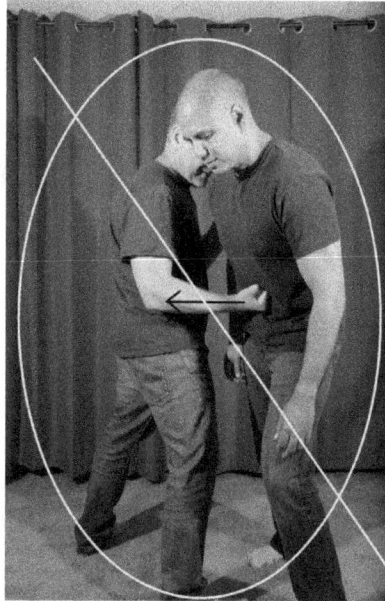

You could slip backward but what does it get you?

You could slip to your right but that requires an immediate strike because you are moving into their weapons and that Dueling Alignment.

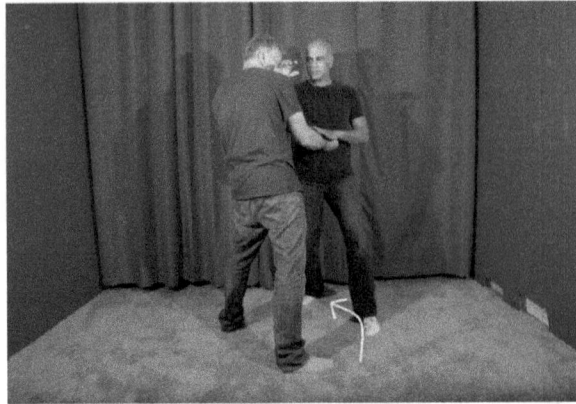

Or you could slip to your left and rotate in close, filling that space, and giving you a far better angle to act from.

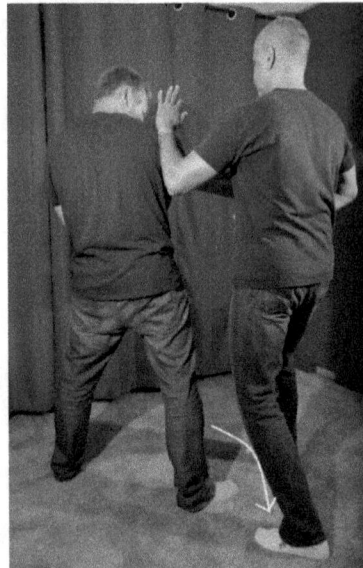

For the first few, simply test where the empty space is and compare what each space gives you strategically.

GO PLAY

STEP TWO: Find three ways to move, and find the next move

After you've done a few, once you have found three spots of empty space and picked the one you feel gives you the best strategic position, then add another move using empty space.

In the picture below clearly you cannot move directly into the strike.

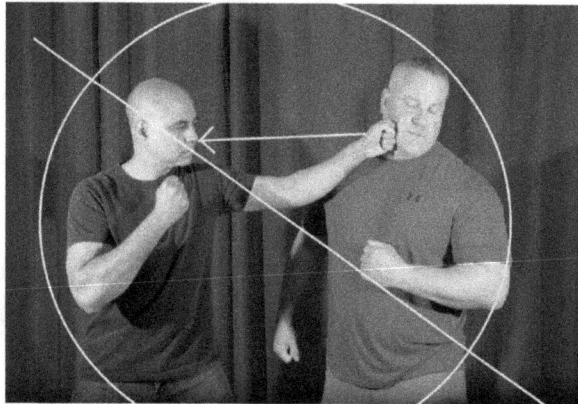

You can move back, and if you are looking to escape then creating distance is a good thing, but in this case, it may have bought you time, but not much more.

Once again moving to the inside is an option, but one that I highly recommend includes a simultaneous strike as in the picture below. However, look at the face to face position it puts you in (Dueling Mentality.)

Once again, you could slip to the outside of the strike as we have in our previous drills.

In this case that is the best spot and now you look for where you can use empty space in a next move. There is empty space between your right hand and the Aggressor's head, so a slide adds a strike and following the line shown below a shear and rotation will move them and begin to drop them into the void indicated.

GO PLAY

STEP THREE: What else can I do with empty space as I step into empty space

The other uses of empty space are to strike through empty space or manipulate your partner through empty space or BOTH. Have a look at what you can do and TALK it through out loud.

Below you are grabbed and once again it makes no sense to go into the grab particularly on a bigger Aggressor.

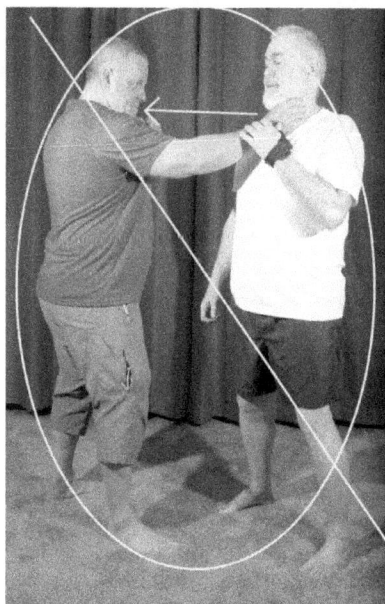

You could try to move back but you would be followed.

Moving to your right doesn't get you anything and, again, you get followed.

You can move to your left outside their arm, but you can also roll your arm over, shearing their arm over as you move and using that shear into empty space to destroy their structure. I think you can all see what might be done from there.

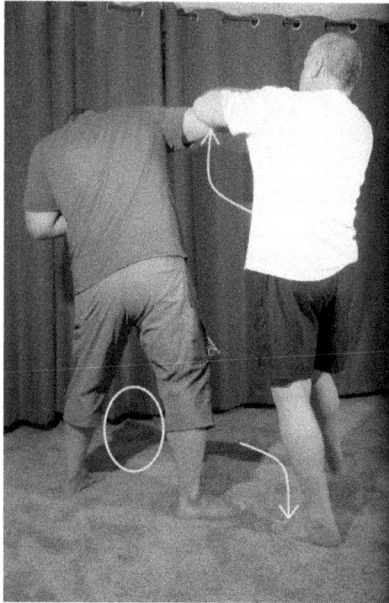

GO PLAY

STEP FOUR: Select only the best empty space

Once you've begun to select the best empty space spot stop looking at others. You want to condition seeing only the best.

In the situation below, the bad spot is being hit with an elbow upside the head. Like it or not, to absorb the blow you will be moving into the empty space circled below.

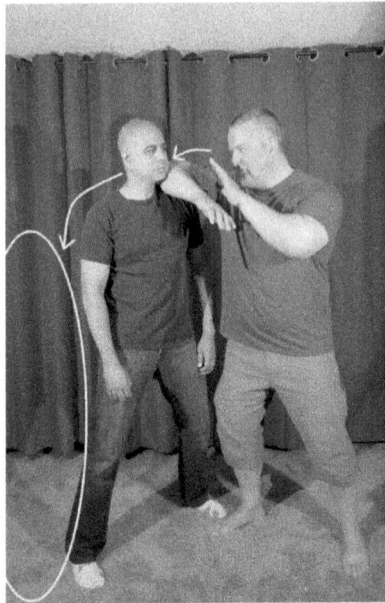

If you are going to be handed empty space, then make the best of it by flowing into it and using the gifts handed to you. In the picture below, you can see where the strike is going to move you so flow with the strike, but also rotate and grab the Aggressor's wrist as you do, taking it with you into empty space.

The end result is extending the Aggressor's arm out into empty space, allowing you to lead him farther and apply an arm bar, driving the Aggressor forward and into the ground or simply opening him up to strikes.

In the example below, you are being driven backwards. A circle in the picture below indicates a spot of empty space and you are going to rotate (see the lines) to your right as you drive your right arm up, which will force the Aggressor's arm up into the empty space above.

As you rotate you will be moved off the line of the push and that will open up empty space behind the Aggressor for you to step into. The goal is to drive the Aggressor into the empty space shown by the circle on the right.

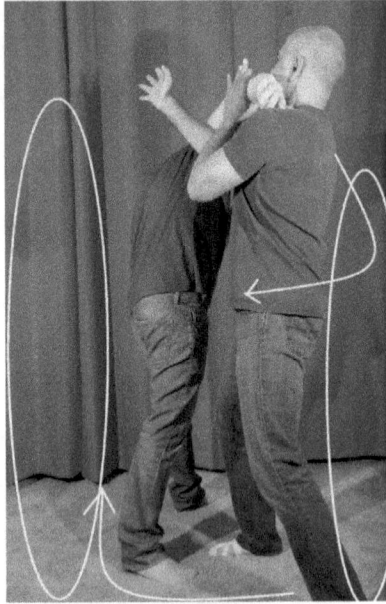

Once again you continue to rotate through empty space and will end in a similar arm bar as the previous example.

GO PLAY

STEP FIVE: Look to attack empty space

You've worked at moving into empty space and what else you can do using empty space, but often, in the beginning, you may forget to attack empty space. Do a few rounds where you not only move into empty space, but also attack into empty space accessing a Major or Minor Void.

In the picture below, you have been struck to your midsection. There are two spots of empty space shown by the circles. Here you are going to go with the strike and use the momentum to rotate to your left. You can rotate away from the force of the strike because of the empty space indicated by the circle behind you. At the same time, you will use the spot of empty space between the Aggressor's legs to shift your foot and fill that jar of marbles.

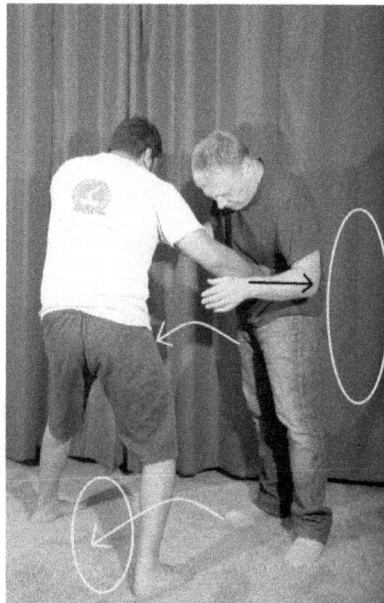

Because there is a path of empty space from the Aggressor's face to your right hand, you can also use the rotation to strike. That strike sets the Aggressor up for an attack into the empty space behind them. Note the circle on the floor indicating that Rear Major Void and the line between the Aggressor's feet and the direction for a strike 90 degrees to that line.

You simply drop an elbow strike into the Aggressor's chest. This is a very good time to add in the thought of Rushing Water and watch what it does to a strike where you want to move the Aggressor.

And down they go.

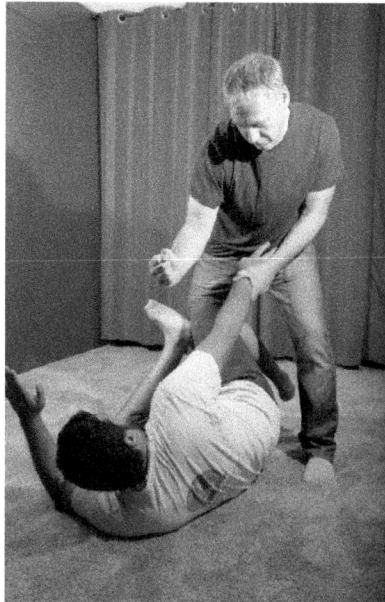

GO PLAY

STEP SIX: Pick Your Preference

Understand that empty space applies to all approaches to self-defence, so make sure you aren't caught up in what "technique" was used in a previous drill or shown in the technique section. Techniques are just a delivery system for the principle of empty space, just as pancakes are the delivery system for syrup.

Here, be yourself. Do what you have trained to do. If you are a striker, strike. If you are a grappler, grapple. If you do it all, then do it all. And if you like to strike from a distance, make sure at the end of your turn you have used striking and empty space to gain distance.

Using empty space applies to all things, so there is no wrong way if you have a different preference. I like to be up close and personal, because I have always aspired to what Moses Powell said, "If I can touch you, I have you." But if that isn't your thing then don't do it. Use empty space to do your thing. Now, as we enter operant conditioning is the time to make empty space your own.

STEP SEVEN: Add/create and play (Don't be afraid)

Let's say you are a Judoka or Jujitsu person.

The Judoka's preferred response might be to find their throw each time through empty space.

The Jujitsu practitioner might like to throw or lock.

Do that but don't be afraid to play.

The Judoka may use empty space to move in for the throw but instead of completing it, pause and allow their partner to find a counter using empty space. The amazing Judoka, Kyuzo Mifune, was a master of using empty space to both throw and counter.

The Jujitsu practitioner might move into the lock position but just before it is applied, pause and allow their partner to seek and escape or counter using empty space.

Make this drill your own.

Be creative and play.

Drill Two: Rory Miller's One Step

This one is from Rory Miller (used with his permission) and is described in much more detail in his book *Training For Sudden Violence: 72 Practical Drills* on page 10 called The One-Step.

> "At its most basic, it is very simple: one partner initiates a move in slow motion and the other partner at equal speed makes one motion to respond. The partners continue this without resetting, winding up wherever they wind up and finding solutions."

There will be two steps in this Drill.

STEP ONE

1. Your Partner takes a turn (one move) and you will allow your partner to complete their move and place you into a bad place.
2. You take a turn (one move) and solve the problem you've been put in using empty space and try to put your partner in a bad place as you do. Your partner allows you to complete your move.

3. Your partner takes a turn (one move) and solves the problem they've been put in using empty space and try to put you in a bad place as they do.

4. You take a turn (one move) and solve the problem you've been put in using empty space and try to put your partner in a bad place as you do.

And so on and so on, back and forth, solving problem after problem.

You can see the shift from the previous drill where you were given only one problem to solve with multiple moves in a row. In this drill, you are taking turns and alternating solving problems with your partner. Once again you will have time to solve the problem.

GO PLAY

STEP TWO

This step adds a little flow to the drill, but it can also lead to competition and speeding up so be cautious of that. Don't do it or stop and restart if you do.

1. Your partner begins to take a turn (one move) and you are allowed to begin to respond as they do (before their move is completed), but that is your move and you only get one.

2. As you respond to their move your partner can adjust and respond to yours (before it is completed), but that is their move and they only get one.

3. You respond to your partner's new move, but that is your move and you only get one.

4. As you respond to their move your partner can adjust and respond to yours, but that is their move and they only get one.

And so on and so on, back and forth, solving problem after problem using empty space.

You may find it hard stay in the drill work slowly and only take one move but do your best to stay there because speed tends to add competition.

Because you are to respond AS your partner is making their move you no longer have the time to pause and figure it out as you did in Step One where he took a turn had to wait until you solved the problem. Even though you are both moving slowly having to problem solve "on the fly" will take your problem-solving skills using empty space to a higher level.

This drill can be hard to keep a proper flow so feel free to stop and restart when the flow has been lost.

NOTE: At the start you may find you can't respond fast enough, and your partner finishes their move before you come up with a response, and that is just part of the learning process. Your partner will wait for you to take your move and begin to respond as you do.

Drill Three: In Chaos

We want to mimic an assault. Your partner will (moving slowly) assault you from up close and personal, and most often from the side or from behind. The impact or contact may be your first clue you have been taken by surprise and attacked.

Your partner, from their position (front, side or behind), will begin to attack slowly.

The moment you see or feel the assault begin you are allowed to move and use empty space to succeed in defeating the assault.

You cannot move any faster than your attacking partner.

What separates this drill from the first two is that as you work this drill you will progressively increase the level of intensity and resistance of the partner playing the role of the Aggressor.

Up the level slowly and in conjunction with your partner's problem solving skills. Remember we are looking to build how to succeed, so moving harder and faster too soon will hamper that. Having said that, you do have to increase resistance at some point or you fall into some really odd fantasy martial arts.

In the assault below, you have been grabbed from the side by an Aggressor. In this case, we want you to show how three different ways empty space can be used at the same time. You will rotate and step into empty space (the circle in front of you on the ground). During the rotation you also drive your arm up to raise the Aggressor's arm into empty space (the circle above). All this to get to and drive the Aggressor into the circle of empty space behind you.

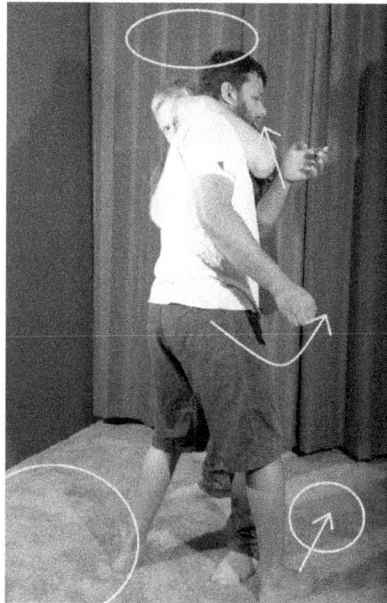

Your success relies on you continuing to rotate and step into empty space, which will open the spot of empty space you have has picked for your Aggressor.

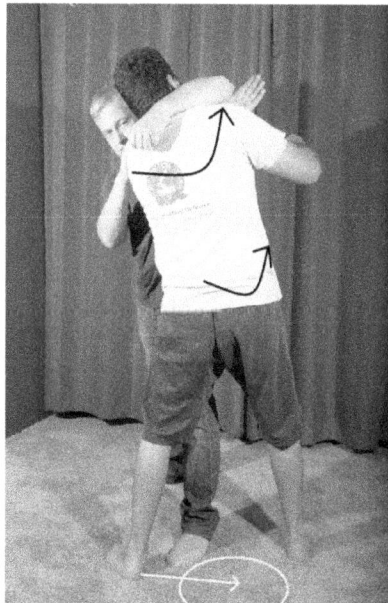

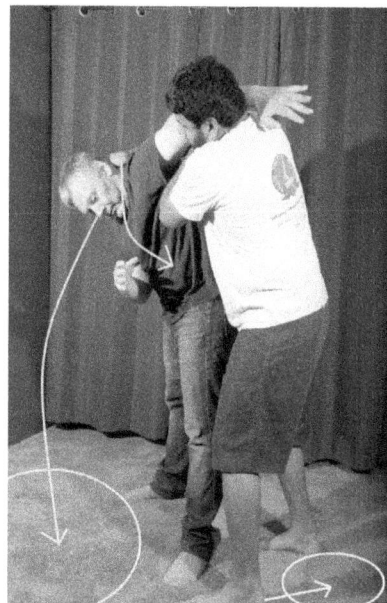

With the last rotation and step into empty space, the Aggressor is driven to the ground.

In the next scenario, you are assaulted from behind. (You need to learn to stay out of bad places.) There is empty space in front of you and up above your heads.

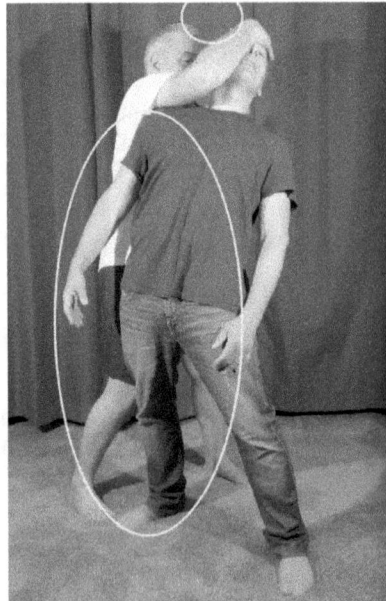

You both drop (sink) down, but also push up into empty space on the Aggressor's elbow (a control point.)

This opens empty space for you to slip under the Aggressor's arm.

This now gives you access to that empty space to step and rotate into.

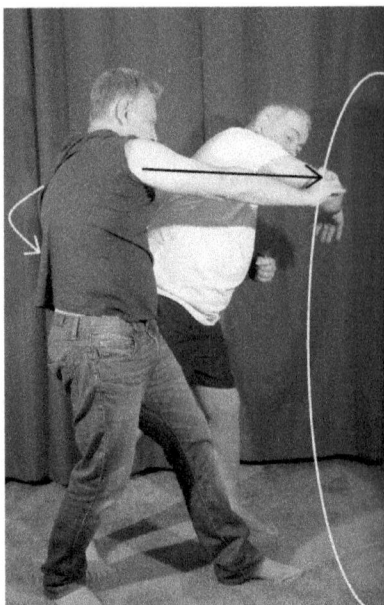

The movement also opens up another spot of empty space in front of the Aggressor. But let's not forget that we also want to set our own maze lines for protect and we defend ourselves. (I've circled your hand now up setting a maze line in the picture below.)

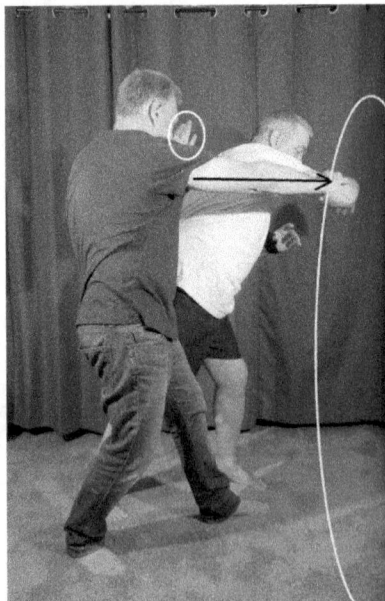

You now want to take the Aggressor's arm into that big open void in front of him and drive the Aggressor to the ground.

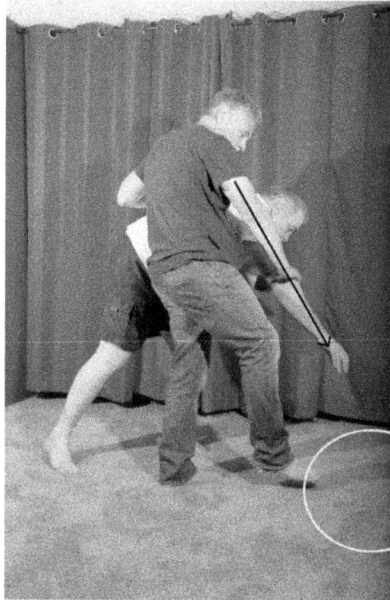

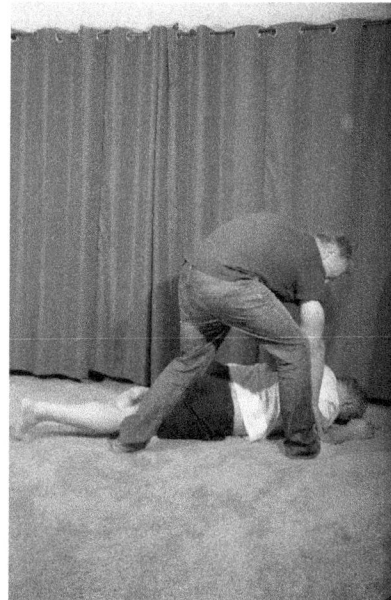

GO PLAY

Drill Four: The Ambush

This drill is an adaptation of Tony Blauer's Night of the Living Dead Drill and attempts to simulate that moment of sudden surprise in an assault. It can also have many layers depending on what you want to work. BUT once again it must be done is slow motion. You cannot move any faster than your attacking partner.

Because once again we want to build that problem solving, begin slowly and then begin to have your partner increase the resistance they give you.

One partner closes their eyes and the other partner begins an assault in slow motion. Either half way through the movement they say "begin" and their partner gets to open their eyes and respond OR the simulated assault involves indexing, which is touching or grabbing the partner in some way, in which case the moment they are touched the person can open their eyes and respond. You can also do this so they do not open their eyes until hit.

Having your eyes closed until you hear begin or you feel contact can be challenging and this is the attempt to simulate the sudden surprise of an ambush.

Below, you have has opened your eyes only to find you are being kicked hard in the thigh with no chance to avoid it. Therefore, you are going to flow along with the kick into empty space by rotating.

By rotating and allowing yourself to be moved you have been given a gift: The Aggressor's arm has been handed to you.

You will continue to flow and allow your knee to drop to the empty space indicated above. Of course, you will keep the gift you were given.

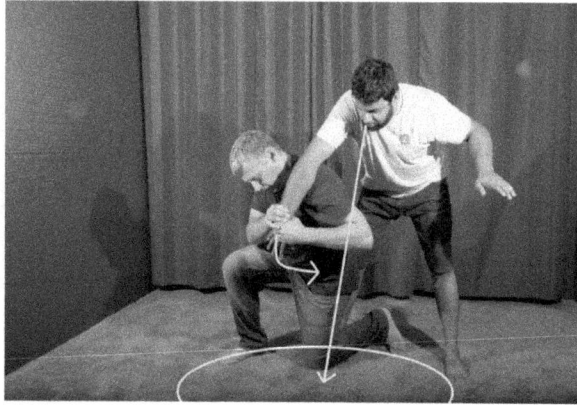

As you can see by the picture above, this is leading the Aggressor out over a big open void. You simply continue to rotate and lead their arm (and therefore them) into the empty space. You can follow the progression below.

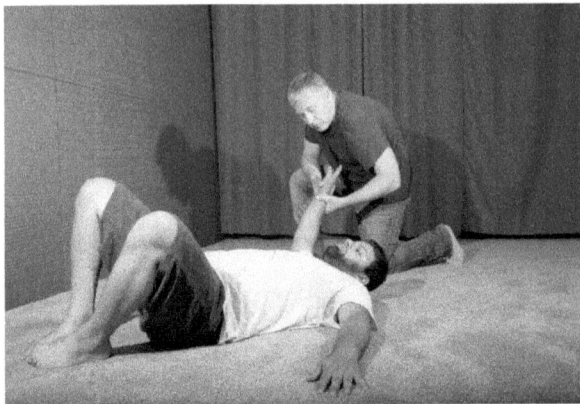

Play and have some fun.

In the next example, the response is to a kick from the side to the thigh. You open your eyes and you are being kicked. Once again, we're using that same spot of empty space as in the previous example, but this time the kick is dropping you, so use that.

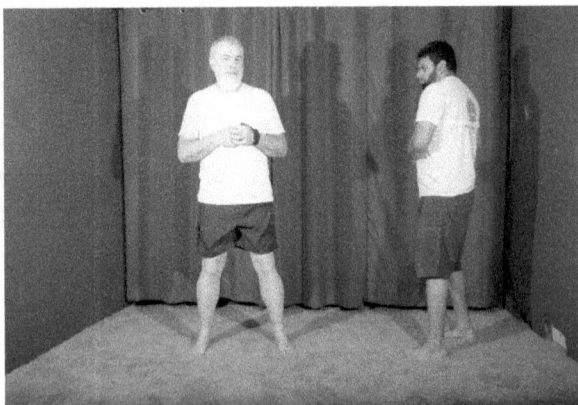

You are going down anyway, so you take advantage of that to drop and roll into empty space. You will note that while you are going into empty space a big spot has opened up for the Aggressor.

Now you drop and roll and allow your left leg (the one kicked) to connect to the lower part of the Aggressor's leg. As your right leg is driven over by the momentum, it connects to the back of their knee, circling it to collapse the knee and drop the Aggressor.

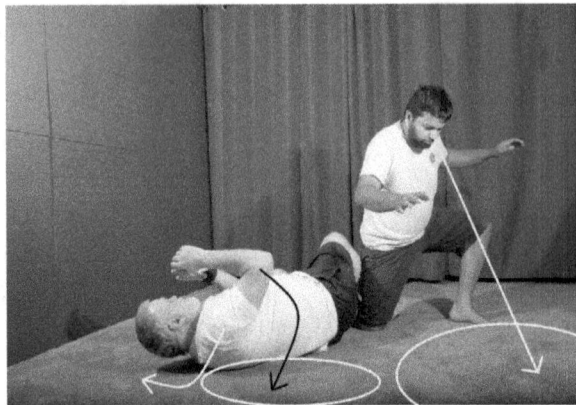

Every move opens another spot of empty space and below you leave your right leg connected to the Aggressor's as you move up into empty space using your leg for a compression lock on theirs.

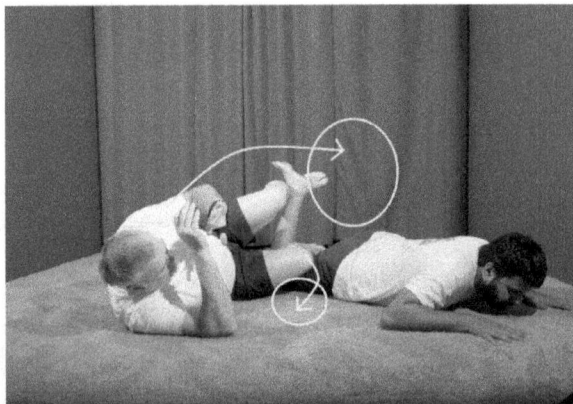

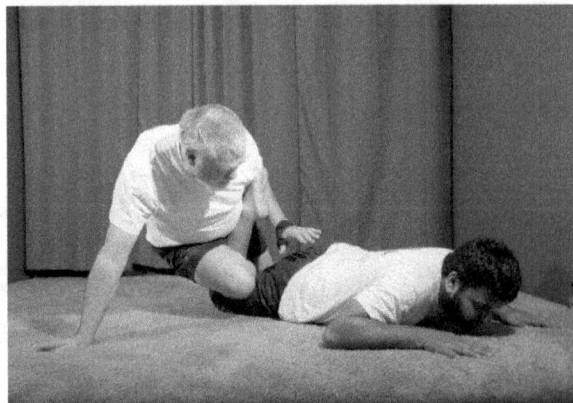

Try this one. Seriously, it is fun.

NOTE: For self-defence it would be better to get back to your feet rather than get entangled on the ground (see my upcoming book, *From the Ground Up.*)

In the next example, you open your eyes and are being grabbed for a knee strike. You see the strike coming (because you opened your eyes on the index – the grab) and begin to move.

You rotate into empty space with the strike, avoiding the impact and connect to the Aggressor's leg with your left hand. The rotation is just like your index finger on your palm in the Helpful Hint Chapter.

Now you rotate back into empty space to set the Aggressor out and over the big empty space on the ground.

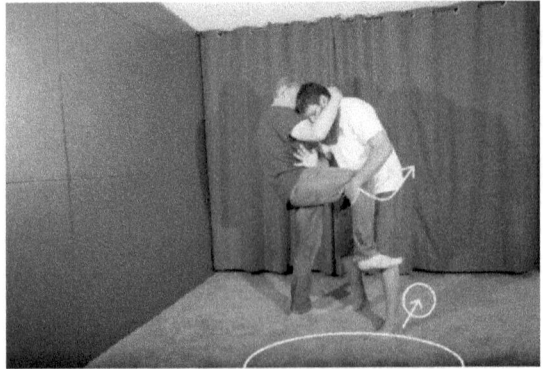

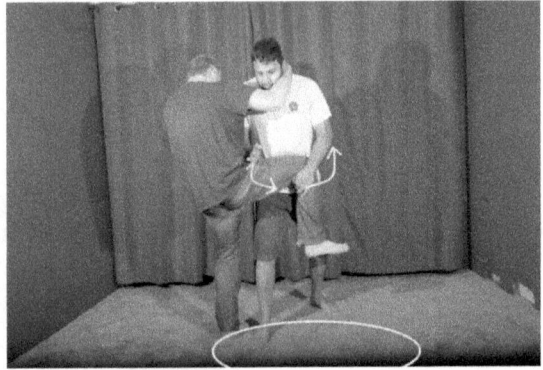

The rotation and stepping into empty space has sucked the balance from the Aggressor. You now attack empty space with a shear, dropping the Aggressor to the ground.

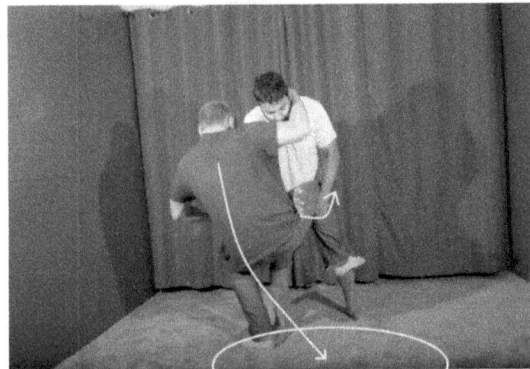

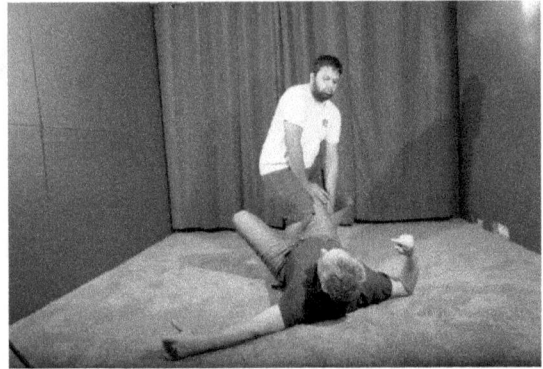

As you play, mix it up:

- You can increase the fun by adding in weapons.
- You can increase the fun by adding in multiple Aggressors.
- You can increase the fun by never opening your eyes.
- You can increase the fun by counting backwards from 100 when your eyes are closed to try and simulate being distracted thinking of other things.

GO PLAY

Be yourself and do what you do.

Just use empty space to do it.

NOTE: A few key points.

1. There is no teaching in Operant Conditioning drills; the experience is the teacher. (If there is no success, return to the Learning Zone.) The only exception is the beginning of "The Bridge" because you will be talking and working with your partner.
2. Never end on a failure. Yes, go back to the Learning Zone when necessary, but return to the Conditioning Zone and call it a day only after success.
3. We all tend to mull over and focus on our failures far more than our successes. This is wrong for operant conditioning. If you are thinking and focusing on your failures, then that is what you are driving into your brain: how you failed. I'm not saying you don't think during the drills about your failures, but afterwards focus on what went right. Think those experiences over. Focus on those experiences and what made them successes. Drive into your brain what worked, not what didn't.

Let's Sum Up

Operant conditioning the use of empty space is the most vital piece of solving the maze. If you cannot use empty space without thinking of it, then it will not be used in the chaos of an assault, exactly where you need it. The steps above introduce you to problem solving with empty space, then using empty space immediately, and then finally and hopefully using empty space when taken by surprise (as much surprise as can be simulated in a drill.)

Conclusion

I know there are a lot of different uses of empty space being presented in this book. I hope that doesn't come across as too much all at once, but I felt if I was going to write a book on how to use empty space then I had to put in everything I've learned (so far.) If it seems too much for one bite, then pick the beginning sections on striking, moving, and manipulating, and work those first before coming back for the rest.

But here is the real thing: while we can use empty space to move into, we can use empty space to strike into, we can use empty space to manipulate the Aggressor and we can use empty space to close our connection, in reality for all of the above you are simply occupying empty space.

If you step into empty space, you occupy it. If you strike into empty space, you occupy it; you just have the Aggressor in your way. If you manipulate the Aggressor, you occupy empty space; you just take a piece of them with you. If you eliminate the empty space in your connection to the Aggressor, you are occupying that small bit of empty space between you.

To use empty space is basically to occupy it no matter what the purpose is or how the effect may change. Therefore, while we have presented many uses and effects we can create with empty space, the actual principle is always to occupy empty space no matter how it is used or what effect we want to cause.

And that is why my wife Andrea's suggestion for the title of this book worked so well: "Now You See it, Now You Don't." You see the empty space, you occupy the empty space, now it is gone.

Empty space is a defining principle and one that I think can take the average practitioner and make them great.

Empty space is the equalizer for size and strength. Let me qualify that and say size and strength will always matter. However, the founder of BJJ, Helio Gracie, was able to use empty space to defeat larger stronger opponents. At the same time, I saw a clip the other day of a power lifter in the bottom of the mount simply throw a smaller person off them like they were doing a bench press. I don't want to give the impression that empty space can eliminate the attributes of size and strength entirely.

There is no magic in self-defence and nothing makes you invincible.

Having said that, however, using empty space can make it seem like you are using magic to others. I have been nicknamed The Dark Wizard by Dillon Beyer, Randy King and Rory Miller. I've been called a magician by an Alberta Sheriff's tactical instructor. At the end of teaching a seminar on using empty space, one of the participant's comment was that some of it just seemed like magic.

I don't want people to think it is magic. I want them to see, understand and know how to do it too.

The use of empty space can be particularly disconcerting for a big strong person whose strength has always allowed them to dominate. When you do things that never challenge their strength, then they do not get to use their strength. (However, beware of the big strong person who has read this book and practiced using empty space, because their size and strength come right back into play.)

When I was deciding which principle to write about first, I choose empty space because it is one that adapts to any style or system and in fact can be seen in any style and system by the best practitioners. Often it is the use of empty space that makes them just that: the best practitioners.

You need to begin to look for empty space all the time and incorporate it in everything. If you have techniques in your system, look for where empty space is used or could be used. Begin to make using empty space in self-defence just what you do, and it will have a profound effect.

The wonderful thing about focusing on empty space are the complimentary bonuses that come with it. It is far better to be indifferent to what the Aggressor is doing, because it allows you to do what you need to. That becomes difficult when someone is trying to take your head off; however, people have found that in focusing on empty space they do become as indifferent to that incoming strike as they can be, like avoiding that single tree in the middle of the African grasslands.

There are many principles that can make you a better martial artist, better at self-defence, but I believe the principle empty space is an exceptional one that can improve anyone's abilities.

There were a lot of techniques used in this book to demonstrate the use of empty space, so I need to say once again that the techniques were only a delivery system. The important thing is what was being delivered: how to use empty space in self-defence.

Addendum One: Understanding Drills and The Three Progressive Zones of Training

Before we get to the three zones, we need to explain what "drills" are and what their purpose is. (Or refresh your memories if you've read *Watch Out For The Pointy End*.)

What is the purpose of a drill?

- Drills are for training or practice.
- They are an artificial device to gain a specific skill.
- They are not real.
- Understanding what a drill is and keeping the goal and purpose of a drill in mind and clear in teaching is important to avoid wavering from the path.
- Always remember a drill is only a teaching tool. It is never real.

I included this section because sometimes people have a few issues with drills:

- People don't grasp it is artificial; therefore, they toss it out when it isn't "real" and fail to gain the skill it would have taught.
- They don't know what the skill is they are supposed to learn therefore never achieve it, or the purpose of the drill is lost over time.
- They start to believe it is real and therefore slip into some fantasy world of delusion.

The Three Progressive Zones of Training

1. Learning Zone
2. Conditioning Zone
3. Testing Zone

It is vital you understand:

1. The purpose of the drill, and
2. Which of the three progressive zones you are working in.

The Learning Zone

In the Learning Zone, you have to understand you are trying to learn and grasp something new. Often to allow that, it is broken down in to smaller parts and even simplified until you begin to learn it. You are trying to digest and take in new facts and see if you have them right. The Learning Zone is where you are taught.

This distinction is very important. At one knife defence seminar I taught, a participant was not happy with how it was being presented. His views helped me formulate the three progressive zones.

He wanted everyone to go just as hard as they would need to go on the street. But that is not how you learn something new. You can't learn anything new going full out. No one teaches you something new in the middle of full contact sparring for example. (Or if they do get a new teacher.) What he wanted to do belonged in the Testing Zone and not the Learning Zone. Going hard and at speed meant his previously conditioned responses would always come out. He didn't complete the seminar because he wasn't willing to let go of what he was good at to create the possibility of becoming better.

The other thing that happens in the Learning Zone is teaching. It is in this zone that your coach, teacher, Sensei will provide feedback and corrections and, if necessary, where they make you repeat a certain part of something until you get it right.

The Learning Zone is vital.

In the Learning Zone, you get to think and ponder and consider and learn to problem solve. You have time; time you will not have in the Testing Zone or real life. You can stop partway through a move and ask if you are in the right place, can you feel if this is working, and so on.

In the Learning Zone, you can intellectually grasp a subject and grasp the physical requirements.

Let go of what you know and allow yourself to be taught and learn in the Learning Zone.

The Conditioning Zone

The Conditioning Zone is where some of what many call "alive training" is introduced. Alive work is even greater in the next zone.

You move into the Conditioning Zone when you think you have enough intellectual grasp of the learning to bring it into your conditioned responses.

There are two types of conditioning drills:

1. Skill Set Conditioning
2. Operant Conditioning

Skill Set Conditioning

Skill Set Conditioning isolates a particular skill set or principle and focuses on developing or obtaining that skill. It allows you to bring that skill set into your responses through total focus on it. Skill Set conditioning should always have some bridge to reintroduce the many other factors involved in the chaotic environment of an assault.

The way I prefer to develop a particular skill is to isolate it. I like to sluff off all the noise and chaos and other things that go on in simulating an assault to simplify a slice of time or a moment where a particular skill is needed and work on that one micro moment by extending the time you are in that moment.

For example, I consider locks to be a gift. It is rude to try and take a gift before it is offered, and it is rude to turn one down. Locks work the same way. They are hard to force on an Aggressor but often the opportunity to apply a lock is offered.

This assumes you can see the gift and take advantage of the offer. Separately working on when you can apply a lock is a skill set conditioning. By limiting what is going on or what can be done, you can focus on when the opportunity to accept the gift of a lock occurs. By focusing on that movement, you condition yourself to recognize it.

To be effective you must begin to add back in the other factors and the chaos so that you still recognize the opportunity. You do this slowly and progressively.

Any skill can be isolated and focused on in Skill Set Conditioning and the drills used are specific to the skill set; therefore, I won't be going into them in this Addendum.

Operant Conditioning

In Operant Conditioning, you do not want to do anything that you do not want to do in real life. You cannot stop part way through to see if you have control. You don't hand the weapon back, you don't stop until you have stopped the threat, you don't help the bad guy up, you don't do anything you don't want to do in a real situation.

There are numerous approaches for how to accomplish this and my approach is to use a number of slow motion drills. Every drill has a safety flaw. The safety flaw I prefer is going in slow motion because it doesn't seem to carry over when shifting to full speed in the Testing Zone.

I use slow motion for the following reasons:

- It gives you time to choose to use your new learning.
- It gives you time to problem solve.
- It allows you to use any move because going slowing protects your partner.
- It allows you to do every move fully. (For example, you can drive your elbow through your partner's head in slow motion without damaging them.)
- It allows you to condition a new and different response by giving you time to recognize the cues.

Some of the drills we use in Operant Conditioning give a little kick juice (adrenaline) therefore I call this Soft Adrenaline Work. Having a little adrenaline helps you condition the responses.

In Operant Conditioning NO TEACHING TAKES PLACE – NONE. It is important for operant conditioning that you allow the student to remain in a particular mind set. Teaching takes them into the intellectual. Instead, here we want them to have experiential learning, where if it worked and felt great, do that again. If it didn't work and felt horrible, don't do that again.

If they continue to fail then you shift out of the Conditioning Zone and back to the Learning Zone, because they had not learned the material well enough to condition it.

Testing Zone

The Testing Zone comes when we think we have conditioned the responses we want, but now we need to see if that conditioning comes out at speed, against resistance and in as much chaos as we can fake.

I call this Hard Adrenaline Work because it usually kicks in more adrenaline than the slow work.

Once again you do not do anything you would not do in the street EXCEPT for whatever safety flaw you have put in place, so you and your partners are not constantly sending each other to emergency or the morgue. There will always be a safety flaw in any drill and SHOULD be. Understand that I call it a flaw because it means the drill cannot totally duplicate real life, but it is required to safely attempt the training.

I like to progress into the Testing Zone in stages from the Conditioning Zone rather than just leaping all the way to testing. I have partners gradually increase resistance and gradually increase the speed until we have shifted out of the Conditioning Zone into the Testing Zone. Once they have done some Testing work you can introduce drills taking them right into testing without a build-up.

Again, should there be constant failure then move back to either the Conditioning Zone or the Learning Zone as needed. For example, if they understand how to respond but cannot do it at full speed, then it is back to the Conditioning Zone. If they cannot do the correct response or do not know what to do, then it is back to the Learning Zone.

The three zones progress through three steps:

1. They teach the student what to do.
2. They make it a conditioned response.
3. They test to see if the learning and conditioning are there when the student needs it, or at least as much as we can in a safe place to train dangerous things.

Often once a student learns something they tend to stay in the Testing Zone but remember nothing new is learned there because of the risk for injury. Constantly going back to the Learning Zone and Conditioning Zone is needed to continue learning and improving.

Author's Note

As an independent writer people often use the reviews of books when deciding to give them a try or not, so if you enjoyed this book and found it useful, I hope you will take the time and do me the favour of writing a review.

I also love hearing from people who have read my books and I am more than happy to respond to any questions you might have so feel free to contact me through my website wpd-rc.com.

About the Author

Rick Wilson began his intense interest in the martial arts when his grandfather, Wallace Wilson, began teaching him boxing as a young child. Wallace Wilson had boxed while serving in World War I. This set off a lifelong interest in self-defence.

Then later, as a young teen, he was briefly taught Judo by Master Masao Takahashi in Ottawa, Ontario, Canada. It was his first hands on experience with the self defence arts of Asia. It was an interest and a love that would carry on throughout his life. Rick learned an appreciation for the devastatingly practical applications of martial arts when for a short period he studied Jiu-Jitsu in his teens under Kyoshi John Therien in Vanier, Ontario.

He gained an understanding of the mental value of forms while training in Tae Kwon Do with Master Hong Park in Edmonton, Alberta, Canada.

All of this experience brought him to become a student of Uechi Ryu Karate Jutsu with Shihan Neil Dunnigan, then with Kyoshi David Mott and now, because of his focus on reality, he is on his own seeking the most effective material he can.

Rick's delving into the reality base of martial arts was heavily influenced by two legendary Seniors of Uechi Ryu, Van Canna and Jim Maloney (both holding 10th Dan in Uechi Ryu) as well as the writings and teaching of Rory Miller.

For Rick Wilson the close quarters combat aspect of Uechi Ryu with its Southern China influences was the style that suited him best. He could bring all his past experience and find a place for it. He continues his lifelong study of Uechi Ryu Karate and has established the International Uechi Ryu Pwangainuun Association (IUPA).

In 2010 Rick Wilson was honoured to be evaluated by Jim Maloney Sensei and promoted to Rokyudan Renshi (6th degree).

Rick also currently studies a version of the Chen Taiji Practical Method from his long time training partner, Rick Bottomley.

Rick closed his martial arts school after eighteen years to devote more time to his grandchildren and now runs the Wilson Practical Defence website (wpd-rc.com) offering instructional videos and seminars and is also a Senior Consultant for Randy King's KPC Self Defense in Edmonton, Alberta, a Krav Maga school.

Rick taught his knife defence system at the Alberta Peace Officers 2017 Annual Conference.

As a trained martial artist would you like more depth of knowledge and understanding in your training?

As a LEO or security would you like to be more efficient and effective using your prescribed techniques?

As a citizen would you like efficient and effective self defence training?

wpd-rc.com

Members receive access to over two-hundred instructional video clips and an interactive forum. Information on seminars and private or semi-private lesson also available.

Our Promise: To increase your efficiency and effectiveness in practical self defence.